D1602880

Criminal Financial Investigations

The Use of Forensic Accounting Techniques and Indirect Methods of Proof

Second Edition

Criminal Financial Investigations

The Use of Forensic Accounting Techniques and Indirect Methods of Proof

Gregory A. Pasco

CRC Press
Taylor & Francis Group
Boca Raton London New York

CRC Press is an imprint of the
Taylor & Francis Group, an **informa** business

CRC Press
Taylor & Francis Group
6000 Broken Sound Parkway NW, Suite 300
Boca Raton, FL 33487-2742

© 2013 by Taylor & Francis Group, LLC
CRC Press is an imprint of Taylor & Francis Group, an Informa business

No claim to original U.S. Government works

Printed in the United States of America on acid-free paper
Version Date: 20120713

International Standard Book Number: 978-1-4665-6262-2 (Hardback)

Library of Congress Cataloging-in-Publication Data

Pasco, Gregory A.
  Criminal financial investigations : the use of forensic accounting techniques and indirect methods of proof / Gregory A. Pasco. -- 2nd ed.
    p. cm.
  Includes bibliographical references and index.
  ISBN 978-1-4665-6262-2 (hardcover : alk. paper)
  1. Forensic accounting--United States. I. Title.

KF8968.15.P37 2013
363.25--dc23   2012028116

Visit the Taylor & Francis Web site at
http://www.taylorandfrancis.com

and the CRC Press Web site at
http://www.crcpress.com

*To my wife and family
for their support, encouragement, and patience.*

To the administrative staff and faculty at Colorado Technical University, Sioux Falls, South Dakota, for the opportunity and assistance in completing this book.

Contents

Foreword

Inherent in every society is an element that comprises that society, for whatever reason, based upon your favorite criminological theory, elects to take advantage of the resources and efforts of other individuals and corporations (for example, Enron, WorldCom, Adelphia Communications). Due to this rather Machiavellian tendency on the part of certain individuals, and in some cases, corporate philosophy, society has responded through legislative enactment, administrative regulations, and an array of other safeguards to regulate this behavior.

This book addresses those financial crimes that are for the most part perpetrated by individuals who are part of the more affluent social and economic sector of our culture. The text provides in-depth, clear explanations of the concepts, and substantive issues that are associated with the financial aspect of the investigation of white collar crime. The text offers a paradigm to develop the necessary mind-set, as well as the investigative understanding in terms of techniques, that may not necessarily be part of a more traditional criminal investigation course directed more to the law enforcement community.

Investigating financial white collar crime dictates a uniquely different set of investigative skills and mind-set. This book explores a historical overview of the topic, the different forms of financial fraud and misappropriation of assets, inclusive of money laundering and transnational financial transactions, logically progressing to the courtroom, litigation, and evidence. It sets out a methodology that provides the foundation to understanding what is necessary to identify, investigatively pursue, and ultimately successfully prosecute financial white collar crime.

The utility of the case study method employed in this text enhances the understanding of the concepts related to such topics as investigative auditing techniques, financial investigative mind-set, and the legal environment that such investigations are ultimately resolved within. By employing the case study method, the book provides the reader, whether a novice or someone with knowledge of forensic investigations, guidance in understanding the mind-set and skill set that is involved in the challenges that are faced in a successful investigation of financial white collar crime.

David W. Schrank
Professor of Criminalistics
Chairman, Department of Criminal Justice
Colorado Technical University
Sioux Falls, South Dakota

Preface

Investigation of the financial aspects of criminal activity has been overlooked in the instruction and practice of criminal investigating. The fact that most crimes are committed for financial gain has been ignored in the field as well as the classroom. Many texts provide insights and practical applications of forensic techniques involving physical evidence but fail to address the benefits drawn from a thorough investigation of the financial motivations behind criminal behavior. From an enforcement standpoint, this type of investigation is probably more beneficial than trying to determine the sociological or psychological reasons for criminal behavior.

For the investigator, the complexities and intricacies of a financial investigation require constant application of mental exercises in logic and reason. At the same time, the investigator must be able to organize and relate a large amount of individual activities to construct the financial profile of the investigation. The ability to work these cases does not require specialization in any specific discipline. It does, however, require a familiarity with a variety of disciplines and an understanding of how those disciplines work together to uncover the truth.

Conducting an indirect method of proof investigation using forensic accounting and financial investigative techniques can be a valuable tool in the enforcement and deterrence of financial crime. As demonstrated in the text, they can also be used to strengthen criminal cases that involve an ongoing criminal enterprise. The methodology can also be applied in a number of noncriminal applications. The same techniques can be used to determine the equity in civil disputes over debt settlement offers and agreements, verification of business values in considering acquisitions and mergers, and civil litigation dealing with financial actions. Once the logic of using these methods is understood, the investigator can view the financial activity of the criminal or civil actions from a broader perspective, and provide the necessary information and advice to resolve the situation.

An ability to follow the money trail allows for the full development of the facts and circumstances involved in the case to be shown in a logical and sequential pattern, and simplifies the understanding of how the financial pieces fit together. For criminal investigations, it gives the investigator the tools necessary to uncover and identify all of the participants in a criminal enterprise. Financial investigating leads the investigator up the ladder in criminal organizations, so that the entire organization can be eliminated. The top players in criminal organizations are no longer insulated from prosecution, but face the same jeopardy of conviction and incarceration as their underlings.

To effectively use these techniques, the investigator must be willing to learn various aspects of several business and financial disciplines, and to incorporate them into a solid investigative repertoire. The application of these methods can range from simple verification and corroboration of criminal acts to the prosecution of the most complicated corporate schemes. In today's world they also have an important place in the tracking, tracing, and interruption of the money flow going to terrorist organizations.

Financial crimes cost our country billions of dollars each year. The harm caused by these crimes is not as dramatic as a single act of murder, rape, or arson, but they can affect thousands of victims year after year until they are stopped. We are all victims when the costs to recover from the fraud perpetrated against insurance companies, medical facilities and providers, social programs, environmental agencies, the Securities & Exchange Commission, banks, businesses, and taxing authorities are added to the prices we pay on goods and services each day.

The purpose of this book is to give insight and incentive to civil and criminal law enforcement agencies, and provide financial investigators in business and industry an understanding on how to approach the investigation of financial crimes.

About the Author

Gregory A. Pasco is a professor of criminal justice at Colorado Technical University's Sioux Falls, South Dakota, campus. He received his B.A. degree from Ohio University, Athens, and his M.A. from the University of South Dakota, Vermillion.

Pasco spent more than 28 years in federal law enforcement as a special agent with the Criminal Investigation Division of the Internal Revenue Service (IRS). During this time, he conducted more than 100 financial criminal investigations. The investigations covered violations of Titles 26, 18, and 21. Three of his investigations involved cases that took him overseas and required extensive research into foreign tax and criminal financial law.

He worked in the IRS Organized Crime Unit in Detroit, Michigan, and with the Narcotics Task Forces in New Mexico and Ohio, and completed his federal law enforcement career in South Dakota. He has 24 years of field investigation experience, and 4 years of management and legal sufficiency review.

During his career, Pasco became qualified as an expert witness in criminal tax computations and was accepted as such in federal district court. He was also called upon to provide electronic surveillance and monitoring assistance in other investigations, and was qualified and testified as an expert witness in this area in federal district court. His other qualification as an expert witness was in the area of money laundering.

Pasco has received a variety of awards and commendations for his efforts as an investigator, not only from the U.S. Treasury Department but also from the Federal Bureau of Investigation (FBI), the Drug Enforcement Agency (DEA), and several states' attorney offices.

In addition to teaching at Colorado Technical University, Pasco has participated in international seminars on forensic accounting techniques. Married to his wife, Deborah, for 40 years, he has four children—Amanda, Rachel, Mary, and Greg, Jr. Pasco enjoys following politics and current events, and has written commentaries on government and public education.

Introduction

1

White collar and other financial crimes cost the U.S. economy billions of dollars each year. Organized crime and drug cartels, often included in this category, add substantially to the economic and social costs. In addition, the development of terrorist activity within the nation's borders employs the same strategies to finance their operation. As these law enforcement problems grow and develop, the role of law enforcement must continue to evolve, and it must adapt to face these threats and ensure the safety and stability of our society.

During the last 50 years, criminal enterprises and corporate criminal activities have become more sophisticated, better organized, and more complex. They have also caused greater harm to the direct victims of the crimes and society overall. Investigation of these criminal activities must constantly adapt to deter, enforce, and prosecute them. Forensic accounting is the means for investigation and prosecution of these crimes.

What Is Forensic Accounting?

Forensics are an integral part of criminal investigative practices and procedures. Analysis of a crime scene provides the information and evidence necessary to determine the method used to commit the crime, the time and place the crime occurred, and the people involved in the crime. Forensics apply a wide range of scientific disciplines to determine the who, what, where, when, and how of the crime that was committed. Chemistry, biology, physics, anatomy, botany, and other disciplines are used to obtain any and all information possible about the crime. This, in turn, provides the best evidence possible for solving and prosecuting the perpetrators of the crime.

The world of business, finance, and economics also uses certain disciplines to accurately reflect financial transactions, transfer and ownership of property, and economic development. These disciplines include accounting, business law, trade and patent regulations, domestic and international tax laws, and commerce regulations. They rely on documentary evidence to support and reflect the financial transactions that occur in everyday life.

The documents created to record and preserve financial transactions are the raw evidence used in forensic accounting. Just as fingerprints and DNA are used in forensic crime scene investigations, documents are used to identify the who, what, where, when, and how of the financial crimes that have occurred. Many crimes of violence and other types of crimes are committed for the purpose of economic benefit. Forensic accounting disciplines are also utilized to determine the profitability of criminal activities and the beneficiaries of the illegal gains. The methodology of general criminal forensics and forensic accounting is the same.

Criminological Theories

Criminologists debate the theories on how, why, what, where, and when crimes occur. They discuss the plausibility of causation, deterrence, and social and political ramifications. In the case of white collar or financial crimes, they struggle with isolating and defining them. Edwin Sutherland made the first attempt to define white collar crime in 1939. He noted that the perpetrators were at the higher end of the social and economic scales in society, and they held positions or occupations that provided the opportunity to commit such crimes. Since then, other criminologists have argued that such a definition is too narrow. It overlooks the individuals who function within criminal networks and organizations, and corporate entities that commit crimes through board decisions and illegal business practices. It also omits the scam artists who use fraud and deception as their means of theft and the individuals who steal through tax, bank, credit card, and Internet fraud, as well as those who commit embezzlement.

For investigative purposes, all of the theories on criminal motivation, crime causation, crime typology, and criminal deterrence can be condensed into one motive for criminal behavior and two categories of criminal acts.

Motive

Most of the criminological debate on motivation is directed at determining outside factors that motivate individuals to engage in criminal activities. This debate is functional to the extent that it can develop the intricacies and relationships between social factors and criminal behavior. However, it often overlooks the basic or root causes for criminal actions. Before criminology existed, these root causes were the topic of debate in social and political philosophy.

Thomas Hobbes may have expressed it best, although quite pessimistically, in *Leviathan*, where he states that, without law, the nature and life of the individual is "solitary, poor, nasty, brutish, and short."[*] He draws this

---

[*] Thomas Hobbes, *Leviathan*, 1651; *Great Books of the Western World*, Encyclopedia Britannica, Inc.

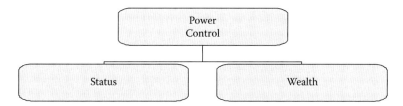

Figure 1.1 Motivation diagram.

conclusion based on the premise that without law there is no peace, without peace man is in a constant state of war with every other man, existing in a society without social, economic, or scientific progress. A simple example would be that of playing a game without any rules.

There are two opposing philosophical views on the nature of man. One is that man is inherently good and getting better. The other is that man is inherently bad and requires laws and rules, backed by punishment for violation, to maintain civility.

The fact that individuals in the higher social and economic status in our society commit most of the white collar and major financial crimes contradicts the first view of the nature of humans. In criminal investigations, it is best to adopt the second view and hope to discover the "exceptions that prove the rule."

Figure 1.1 is a diagram of the simplified explanation for the motivation of criminal behavior. In the diagram, power or control or both are the motivation for all crimes. This lust for power can be manifested in physical power or control over another individual or group of individuals. The means to achieve or fulfill this motivation can take the form of either of two types of criminal behavior.

One means would be to increase one's status over others through violence and intimidation. Such criminal dominance is exemplified in the commission of crimes such as murder, rape, assault, battery, arson, and vandalism. The goal would be to increase one's status over others by violence or threat of violence, and thus gain illegitimate control over them. In politics, it would equate to tyranny or control by use of force or fear. The use of force to coerce the behaviors desired by those in power limits the freedoms of the people in that society. When physical force is not possible or plausible, as in a democracy or republic, the instillation of fear of ostracism or of an external disaster is often employed to intimidate enough of the population to accept restrictions of their freedoms by law or regulation.

The other means would be to gain wealth through illegitimate methods so as to surpass the economic standings of others, thereby being in a position to buy control over them through the use of excessive wealth. These financial crimes would include tax fraud, insurance fraud, welfare fraud, and any other crimes of theft by fraud. It would also include corporate crimes such as price fixing, securities fraud, environmental crimes, consumer fraud, and market manipulation.

In viewing crime and its motivation, we have distilled the problem. The motive is power, and the means are violent crimes and financial crimes. We must also recognize that often violence may be incorporated into the commission of financial crimes.

Murder for hire is a violent crime, but it does not seek control over the victim but rather the financial gain derived in fulfilling another person's desire for power. Similarly, the professional arsonist has little, if any, interest in the property to be destroyed, and is only interested in his or her financial gain. Extortion uses violence as the incentive for others to submit to the theft of their money rather than face physical harm. Even the street mugger is concerned more with the amount of the take from the victim than the actual assault.

The motive shown in Figure 1.1 is the same for all people. Everyone wants a degree of status and wealth, and to have a comfortable position in society. The differentiation between crime and personal industry is whether society accepts the means of attainment as legitimate or illegitimate. The simple analogy would be whether the individual follows the rules or cheats to win the game.

Opportunity

One distinction that separates white collar financial crimes from other financial crimes is the opportunity to commit the crime. This distinction is the sticking point for many criminologists in trying to define white collar crime. These crimes are often crimes of opportunity that can only occur if the perpetrator has sufficient position, control, or power over the situation. As an example, an individual must have a position of control within a bank to embezzle funds from it. The more intricate the fraud scheme is within the business, the greater is the need for influence and control of the record keeping and financial activity of the business.

Intricate financial crimes require the perpetrator to have a detailed understanding of the industry in which the business operates, the way in which financial activities are recorded, and the areas in which manipulation of record keeping could generate illicit or unreported income. These requirements place an additional burden on the investigator. Research into the general business operations for the type of business being used to commit the fraud is often needed. In addition, the investigator needs to understand the record-keeping procedures of the specific business in which the fraud occurs.

Another path of opportunity is found in the victims of financial crimes. In financial fraud schemes, the victims may also provide opportunity to the perpetrator. Most financial fraud schemes involve convincing people to give their money to the perpetrator in anticipation of receiving a far greater return on their investment than would be available through legitimate investments. When the deal is "too good to be true," it is almost always too good to be true, and because of their own greed, the victims are taken. The investigator must realize that the power of greed is as strong over the victim as it is over the perpetrator. The only difference is that the perpetrator will act using illegal means to fulfill the desire for more and more wealth.

A final difference between financial crimes and violent crimes is that the former will often be continuing while the investigation is in progress, whereas the latter is usually over after it is committed. This gives the financial investigator an advantage in that the financial criminal is less apt to try to lay low or hide out from enforcement. This criminal would rather try to use loopholes or elaborate defenses to convince authorities that no crime was committed.

Financial Crimes

Financial crimes have existed as long as men have had financial dealings with each other. These crimes have been categorized separately from other crimes and criminal activity due to the use of fraud (and often conspiracy) to commit the crimes. The heavy thumb on the scales by merchants, the misrepresentation of the quality of livestock sold, the "salting" of mineral deposits in mining, and the street games of hucksters are all examples of man's willingness to take the earnings of others by fraud and deception to enhance their own wealth. A large part of our codified system of law was written to protect the unsuspecting and the unsophisticated from loss of property and personal well-being.

As society and industry matured over the past century, and the economy and standards of living expanded and developed, illegal financial schemes became more innovative and complex. The study of criminology began to address the differences and distinctions of financial crimes in comparison to the standard studies in the past. From the initial identification by Sutherland, criminologists have struggled to contain and clarify the definition of white collar and financial crimes.

From the field investigation perspective, there is little need to go beyond the single motive and dual access to the motive already put forth. The variations of the crimes are of importance, but the underlying social and psychological justifications are weighed for their value by judges and juries. The investigator is responsible for presenting an accurate account of the financial activities that occurred, and sufficient evidence for establishing intent to commit the crime and the elements of the crime alleged.

The white collar or financial criminal has the same motive for crime, but through official position, status, sophistication, or professional acumen is able to effect the crime without the use of violence. This has resulted in severe sentencing discrepancies between the white collar criminal and the street thug. A convenience store robbery that nets the thief $100 usually results in a jail sentence that can range up to several years. The corporate executive who bilks his company of millions of dollars usually receives a much lighter sentence, if he goes to prison at all.

Our country's history is replete with financial schemes, some legal, some illegal, but all unfair to the victim in some degree. In a democratic republic, as schemes and practices spread and gain notoriety, public outrage peaks, and government intercedes to regulate or make the actions illegal by legislative, judicial, or executive response.

The industrial and scientific revolutions, beginning in the 1800s, sparked dramatic changes in the U.S. economy. Major corporations were formed, and the government raced to regulate and control their actions toward customers and employees. This economic boon also inspired waves of immigration into the United States as people sought to improve their economic opportunities.

Laws were written to limit the ways in which corporations could operate. Regulations against monopolies, unfair labor practices, price fixing, and false or deceptive advertising were put in place. Consumer rights and environmental protections were also instituted. As these bodies of law grew, the government established enforcement and regulatory agencies to ensure compliance. The judicial branch of government participated in adjudicating unfair practices and actions, and clarifying the laws and regulations that were adopted.

Legal Requirements

The United States functions under a codified or written system of laws. In this system, each prohibited criminal act is defined, and the requirements for prosecution and conviction of the crime are delineated. The requirements are referred to as the elements of the crime and must be proven by the investigator for successful prosecution of the perpetrator. The investigator in any criminal case must be familiar with the elements of the crime he or she is investigating. This familiarity will assist the investigator in determining the direction of the investigation and the sequence of leads to be followed to prove the case. As financial crimes are often very intricate, the investigator must consider possible variations in the scheme employed and the potential for multiple criminal violations.

Financial crimes are expressed in a similar fashion. Each action necessary to complete the crime is delineated. The complexity of financial crimes often requires the investigator to piece together several facts to establish a single element of the crime. For an action to be elevated from the ranks of an accident or negligence to that of a criminal violation, certain factors must be present. Most criminal statutes require that the perpetrator intended to commit the crime and that it was a willful commission.

Statutory laws define each crime and identify the factors that must be present for the perpetrator to be in violation of the law. These factors are called the *elements* of the violation. In litigation, it must be shown that the individual charged performed each of the elements of the violation and did so with the intent to violate the statutory provisions. As an example, a statute may define robbery as the taking of property rightfully owned by another person with the intent to keep possession of the property for oneself. The prosecution would have to prove that the accused

1. Took the property.
2. The property belonged to another person.
3. The accused intended to take and keep the property.

In this example, it is easy to imagine that the prosecutor would have a witness or witnesses who could place the defendant at the scene, forensic evidence (footprints, fingerprints, fibers, etc.), or other evidence (possession of property from the store) to prove that the defendant took the property. The prosecutor would also have the complainant's testimony and documentation as to ownership of the property to prove element 2. The difficulty lies in proving element 3. The state of mind of the defendant at the time of the theft requires circumstantial evidence. The evidence must be sufficient to convince the judge or jury that the defendant had the intent to steal. If the defense had sufficient evidence to refute elements 1 or 2, the case would not have gone forward for prosecution. For example, if the defense provided a verifiable alibi for the defendant at the time the offense occurred or proved that the defendant was a co-owner of the property taken, the charges would have to be dropped.

Therefore, the defense must attempt to refute the state-of-mind contentions presented by the prosecution. This is where the diligence and deductive reasoning of the investigator becomes crucial to the success or failure of the case. The investigator must have obtained proof beyond a reasonable doubt that the defendant committed all of the acts required for a violation of the statute. In the example, possession of goods from the store by the defendant, prior criminal history of burglary, negation of alibis, possession of tools or items used to enter the structure, and the defendant's familiarity with the store could all be used to establish and support the alleged state of mind of the defendant. In a case such as this, forensic accounting techniques can also be utilized if the profits from the theft have been realized (the stolen property sold through a fence). Analysis of the suspect's finances could show income or gain for which there is no legal explanation or source.

Financial crimes require more planning, intricate concealment of the means and fruits of the crime, and, in most cases, more than one individual to effect the crime. These crimes are also perpetrated over time, and need to be presented in a historical or chronological format. Therefore, the majority of evidence used to prove criminal financial violations is circumstantial in nature. The investigator must be diligent and innovative in assembling the evidence to ensure that the "weight" or preponderance of the evidence is sufficient for successful prosecution of the alleged crimes.

The investigator needs to have an understanding of the legal definitions and elements of the crimes of fraud and conspiracy as well as of the specific crime under investigation. The next step would be to acquire a basic understanding of the business or activity in or through which the financial crime was perpetrated.

In addition to the legal aspects of the crime or crimes under investigation, the investigator must also develop a familiarity with the business or industry through which or in which the crimes have been committed. The investigator must understand, at least in a general way, how the business or industry is supposed to function to be able to identify the methods used to corrupt the system. In a way, it is like being an automobile mechanic: the normal functioning of the automobile must be understood before the mechanic can identify and solve what is wrong.

The Financial Disciplines

2

General Business Operations

In the area of personal finance, there are two ways to increase wealth. The first is to make more money, and the second is to spend less of the money you make. In business the same two principles apply. You can increase income or reduce expenses. Businesses make money in different ways, depending on the sector of business they are in. It is important to understand the general operations of a business to be able to conduct a financial investigation of that business.

Businesses are no more than organized efforts to gain profit from providing goods, ideas, or services to others. Providing goods can be broken into two categories: (1) manufacturing and wholesale, and (2) retail sales.

Providing Goods

Manufacturing involves the production of a large amount of a single product. Some major businesses expand to include several related products. These products are sold in bulk to a variety of stores and distributors. Manufacturing takes raw materials, such as farm produce, oil, steel, or plastics, and creates a product. Manufacturing usually requires specialized equipment to produce and package the specific product.

As an example, a cereal company will purchase grains and other ingredients to make the cereal. These raw materials are processed in equipment specifically designed to grind, blend, bake, and shape the cereal. The cereal is then conveyed to a packaging machine that prepares the cereal boxes and liners, and then to a machine to fill and seal the boxes. The individual boxes are then conveyed to larger boxes that hold several boxes of cereal to be shipped to stores and distributors. These quantity purchases by distributors and stores are referred to as wholesale sales.

The cereal company has invested substantial capital to buy the specialized equipment needed to produce, process, and package the cereal. For the cereal company to add a prize inside each package, it would purchase the prizes from another manufacturer and modify the equipment to include the prizes in the cereal boxes. The other option would be to purchase an entirely different set of machines to make the prizes themselves. This would be a costly and inefficient way to operate and would reduce business profits. For a business to consider the second option, a cost–profits efficiency analysis would be made to determine the costs that would be incurred versus the savings that would be made in not paying the markup charged by the prize-manufacturing business.

The other category for providing goods is in retail sales. These are the sale of manufactured products to the public. Examples of retail businesses would include department, grocery, hardware, and convenience stores. These businesses purchase a small amount of products from a wide variety of manufacturers, add a markup to the products, and offer the products for sale to consumers.

Retail sales businesses face the problem of maintaining sufficient inventory to keep the shelves stocked and to ensure that they do not overbuy perishable products or products whose popularity may quickly end. Retail sale involves a lot more educated guessing as to what items will become popular, what items will turn over rapidly, and what will be in demand for each seasonal change. The differences between these two ways of providing goods involve variations in accounting to track, analyze, and predict market activity for their products.

Providing Services

Service industries earn their money by performing tasks that businesses and individuals cannot or do not want to do for themselves. Professional service providers such as doctors, lawyers, accountants, and scientists apply extensive training and expertise in their fields that are not widely held by the general public or private business. Other service providers fill the needs for transportation of people and goods, and for construction, repair, and maintenance.

Government employees provide services in the areas of infrastructure management and oversight, safety and law enforcement, and in regulatory and assistance programs. Still other service providers are involved in the arts, sports, entertainment, convenience, education, and information fields. These services can be provided by an operation of any size, from a single individual, such as a dentist, to a major corporation such as AT&T.

Providing Ideas

Another area of endeavor that creates income is in the development and sharing of ideas. Inventors develop new products or improve upon existing ones for the betterment or convenience of industry and the public. Researchers expand the knowledge in their fields to produce a greater or better understanding of the world we live in. Writers, journalists, and professional speakers offer their insights, ideas, and opinions on a wide variety of topics by means of several platforms and media outlets.

The reason for briefly discussing the various means of gaining wealth is to keep the forensic accountant or financial investigator aware that each area of employment or field of endeavor within the general areas requires an understanding of how money is earned. To investigate a real estate agent, the investigator must understand how commissions are earned, what expenses are involved, and what areas of bookkeeping or accounting are most susceptible and prone to fraud. This familiarity with the business operation is just as important whether the business activity is legal or illegal in the eyes of the law.

Sales can be legal on the surface and still be illegal if fraud and deceptive practices are employed. Sales can also be illegal in their nature as in the cases of controlled substances, child pornography, or the sale of stolen property. In the same way, providing services is a legitimate way to earn a living but requires certain certifications and licensing. Some services are prohibited by law, such as murder for hire or prostitution, for the protection of the public.

Whether the investigation involves finding the profits of illegal operations for civil or criminal forfeiture, or profits from fraud in a legitimate business, the investigator must know how the business operates and what generates its profits.

Record Retention

Laws and regulations require businesses and individuals to record financial transactions and to keep those records for various periods of time. Tax laws require businesses and individuals to maintain their records for a period of 6 years to accommodate the criminal statute of limitations. County offices keep real property records virtually forever. Other businesses are under varying time requirements set by the regulatory agencies that oversee their operations. In addition to the time requirements, government and industry regulations restrict access to these records to ensure individual and business confidentiality and privacy. Public records such as property ownership, mortgages, loans, liens, corporate filings, and others are available for review by the public. Tax return records and information are kept in strict confidence to ensure the privacy protection of taxpayers and to maintain public confidence in the voluntary tax system.

The investigator is responsible for obtaining the restrictions information on the financial records needed in the investigation. The investigator must also keep in mind that an individual or entity may voluntarily provide its records by waiving the right to regulatory privacy protection. This applies to records of the person's transactions. Enterprises such as banks that maintain the records of other people and businesses are considered third-party record keepers and cannot disclose information without the permission of the account holder or without being required to make the records available by court order.

Good interviewing techniques and a knowledge of what records exist can facilitate obtaining the records needed. In situations where a subpoena or court order is required, the investigator must explain the relevance of the information sought to the investigation. In those cases where there is a high probability that illegal income is unreported, the state, local, or federal taxing authorities can be asked to enter into a joint investigation.

Basic Accounting

Basic accounting practices are used to compute and prepare the documents used to record financial transactions. This provides a common standard for the preparation of financial records. The financial investigator needs to understand the vocabulary and the basic reasoning used in accounting. The following is a short list of terms that are most commonly used in financial records preparation.

Asset—Ownership of a possession having monetary value.

Current or liquid asset—Things owned, cash, or things that can be quickly converted to cash, for example, stocks, bonds, collectibles, and jewelry.

Long-term asset—Things owned that are not easily converted to cash, for example, buildings, real estate, and equipment.

Liability—A legal debt owed by a business or individual.

Income—What a business or individual earns.

Expense—A cost that is incurred.

Gross income—Total money coming in.

Net income—Gross income minus all expenses; the result is profit or loss.

Credit—An increase to an income or liability account, or a decrease to an asset or expense account (money coming in).

Debit—A decrease to an income or liability account, or an increase to an asset or expense account (money going out).

Receivables—Items due to be paid to you.

Payable—Items you are to pay.

Account balance—The total difference between debits and credits to an account (Deposits – Checks written = Checking account balance).

Calendar year—January 1 through December 31.

Fiscal year—One year beginning and ending on other set dates (e.g., July 1 to June 30) used in business to record income for tax purposes.

There are two methods of accounting used in business: cost and accrual. Each method takes into consideration all of the income and expenses but identifies situations when they occur differently. Cost basis accounting identifies income when payment is received, and records expenses when they are paid. Accrual accounting identifies income when payment for goods or services or both is promised, and expenses when the promise for payment is made. A contractor might find accrual better for the business if payments are received after the job is completed. A retail store would most likely use cost accounting because payment for goods is received when sales are made. For tax purposes, individuals are considered on a cost basis unless they can show a compelling reason to be on accrual basis. Once a method is chosen that method must continue to be used unless a formal change procedure is followed.

Books and Records

The books and records of businesses are constructed using a separate account for each item of income or expense. All accounts have two columns to enter financial data: debits and credits. Debits are entered in the first column, and credits in the second. A widely used way to remember this construction is, "debits on the left, credits on the right." The individual accounts keep a running total of financial activity for each item of asset or liability, income or expense, for a set period of time (usually, the calendar or fiscal year is selected for reporting purposes). Remember that the type of account determines whether the debit or credit entered is an increase or decrease to the account (debit is a decrease to an income or liability account, or an increase to an asset or expense account; credit is an increase to an income or liability account, or a decrease to an asset or expense account).

As an example, a shoe store buys $5,000.00 worth of sandals from a wholesaler. The store owner writes a check for this purchase. Both inventory (the sandals) and cash (in checking) are asset accounts. The account entries would be a debit (increase) of $5,000.00 to inventory and a credit (decrease) to cash in checking.

	Debit	Credit
Inventory	$5,000.00	
Cash in checking		$5,000.00

Every financial event in the business requires a debit and a credit entry to the accounts affected. The same amount has to be entered in each category, or the final summary (general ledger) will not balance. This is how the system receives its name as a double entry system of accounting.

If the store sells all of the sandals for $10,000.00 and deposits the money to the checking account, the following account entries would be made:

	Debit	Credit
Sales		$10,000.00
Cash in checking	$10,000.00	
Inventory		$5,000.00
Cost of goods sold	$5,000.00	

The accounts are then combined in a general ledger. The general ledger becomes the summary of all the financial activities of the business. The general ledger lists all of the business accounts by category of accounts (asset, liability, etc.). The entries to the general ledger are the balances of the individual accounts as of a certain date. Annualized entries are used for tax purposes, quarterly entries for employment tax purposes, and monthly entries for profit and loss statements. The business needs and circumstances may require other summaries to be prepared. Each account is kept on a separate sheet, and the activities are computed to show increases or decreases in the account for the set period of time. To close the books, each account sheet would be balanced to determine the increase or decrease, and the balances will be taken to the general ledger. The account sheets would look like this:

Inventory

Inventory	Debit	Credit
Beginning balance	0	
Purchase		$5,000.00
Cost of goods sold	$5,000.00	
Ending balance	0	

Cash in Checking

	Debit	Credit
Beginning balance	$5,000.00	
Inventory purchase		$5,000.00
Sales	$10,000.00	
Ending balance	$10,000.00	

Cost of Goods Sold

	Debit	Credit
Beginning balance	0	
Inventory sold	$5,000.00	
Ending balance	$5,000.00	

If these transactions were the only financial activities for the shoe store, the books would show gross income (sales) of $10,000.00, and cost of goods sold (expense) (inventory) of $5,000.00, resulting in net income of $5,000.00. The profit and loss statement would show the financial information in the following manner:

Shoe Store P&L

	Debit	Credit
Sales		$10,000.00
Cost of goods sold	$5,000.00	
Net income		$5,000.00

These summaries fulfill regulatory requirements, provide investors with information, and give the business managers information on trends and ways to increase profits. They also provide the investigator with a wealth of information. Drastic changes in account activity and balances may indicate areas of financial activity that are being misused or manipulated by the business owner.

In addition to the account sheets and general ledger, the business will also have the source or supporting documents that prove the transaction actually occurred. In the previous example, the business would have the purchase order for the sandals, the receipt for delivery of the sandals, the check stub for payment, the canceled check, and the bank statement showing the check was paid. If there appears to be too much or too little activity in a certain account, the investigator can review the source documents to ensure that the financial activity is accurately recorded.

The amount and complexity of the accounting system used in the business is proportional to the complexity and volume of the business the company has. No matter how complicated the accounting appears, the investigator has to remember that the perpetrator can only commit a financial crime by understating the income or overstating the expenses in a business operation.

Basic Tax Law

Tax laws have become more and more complicated as innovative businessmen and individuals have discovered loopholes in the laws, and legislators have scurried to close those loopholes and to be just as innovative in finding new ways to tax the population. The tax laws and Internal Revenue Service (IRS) regulations set the framework for accounting practices.

There are thousands of pages of tax law (the Internal Revenue Code) and tax regulations. These rules define business practices and set the parameters for financial activity for individuals, businesses, and organizations. Due to the volume of information contained in these documents, the investigator is best served by being familiar with the documents as a research tool for specific regulations that apply to his or her investigation.

As ironic as it may seem, the federal income tax system is considered to be a voluntary system of taxation. If you meet certain criteria, you are required by law to file tax returns. However, the information you provide is given voluntarily to the government. In a way, it is similar to driving a car. If you meet certain criteria, you can drive. It is presumed that you will follow the driving rules and regulations voluntarily. If you violate the driving regulations by speeding or running stop signs and red lights, you are subject to legal fines and penalties.

To maintain confidence in the system, the government has imposed strict disclosure regulations that apply severe penalties if tax return or return information is released without legal cause. These restrictions prohibit the IRS from sharing tax information with other law enforcement agencies unless they are working in a joint grand jury investigation or are legally required to provide the information. This protects members of the public from having their financial information made available to others. However, the individual can waive the right of protection for the information he or she provides.

Familiarity with a few general rules in taxation can be of help to the investigator. Income from any source is required to be reported on federal income tax returns. This requirement affects not only the person receiving the income but also those who pay the income. Banks, brokerage firms, employers, and other businesses paying interest, dividends, wages, or fees for services in excess of a certain dollar amount are required to notify the recipient as well as the IRS.

Employers must also file employment tax returns that show the wages paid, tax withheld, and other information quarterly, as well as W-2 forms that show this information for the entire year.

Regulatory Agencies

When we think of laws and law enforcement, we often focus on crimes of violence such as murder, kidnapping, assault, and robbery. It is interesting to note that throughout history most of the laws written—from the Code of Hammurabi to our current U.S. Code—deal with property and financial transactions. Even the teachings of major religions include teachings on property, ownership, and fair and equitable financial dealings. Several references can be found in the scriptures of major world religions.

Governmental regulations are contained in the law, and penalties are applied for violation. In addition, other governmental regulations are enforced through allowing specific privileges and applying licensing regulations. Businesses and independent contractors that provide goods and services to the public, both directly and indirectly, must meet certain criteria and submit to periodic inspections to obtain and keep a license to operate. The penalty for violating these regulations is the suspension or revocation of the business license and the loss of the privilege to do business.

Even the public at large is subject to licensing and permit regulations to exercise the privilege to drive or alter their property. Contractors and land developers are required to follow building codes and zoning regulations. All of these regulatory provisions serve to protect the community and to regulate commerce. The primary goal is to provide public safety and equal access and treatment in financial transactions; however, these regulations also provide an extensive paper trail of the financial dealings of the individuals and businesses conducting the financial transactions.

The IRS is the largest regulating agency in the United States, and it affects the entire population. The IRS requires that all citizens and businesses obtain social security or employee identification numbers for tax reporting and collection purposes and to be able to claim dependents. Businesses are also required to maintain identification numbers for employees and contract labor to monitor wages paid.

For auditing purposes and verification, the IRS requires that documentation be maintained by taxpayers for the items reported on their returns for a period of 3 years. This time frame coincides with the civil statute of limitations (the period for which civil claims or lawsuits may be filed). The criminal statute of limitations is 6 years, and many financial businesses are required to keep transactional records for that period of time. Banks and brokerage firms are two of the financial types of businesses that fall under the 6-year retention period. These are the major general requirements imposed by the government for purposes of taxation. The Internal Revenue Code (IRC) also has a multitude of other rules and regulations that relate to a wide variety of business activities but are applied to specific types of income and business activities.

The U.S. Treasury also has specific rules and regulations for financial institutions and other businesses. Cash transactions in excess of $10,000.00 occurring in the United States are required to be reported by the business or individual conducting the transaction. A $3,000.00 limit is applied for currency crossing the U.S. border. In addition to governmental mandates, major industries have self-imposed additional rules and regulations to protect themselves and their customers, and to deter waste and fraud.

Land and buildings are usually the largest investment made by individuals and businesses. If you have ever sat through the closing of a real estate transaction, you are aware of the pile of documents that are reviewed and signed by buyers and sellers. These documents are prepared and maintained to protect the parties involved in the sale, and the lender and insurer of the property. In addition, transfer of ownership, as well as mortgages, liens, and easements, are officially recorded in the Registrar of Deeds office in the county where the property is located. Any additional financial transactions, second or third mortgages, building permits and contractor liens, and right-of-ways that affect property valuation are also recorded.

Even the public at large is required to follow a variety of rules and regulations if they want to exercise certain privileges that are allowed through government licensing requirements. Owning and operating an automobile, boat, or other motorized vehicle requires a government-issued license, annual registrations, and compliance with driving laws. Businesses are also required to obtain licenses to operate. The requirements vary by type of business and include health, safety, fire, and access inspections to maintain government standards. Building contractors are also regulated through licensing regulations and zoning laws that limit the type of construction for the location, and the quality of the construction and materials used.

The reporting and verification for these rules and regulations serve a dual purpose. The primary goals are to provide public safety and access, and to facilitate government funding through taxation and fees, but they also provide an extensive paper trail of the financial transactions of businesses and individuals.

There are thousands of courts in the United States. These include municipal, city, county, state, and federal courts. There are also specialized courts that handle tax, traffic, commerce, and international cases. Records of the proceedings are maintained as an integral part of our legal system. Court cases and judicial decisions from cases that have decided similar issues are used as precedents for arguing current cases. They are also used in law enforcement to prepare, maintain, and review criminal histories. These records often hold a wealth of information about financial transactions and the actions of both businesses and individuals.

Open court proceedings are considered public records unless sealed by the court. The general public has the right to inspect and review these records. Civil and criminal cases from small claims, divorce, and custody hearings up to major financial fraud cases can provide evidence and leads in forensic accounting investigations. As the information is taken from a legal proceeding, the information is substantiated by the fact that it is provided under oath.

With the mountains of records prepared, filed, and kept by businesses, individuals, and agencies, all the investigator needs to do is sort through and obtain all of the pertinent information to reconstruct the financial activities of the entity under investigation.

Characteristics of Financial Crimes

3

Because financial crimes incorporate planning, business acumen, and deception, they often take place over a long period of time before the effects are recognized. There are two main reasons why detection of financial fraud takes a longer period of time. The first is that the plan for the fraud is designed to be concealed from the victim. The second is that financial crooks will usually start small and as time passes without detection they will be emboldened to take more and more. When the amounts of the financial fraud become greater, the victims will realize that something is wrong even if they do not know what it is or the perpetrators' gain will begin to appear way out of line with their legitimate earnings.

Due to the time frame involved, the investigator works on two aspects of the same crime: the effect of the crime in the past and the ongoing crime as it is occurring. This can cause difficulty in the presentation of the case. Just as business plans are modified to maximize profits, fraud schemes may be modified to increase illegal gains. Also, the laws may change over time and mitigate or accentuate the criminal activity. Therefore, the investigator needs to be able to present the logic and reasoning behind any modifications, and be alert to legal changes that may take place.

Forensic accounting is the methodology used to investigate financial crimes that have taken place over time. Just as other forensic sciences analyze the current evidence and work backward to determine what took place, the forensic accountant begins with a current financial status and works backward to determine how the status was obtained.

To investigate financial crimes or to discover the proceeds of illegal activities, it is necessary to analyze the documents and testimony obtained that reflect all of the financial transactions of the suspect entity and determine the extent of the income derived. To make this determination, total income earned must be established, and then the income from legitimate sources must be removed or subtracted. The balance will reflect the proceeds concealed or gained from the illegal activity. As an example, a bartender is believed to be selling narcotics. He earns $500.00 a week from his job. The financial investigation shows that he spent $90,000.00 in the past year. The gains from narcotics sales would be $64,000.00: the $90,000.00 less his legitimate income of $26,000.00.

In the same way that crime scene investigations analyze the physical evidence to find out what actually happened in a crime of violence, the financial investigation must analyze the documentary evidence to find out what took place to leave the subject of the investigation in his or her current financial position.

Most people want the reassurance of proof of ownership of the items they buy. Businesses want accurate records to strengthen and expand their operations and to decide whether changes in their business practices are required. Even people who are lying about their finances will usually keep hidden records (often a second set of books) to know exactly how they are doing. Some people do not keep good or even adequate records. In these cases, they still remember facts surrounding major purchases or investments. In a situation where one party does not have records of a transaction, it is likely that the other party or parties to the transaction will.

Such documents and testimony become the physical evidence that is used to determine what financial activity occurred to result in the subject's current financial position. The paper trail replaces the footprints, fibers, and other physical evidence used in investigating violent crimes. Because the evidence in financial crimes is preserved and maintained for long periods of time, and it is usually kept by each of the persons involved in the transaction, it is less likely to deteriorate or be lost. It is, however, subject to being destroyed or concealed in the same way that a perpetrator of a violent crime may try to destroy evidence. In addition to potential destruction of evidence, the investigator is faced with time limitations for maintaining documents. Although records are kept for a long time, the crime may not be discovered until after it has been ongoing for a long time. It also takes a lot of time to get all of the evidence needed to completely reconstruct a financial history.

People are limited in what they can do with the money they receive. Money can be spent or saved. If the money is spent, it will be reflected in the possessions and lifestyle of the spender. How people spend or save offers a wide variety of options.

Spending

A person can spend money on perishable goods such as groceries and entertainment, on short-lived items such as clothing and housewares, on recurring expenses such as utility bills and rent, or to continue personal lifestyle choices such as drinking, smoking, and gambling. These expenditures are the most difficult to ascertain in a financial investigation due to the lack of or the short-lived nature of the record keeping. These types of transactions are often done using cash and receipts that do not always identify the person conducting the transaction.

An individual can also purchase durable goods such as an automobile, boat, airplane, house, or home improvements. These purchases are easier to track and document because the transaction records are thorough in identifying the parties to the transaction and are maintained for a longer period of time. In addition, each party to the transaction, and often the government, maintains copies of the transaction.

People can also keep their gains in liquid assets such as bank accounts, certificates of deposit, securities, commodities, or other assets that can be quickly converted to cash. The paper trail for these transactions is usually the easiest to follow because the precautions taken to ensure accuracy and verify balances are greater due to the fluid nature of the asset.

In addition to acquiring new assets, money can be used to pay off existing debts or liabilities. Both the reduction of debts, such as mortgages and loans, and the acquisition of assets increase a person's net worth.

Saving

People can save the money they receive by placing it in cash account liquid assets such as bank and brokerage accounts, or other interest-bearing or growth accounts. This type of saving is very well documented due to the nature of the asset and all of the regulations concerning financial businesses. Those wishing to conceal savings may open accounts in states or even countries outside where they reside or do business. Others may use a money-laundering scheme to make the money appear to be coming from a legitimate source. Some people have been shown to hide the money in loose floorboards, attics, mattresses, or even bury it in glass jars. Hoarding is the least traceable way to conceal accumulated money. It also is the way that is the least secure; it is susceptible to theft, destruction, and decay. Although financial crimes are committed to improve one's standard of living and provide the finer things of life, it is rare for a financial criminal to hoard the ill-gotten gains for long.

The Structure

One of the first determinations made in a forensic crime scene investigation is when the crime occurred. To establish the time the crime was committed, investigators analyze all of the current evidence, then go back in time until they reach the time just prior to the commission of the crime. Forensic accounting uses the same methodology to identify when the financial changes in the investigation started to occur. Because financial crimes are usually ongoing or continuous in nature, the investigation sets time frames for the financial changes. These time frames are selected to best reflect the illegitimate gains in shorter segments of the total duration of the financial crime.

As an example, a criminal tax case will present the unreported income for each period of time that the individual filed a separate return. When a financial crime occurs over several years, it is easier for the prosecution to present the case and a jury to understand the case if it can be presented in sequential blocks of time. The evidence in a financial case is presented using accounting techniques. Summaries of financial transactions are used to show the total financial picture of the defendant's financial status at specific points in time. These financial "snapshots" are then compared to show the changes in the defendant's financial status. The time frames used in the investigation will coincide with the business' or individual's reporting or record-keeping periods.

The beginning financial snapshot is referred to as the *starting point* of the investigation. The subsequent financial pictures show the extent of the gains from illegal or illicit activities over the duration of the crime.

Financial crimes and the concealment of illegal gains require extensive preparation, planning, and deception by the perpetrator for the scheme to be successful. It is often the case that more than one individual is involved in the financial fraud scheme. Because the plan involves fooling the victims so that the scheme can be used for a long period of time, the perpetrators also need to make the scheme appear legitimate and beneficial to the victims. Financial criminals often play on their target's weaknesses, greed, and pride. Two frequent characteristics that arise in financial or white collar crimes are conspiracy and fraud.

Conspiracy

White collar financial crimes are unique in that they require planning, organization, and a form of deception. The planning, or premeditation, of the crime can be simple or complex. The professional thief must plan the theft and the getaway, and have a market for the stolen goods. The bank officer who schemes to run fictitious loans through the bank has to devise a method to create the loans, make them appear legitimate and created in the normal course of business, divert the proceeds from the loans to his or her own accounts, conceal the funds taken through bank write-offs, and make the newfound wealth appear legitimately earned.

Organizing white collar financial crimes requires that the crimes be effected, and the series of events and activities that will conceal the method of trickery or deception employed be created. The thief must have a "fence" or outlet for the stolen goods to remove the evidence of the crime, convert the goods to cash, and to distance himself or herself from the theft. The association between the thief and the fence is a conspiracy to accomplish and facilitate the crime. The bank officer needs access to the forms for creating loans, the means or authority to approve loans, and be in a position to conceal or write off the loans within the bank. He or she would also need the information and the ability to dismiss the loans within the scope of the bank's internal operating procedures. The banker would need to establish a conduit for the funds taken and a means to conceal his or her receipt of the monies received. False identities would have to be established for the nonexistent loan customers, and one or more false or sham business entities through which the monies could be laundered. There might even be a need to falsify financial statements and bankruptcy documentation. The banker would then need to create a legitimate (appearing) source for the newfound wealth and, finally, a way to disguise the illegal proceeds from detection by government and regulatory review. In this example, the banker would need a much larger conspiratorial group to effect and conceal the crime than the professional thief. The following is a legal definition of conspiracy:

> Conspiracy—18 U.S.C. 371 makes it a separate federal crime or offense for anyone to conspire or agree with someone else to do something which, if actually carried out, would amount to another federal crime or offense. So, under this law, a "conspiracy" is an agreement or a kind of "partnership" in criminal purposes in which each member becomes the agent or partner of every other member.

In order to establish a conspiracy offense it is not necessary for the government to prove that all of the people named in the indictment were members of the scheme; or that those who were members had entered into any formal type of agreement; or that the members had planned together all of the details of the scheme or the "overt acts" that the indictment charges would be carried out in an effort to commit the intended crime.

Also, because the essence of a conspiracy offense is the making of the agreement itself (followed by the commission of any overt act), it is not necessary for the government to prove that the conspirators actually succeeded in accomplishing their unlawful plan.

What the evidence in the case must show beyond a reasonable doubt is that

1. Two or more persons, in some way or manner, came to a mutual understanding to try to accomplish a common and unlawful plan, as charged in the indictment.
2. The person willfully became a member of such conspiracy.
3. One of the conspirators, during the existence of the conspiracy, knowingly committed at least one of the methods (or overt acts) described in the indictment.
4. Such overt act was knowingly committed at or about the time alleged in an effort to carry out or accomplish some object of the conspiracy.

An overt act is any transaction or event, even one that may be entirely innocent when considered alone, that is knowingly committed by a conspirator in an effort to accomplish some object of the conspiracy.

A person may become a member of a conspiracy without knowing all of the details of the unlawful scheme and without knowing who all of the other members are. So, if a person has an understanding of the unlawful nature of a plan and knowingly and willfully joins in that plan on one occasion that is sufficient to convict him for conspiracy. Even though the ultimate criminal object of the conspiracy may not be accomplished or carried out, the conspiracy is established.

Of course, mere presence at the scene of a transaction or event, or the mere fact that certain persons may have associated with each other and may have assembled together and discussed common aims and interests does not necessarily establish proof of a conspiracy. Also, a person who has no knowledge of a conspiracy but who happens to act in a way that advances some purpose of one does not thereby become a conspirator.

Conspiracy is the combination or agreement of two or more persons joining together to attempt to accomplish some unlawful purpose. It is a kind of "partnership in criminal purposes" and willful participation in such a scheme or agreement followed by the commission of an overt act by one of the conspirators is sufficient to complete the offense of "conspiracy" itself even though the ultimate criminal object of the conspiracy is not accomplished or carried out.

An agreement between two or more persons to do an unlawful act or an act that may become by the combination injurious to others—formerly, this offense was much more circumscribed in its meaning than it is now. Lord Coke describes it as "a consultation or agreement between two or more to appeal or indict an innocent person falsely and maliciously, whom accordingly they cause to be indicted or appealed and afterwards the party is acquitted by the verdict of twelve men."

The crime of conspiracy, according to its modern interpretation, may be of two kinds: (1) conspiracies against the public; or (2) such as endanger the public health, violate public morals, insult public justice, destroy the public peace, or affect public trade or business. To remedy these evils, the guilty persons may be indicted in the name of the commonwealth. Conspiracies against individuals are such as they have a tendency to injure them in their persons, reputation, or property. The remedy in these cases is either by indictment or by a civil action.[*]

In the legal context, conspiracy is involved in a major portion of extended or ongoing white collar financial crimes. Therefore, the investigator must be

---

[*] The 'Lectric Law Library, "Conspiracy," lectlaw.com/def/c103.htm.

familiar with the elements, statutory provisions, and judicial determinations that relate to conspiracy.

The preceding definition of conspiracy identifies the elements of the crime, which must be proved for conviction of the crime.

Conspiracy requires two or more people to be involved in the planning and attempt to commit another crime (the object crime must be included in the indictment). The object crime is not required to be successful. As an example: Four individuals attempt to rob a bank. Three enter the bank and demand money from the teller. One remains in the getaway car. The teller sets off a silent alarm, and the police arrive before the robbers get the money. The robbers can be charged with attempted robbery (the object crime) and, if the evidence to support the elements is obtained, conspiracy to commit bank robbery.

At times, corporations and other functional entities are treated as individuals. Therefore, they can be charged as coconspirators. To be included in a conspiracy, the person or entity must willingly agree to participate. Coercion, not being aware of the plan, and incompetence are valid defenses to a charge of conspiracy. However, the members of a conspiracy are not required to know the plans of the conspiracy in their entirety.

The conspiracy is not consummated until at least one overt act is committed by one of the members in furtherance of the conspiratorial goal. People may get together and plan an elaborate scheme to break in and steal the gold in Fort Knox; but if it is merely an intellectual exercise and no steps are taken to bring the plan about, no conspiracy exists.

Another factor that must be addressed is that the overt act committed was done knowingly to accomplish some part of the conspiracy plan. For example, three partners may plan to burn their store and relocate to a new mall. Until a direct step is taken to implement the plan, such as tampering with the electrical system or buying flammables and storing them in an unsafe location, the conspiracy is not complete.

Although conspiracy is common in white collar financial crimes, it is not required. Many schemes are developed and implemented by single individuals. Crimes of tax fraud, forgery, and theft by fraud are often perpetrated by individuals without help or assistance.

Fraud

Fraud is a necessary factor in the commission of white collar financial crimes. It is the shell of the crime that the investigator must penetrate. Fraud is used to conceal, distort, mislead, and confuse the investigation of financial crimes. It may be used multiple times and at any point in the criminal plan, execution, and concealment of the crime. Trickery, deceit, and false representations are all part of fraud. The following is a general definition of fraud:

> Fraud, To Defraud—The term "fraud" is generally defined in the law as an intentional misrepresentation of material existing fact made by one person to another with knowledge of its falsity and for the purpose of inducing the other person to act, and upon which the other person relies with resulting injury or damage. (Fraud may also include an omission or intentional failure to state material facts, knowledge of which would be necessary to make other statements not misleading.)

To make a "misrepresentation" simply means to state as a fact something that is false or untrue. (To make a material "omission" is to omit or withhold the statement of a fact, knowledge of which is necessary to make other statements not misleading.)

Thus, to constitute fraud, a misrepresentation must be false (or an omission must make other statements misleading), and it must be "material" in the sense that it relates to a matter of some importance or significance rather than a minor or trivial detail.

To constitute fraud, a misrepresentation (or omission) must also relate to an "existing fact." Ordinarily, a promise to do something in the future does not relate to an existing fact and cannot be the basis of a claim for fraud unless the person who made the promise did so without any present intent to perform it or with a positive intent not to perform it. Similarly, a mere expression of opinion does not relate to an existing fact and cannot be the basis of a claim of fraud unless the person stating the opinion has exclusive or superior knowledge of existing facts that are inconsistent with such opinion.

To constitute fraud, the misrepresentation (or omission) must be made knowingly and intentionally, not as a result of mistake or accident; that is, that the person either knew or should have known of the falsity of the misrepresentation (or the false effect of the omission), or that he made the misrepresentation (or omission) in negligent disregard of its truth or falsity.

Finally, to constitute fraud, the plaintiff must prove that the defendant intended for the plaintiff to rely upon the misrepresentation (and/or omission); that the plaintiff did in fact rely upon the misrepresentation (and/or omission); and that the plaintiff suffered injury or damage as a result of the fraud.

In some cases (depending on the specifics of the case and the law), when it is shown that a defendant made a material misrepresentation (and/or omission) with the intention that the plaintiff rely upon it, then, under the law, the plaintiff may rely upon the truth of the representation, even though its falsity could have been discovered had he or she made an investigation, unless he or she knows the representation to be false or its falsity is obvious to him or her.

In other cases, when it is shown that a defendant made a material misrepresentation (and/or omission) with the intention that the plaintiff rely upon it, the plaintiff must prove that his reliance was justified. If, in the exercise of reasonable care for the protection of his own interests, the plaintiff could have learned the truth of the matter by making a reasonable inquiry or investigation under the circumstances presented but failed to do so, then it cannot be said that he "justifiably" relied upon such misrepresentations (and/or omissions).

For injury or damage to be the result of fraud, it must be shown that, except for the fraud, the injury or damage would not have occurred.

The word "material" means that the subject matter of the statement (or concealment) related to a fact or circumstance that would be important to the decision to be made as distinguished from an insignificant, trivial, or unimportant detail (e.g., regarding insurance fraud). To be material, an assertion (or concealment) must relate to a fact or circumstance that would affect the liability of an insurer (if made during an investigation of the loss), or would affect the decision to issue the policy, or the amount of coverage or the premium (if made in the application for the policy).*

The degree and number of misrepresentations in financial crimes may vary depending on the size and complexity of the scheme. This can be shown through our examples of the thief and the banker. The thief has to conceal the stolen property, and the fence needs to misrepresent that the property is not stolen. This may happen through the altering or removal of property identification numbers or tags. In contrast, the banker has to misrepresent the legitimacy of the loans, disguise the loan-processing system, trick the bank into writing off the loans, conceal the true nature of the source of the funds, and make the illegal funds received appear as a legitimate source of income.

How does this part of the financial crime affect the preparation, direction, and sequence of the investigation? The investigators have to familiarize themselves with the business or industry, and identify the frauds employed to complete the crime. Then, evidence has to be collected, analyzed, and presented, which proves not only the crime but also the fraud schemes used to commit the crime. The investigation must clearly show that all of the elements of fraud were met and present it in a manner that is easily and readily understood. "An intentional misrepresentation of a material fact" becomes intentionally lying about something that will make others act in a way that will injure themselves. The lie can be an open falsification (commission) or a failure to give other information that would alter the victim's decisions (omission).

---

* The 'Lectric Law Library, "Fraud, to Defraud," lectlaw.com/def/f079.htm.

Categories of Theft

4

In Chapter 1, the motivations for financial crimes from the investigative perspective were discussed. We also need to address how wealth can be increased and accumulated. In general, there are only two ways to increase wealth: increase the flow of income or decrease the flow of expenses. Figure 4.1 is a simple diagram.

As simplistic as this seems, the methods used to accomplish accumulating wealth by either means are limitless. From the standpoint of the investigation, a financial crime can use either avenue to gain wealth by concealing what has taken place and is actually taking place. The receipt of income can be understated or the payment of expenses can be overstated. Either of these would constitute a willful misrepresentation or (if the amount is substantial or the income is concealed) a criminal act. Keep in mind that for criminal prosecution the investigation must show harm, knowledge, and intent beyond a reasonable doubt. A business can thrive and expand, and individuals can increase their wealth using legal or illegal means. One of the first steps in a financial investigation is to determine which way gains are being concealed.

Legal ways for an individual to increase wealth by increasing income would include getting a raise in pay, changing to a better paying job, or getting a second source of income. Increased income for businesses could be generated legally by raising the price of their product or service, expanding their customer base to increase sales, or selling off obsolete equipment or materials. An individual can legally decrease expenses (to increase wealth) by purchasing similar products at a lower price, conserving items such as utilities and gasoline, better budgeting, and reducing consumption. Businesses can legally decrease expenses by improving technology to reduce production

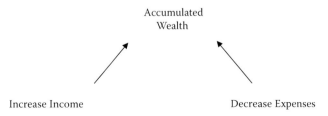

Figure 4.1 Two ways to increase wealth.

costs, reducing overhead costs through improved efficiency, or finding the materials they need to do business at a lesser cost.

There are also illegal means of accumulating wealth, which include the general categories of theft, fraud, and unfair practices. The methods used to accomplish these criminal activities are only limited by the imagination of the perpetrators. New laws and innovative law enforcement tactics may put a stop to some of the schemes used, but inventive criminal minds will find new schemes to replace them.

Theft is a common thread found in financial crimes. In general, it is the willful taking of property from another (without his or her permission or knowledge) for your own use. From the criminal standpoint, it is the illegal taking of the legal property of another. The law has separated and distinguished several variations in theft. The following are some of the definitions.

Theft

Theft is the generic term for all crimes in which a person intentionally and fraudulently takes personal property of another without permission or consent and with the intent to convert it to the taker's use (including potential sale). In many states, if the value of the property taken is low (for example, less than $500.00), the crime is "petty theft," but it is "grand theft" for larger amounts, designated misdemeanor or felony, respectively. Theft is synonymous with "larceny." Although robbery (taking by force), burglary (taken by entering unlawfully), and embezzlement (stealing from an employer) are all commonly thought of as theft, they are distinguished by the means and methods used, and are separately designated as those types of crimes in criminal charges and statutory punishments.

Burglary

Burglary is the crime of breaking and entering into a structure for the purpose of committing a crime. No great force is needed (pushing open a door or slipping through an open window is sufficient) if the entry is unauthorized. Contrary to common belief, a burglary is not necessarily for theft. It can apply to any crime, such as assault or sexual harassment, whether the intended criminal act is committed or not. Originally under English common law, burglary was limited to entry in residences at night, but it has been expanded to all criminal entries into any building or even into a vehicle.

Larceny

Larceny is the crime of taking the goods of another person without permission (usually secretly) with the intent of keeping them. It is one form of theft. Some states differentiate between grand larceny and petty larceny based on the value of the stolen goods. Grand larceny is a felony with a state prison sentence as a punishment, and petty larceny is usually limited to county jail time.

Robbery

Robbery is the direct taking of property (including money) from a person (victim) through force, threat, or intimidation. Robbery is a felony (crime punishable by a term in state or federal prison). "Armed robbery" involves the use of a gun or other weapon that can do bodily harm, such as a knife or club, and under most state laws carries a stiffer penalty (longer possible term) than robbery by merely taking. However, the term "robbery" is improperly used to describe thefts, including burglary (breaking and entering) and shoplifting (secret theft from the stock of a store), expressed: "We've been robbed."

Embezzlement

Embezzlement is the crime of stealing the funds or property of an employer, company, or government, or misappropriating money or assets held in trust.

Swindle

Swindle is to cheat through trick, device, false statements or other fraudulent methods with the intent to acquire money or property from another to which the swindler is not entitled. Swindling is a crime as one form of theft.[*]

"To swindle" in current dialog is often referred to as theft by fraud or theft by deception. This definition applies to most of the white collar financial crimes.

As the foregoing partial listing of the types of theft indicates, the methods used to perpetrate a theft are almost limitless. Some of the ways the individual can perpetrate a theft is by committing robbery, burglary, shoplifting, pickpocketing, embezzlement, tax evasion, or by running a financial fraud scheme.

---

[*] Reprinted with permission from the 2008 edition of Law.com. © 2008 ALM Properties, Inc.

Thefts perpetrated by businesses include copyright infringement, securities fraud, tax evasion, industrial espionage, and unfair business practices. Consumer fraud and environmental violations are often categorized as a separate type of white collar criminal activity. The root cause of these crimes would still meet our greed motive criteria in that the company attempts to overcharge for a product or reduce expenses through violating pollution standards.

As mentioned earlier, fraud and theft by fraud are involved in the majority of financial crimes. Federal criminal statutes have identified several specific types of fraud by major financial categories and written specific laws to identify the crimes and institute penalties. Federal law is specific to tax fraud, bank fraud, and securities fraud. There are also statutory references to fraudulent practices throughout the United States Code.

Theft can be perpetrated at any time by any entity. Forensic accounting is used to investigate the crimes of theft over a specific period of time and a wide scope of victims. White collar financial crimes against the government and certain other industries have often been erringly described as victimless crimes. Similar to pornography, illegal gambling, and prostitution, these crimes are now being viewed in context to the harm they cause to the general public. Insurance fraud, tax evasion, and credit card fraud increase the costs of these services to all the people who participate in or use them.

Financial fraud can be directed at the victims in different ways. The perpetrator can target a large number of victims for a single theft each, a single or limited number of victims repeatedly over a period of time, or target a specific type of business or industry.

In the first situation, the perpetrator could target a large number of victims through fraudulent telephone or mailing offers. After the monies are received, the perpetrator can move on to a new location and repeat the scheme. The victims in this type of scheme vary by the demographic group targeted. The elderly may be targeted in a phony social security or insurance scam, teens in a phony credit or association plan, investors in a bogus investment or financial planning scheme, or any other group that a specific scheme can be designed for. Often, the victims may not realize that they have been swindled, or they may feel that there is no recourse they can take.

In the second type of victimization, the victims will usually be individuals who have high incomes but limited business knowledge. Investment scams alleging to offer high-interest returns and schemes to avoid or defer taxes, and offshore-banking schemes have been targeted at professional athletes, doctors and medical professionals, politicians, and even lawyers. Embezzlement from a bank or other business is another example of the single target that is victimized over an extended period of time. Often these victims will not report the theft to avoid embarrassment or adverse publicity.

In the third fraud example, a specific type of business can be the target. Filing false insurance claims and arson-for-hire target insurance companies. Filing bogus lawsuits for allegedly defective or tainted products can be targeted against food service industries or manufacturing companies. These victims may absorb the costs of the claims (and pass them on to their customers) to avoid bad publicity and the high costs of litigation.

If the scheme of the financial criminal succeeds initially, the perpetrator usually develops a confidence that the scheme is undetectable. As this confidence increases with each fraudulent theft, the thief expands the scheme to more victims or steals more and more money from them. This progression of greed and pride in the scheme are the factors that bring the theft by fraud to the attention of law enforcement. Forensic accounting is an effective method to combat financial crimes that have been running for extended time periods because the criminal activity can be presented sequentially over regular periods of time.

Complex financial frauds involving several coconspirators are designed to conceal the theft by fraud deep within the financial operations and to split the criminal culpability between the conspirators. Having multiple coconspirators reduces the legal exposure for culpability by separating and limiting civil or criminal liability for each of the participants. It also provides a basis for deniability of intent to violate any given law or regulation.

The drawback of conspiratorial crimes is that a weak link will break the chain. Any one of the coconspirators may decide to give the others up for leniency if he or she believes that the investigation will be successful. Forensic financial investigations identify the total amount of theft by fraud and each coconspirator's share in the illegitimate gains from the scheme. Receipt of a share of the ill-gotten proceeds is a powerful piece of evidence in both jury and bench trial litigation. It shows the conspirators' knowledge of the scheme and the financial gains that weigh heavily to the individual's intent to participate in the conspiracy.

The following is an example of a forensic accounting investigation that was used to successfully prosecute all three coconspirators in a loan fraud scheme.

The three conspirators were an owner of a bank, the president of the bank, and a prominent local businessman. They formed a high-risk business loan company that received federal insurance on loans to businesses that could not qualify for conventional financing. The company was allowed to charge a higher rate of interest on the loans it made to these businesses. The theory behind the government insuring some of these loans was to encourage new and minority business development. For the customers (businesses that could not obtain financing anywhere else), this was their last and only opportunity to get the financing they needed.

The scheme involved selecting borrowers with the best potential for repayment and to accept others through the federal guarantee programs. In discussions with the borrowers, the conspirators would require the borrower to pay a substantial loan origination fee. They would include the fee, usually between 15% and 30% of the principal the borrower was seeking, in the original loan amount. The conspirators would file the required paperwork with the government without disclosing the loan origination fee. When the loan was completed, they would take their fee off the top of the loan proceeds. The borrower was required to pay interest on the total loan amount and the fee paid. This scheme was in direct violation of banking laws and lending regulations. A sample transaction would look like this:

Loan needed by victim	$125,000.00
Loan issued	$150,000.00
Kickback to conspirators	$25,000.00
Proceeds to victim	$125,000.00

This was not the end of the scheme devised by the conspirators. The prominent businessman used losses in his legitimate business to offset the personal taxes that would be owed on the illegal income. He reported all of the kickbacks and used losses he was entitled to from prior years (loss carry forwards) to avoid paying income taxes on the kickbacks. This also made the kickback money appear to be generated from a legitimate business (money laundering). The kickback amounts were split equally among the three conspirators. The bank owner and the bank president did not report any of this income on their personal returns.

This appeared to be a perfect scheme with the kickbacks being received when the loan proceeds were given to the borrowers. If the borrower did default, the payments were insured through government programs. The borrowers were not likely to complain about the "origination fee" because they had no other means of getting financing. Finally, the illegal funds were being laundered through an unrelated business, and no discrepancies needed to be made to the loan company books. This was important because federally insured financial businesses may undergo more frequent and rigorous audits than other types of businesses.

A complaint was received from one of the borrowers. The complaint related to the interest rate being charged on the loan. Ironically, the origination fee was not mentioned. The forensic accounting investigation disclosed:

1. The books and records of the high-risk loan company identified the borrowers.
2. Bank records for the loan company disclosed that the funds to borrowers were for the full amount of the loans made.
3. Interviews with the customers did not provide any kickback information.
4. Inspection of borrower repayment records showed the initial kickbacks.
5. Follow-up interviews with the borrowers uncovered the kickback scheme.

A review of the financial records of the bank owner and the bank president showed a substantial increase in wealth since the loan business started. The bank records of the businessman showed some checks in the same amount as the kickbacks being cashed on the same day or the day after they were paid. On the same day that these checks were cashed, there were cash deposits made to the accounts of the other two conspirators in one-third portions of the amount.

A cursory review of the businessman's records for his business showed a sharp rise in income while the loan business was in operation. The businessman had loss carry forwards for prior years that were used to offset the increased income reported. These prior year losses were large enough to ensure that the extra income would not be subject to income taxes. This served a dual purpose in making the kickbacks virtually tax free and in laundering the money received to appear to be generated from legitimate operations. A further review of his records showed that the income could not be generated from his regular business operations. This was shown by analyzing his prior year inventory and cost of goods sold (the result being gross profit) and comparing them to the years the loan scheme was in operation. His markup on sales averaged 15% before the loan scam, and it jumped to 65% while the loan company was operating. There were no significant changes in the prices he paid for the goods he sold or in the prices he charged his customers. Inventories did not increase, and in one year he would have had to sell more than he had to justify the income reported.

During the three trials (the defense motion to sever the cases was granted) the forensic accounting investigation results were presented to the jury. The defense argued that the kickbacks were origination fees that were agreed to by the borrowers, and that these were legitimate transactions. The financial evidence showed that the origination fees were not reported in the loan company books and records, that the kickbacks were diverted and laundered through an unrelated business, and that the three conspirators each received a third of the kickbacks. This was sufficient to convince the jury that the conspirators intentionally committed loan fraud and were in conspiracy together. Each defendant received a 10-year sentence and a $10,000 fine. Civilly, they were required to repay the origination fees, and they were assessed income taxes on the ill-gotten gains. Ironically, the businessman received a tax refund for a few hundred dollars for one tax year. This was because he had overreported his income trying to launder the kickbacks. He received the check while in federal prison.

The case provides several good examples of how forensic accounting can enhance and fortify a criminal prosecution and some of the problems encountered in presenting a circumstantial case. When one or a few individuals have total control of the business operation and record keeping, it is easier to conceive and execute a criminal conspiracy. The three conspirators had backgrounds in the areas of banking and business. These provided them a special knowledge of how the loan business should look to people outside of business. The three were prominent individuals in the community, and their customers relied on them to accurately and honestly conduct the transactions.

The loan documents prepared and given to the customers were official and legitimate in appearance. The loan fraud victims were not aware of the fact that they were being victimized. Several customers were reluctant to provide information based on allegiance to the loan company, which was their only hope.

Regulation of loan fees and charges are complicated enough to sway a jury into believing that violations could occur unwittingly and could be honest mistakes. The financial association between the three individuals had to be established beyond a reasonable doubt. The dollar amounts of the financial crime had to be substantial to show motive. The concealment of the kickbacks and the ability to trace the funds through the unrelated business were crucial to establish intent to commit the crimes. The laundered funds had to be shown as not being generated through normal business activity. Most important, it shows the benefits in "following the money."

The preceding case is an example of financial criminals targeting victims who are in desperate situations. Schemes are also developed that play on the natural greed of their victims. One of the first schemes used to defraud people of their money using the promise of high returns on an investment was developed by Charles Ponzi. This scheme was so innovative at the time that this type of scheme is still referred to as a Ponzi scheme.

From *Ponzi Scheme: The True Story of a Financial Legend,* by Mitchell Zuckoff

Charles (Carlos) Ponzi arrived by boat in the United States in 1903. He sailed with a few hundred dollars to his name. He gambled during the voyage and had two dollars and fifty cents left when he arrived. At first he did not speak English, but quickly picked it up while working a variety of menial jobs. He worked as a dishwasher for a while and was promoted to waiter. He was later fired for cheating the customers and gambling.

In 1907, Ponzi moved to Montreal, Canada, and worked as an assistant teller in the Banco Zarossi. This bank was started by Luigi Zarossi to accommodate the growing number of Italian immigrants arriving in Montreal. At the time, banks were paying two to three percent interest on deposits. Zarossi began paying six percent and his bank was growing rapidly. The high interest rate and a series of bad real estate loans put the bank in serious financial trouble. Ponzi was trying to find a way to go back to the United States. He found out about the bank's problems and forged a customer's check for $423.58. His large expenditures after the forgery drew the attention of the authorities. When confronted by the police, he held out his hands in the gesture of being ready to be hand-cuffed and said, "I'm guilty."

Ponzi spent three years in a Quebec prison for his crime. He was released in 1911 and returned to the United States. He became involved in an immigrant smuggling scheme, was caught, and spent another two years in prison in Atlanta, Georgia. When released, he eventually returned to Boston, Massachusetts. He met an Italian girl, Rose Gnecco. She was captured by his charming ways, and they were married in 1918. He continued to work at a variety of jobs. After several months, he came up with the idea of compiling a trader's guild directory of companies. He was unable to make the venture work, and his first attempt at business failed.

A few weeks passed when Ponzi received a letter from a company in Spain inquiring about the directory. Contained in the envelope was a postal reply coupon. Ponzi had never seen one before and researched the coupon. The postal reply coupon was a form of including a return enve-lope with postage paid, for foreign mailings. As an example, a person in the United States could purchase the coupon and include it in a letter mailed to Europe. The coupon could then be redeemed in Europe for their stamps to cover postage for the reply.

The rates for the coupons were originally set during an international postal union agreement in 1907. This established a set rate of exchange on postage for international mailings. The costs of the coupons were equiva-lent between the currencies of the different countries. You were able to buy the coupon at the original 1907 rate and exchange it for stamps at that rate.

After WWI, several foreign currencies were highly devalued, but the exchange rate had not changed. Ponzi noticed that he could purchase the coupon for about a penny (US) in Europe and cash it in the United States for about 6 cents. His first step was to exchange American currency for a foreign currency at a good rate. His agents in the foreign country would purchase the coupons where the currencies were devalued and send them back to Ponzi, who would then cash in the coupons. Ponzi claimed to be making an investment return, after costs and expenses, of more than 400%.

Ponzi began recruiting friends and associates to invest in his new ven-ture. He offered a 50% return in 90 days. Quickly he reduced the time for the return to 45 days. He explained that the coupon redemption plan made these profits easy. He began the Securities Exchange Company as his business. Ponzi was a good salesman. He obtained his first investors and paid them off as promised. As the word spread his business grew and grew. He hired employees and paid them commissions on the investments they brought in. By February of 1920, Ponzi had deposited $5,290.00 in profits.

The following month he had increased his profits to about $30,000.00, and people were lined up to invest. He sent agents out to other parts of

New England. His persuasive sales pitch and the huge profits offered gave him thousands of investors. By May he had several hundred thousand dollars. He deposited a lot of his money in the Hanover Trust Bank in hopes of becoming its president. He did manage to gain a controlling interest in the bank.

By July, Ponzi had more than two million dollars. Most of his investors were so confident, that they rolled over their investment with interest, as the investments matured. Ponzi began a lifestyle of wealth. He purchased a huge home, brought his mother to America from Italy on a first class passage ocean liner, and became a local hero in the Italian community.

Although money continued to come in, his expenses and lifestyle drained more than was being received. A lawsuit was filed for prior debts. Although unsuccessful, the suit caused doubts and fears in the investors. Soon there was a run on the Securities Exchange Company. Ponzi calmly paid the investors that wanted out and the run ended. Business went back on the upswing after good publicity and he was again bringing in thousands of dollars a month.

Curiosity and possibly envy drove the newspaper to assign investigative reporters, and the Commonwealth of Massachusetts began an investigation. He appeared to be cooperating with the investigation and was able to delay their efforts. Ponzi had no real records of his financial transactions.

Near the end of July, the newspaper began a series of articles questioning Ponzi's investment scheme, and was able to get Clarence Barron, a financial analyst and publisher of Barron's financial paper to look into the scheme. Barron noted that, although Ponzi promised phenomenal returns, he did not invest any of his own money into the scheme. It was estimated that 160 million coupons would be needed for the scheme and only about 30 thousand were in circulation.

These stories caused another panic for the investors, and another run on the Securities Exchange occurred. He began paying off investors again and tried to reassure them of their investments. Many believed him and left their money in. The newspaper reported on Ponzi's prior criminal record, and in August he was arrested on 86 counts of mail fraud. Many of the investors refused to believe his guilt, either from blind faith or the inability to accept their own foolishness.

On November 30, 1920, Ponzi pleaded guilty to mail fraud and was sentenced to five years in prison. He was released after three and a half years to face the State charges that were pending. He was found guilty and sentenced to nine more years. Ponzi was released on parole in 1934 and immediately deported to Italy.

Source: Zuckoff, Mitchell, *Ponzi's Scheme: The True Story of a Financial Legend*, Random House: New York, 2005.

Variations on this scheme have been used ever since. The key ingredients are to offer a phenomenal return on an investment, find investors anxious to make large profits with little or no effort on their part, make the scheme appear to be on a new undiscovered investment opportunity, and an understanding on when to close up shop and take the profits. The following section on schemes has examples of this type of crime and the forensic accounting investigation used to prosecute it.

Schemes

In this case, there were two men involved in setting up a get-rich-quick scheme involving investments in genetically superior cattle. Major cattle breeders invest up to hundreds of thousands of dollars for the very best bulls and cows for breeding purposes. If the bull and cow pair can produce calves that have less fat, more meat, and mature quicker, they can greatly increase the profitability of a cattle-raising enterprise. In this case, a medical school dropout and a person who was a veterinarian assistant came up with the scheme that a fertilized egg from a prize pair of cattle could be placed inside the womb of any other cow and be calved with the same genetic qualities as the prize pair. They realized that obtaining the egg and sperm would be possible at a high price (about $3,000.00 each), but the owner of a prize pair would not risk the health of a prize cow by allowing fertilized eggs to be removed. The two devised a scheme to sell to investors:

They would rent a small extra barn from a rancher and buy a dozen
   breed cows.
They set up an elaborate veterinarian work area in the barn.
They rented a very nice office in a nearby town and set up a business front.
They attended several cattle auctions and solicited customers from
   the crowd.

The investment plan they proposed was that they would purchase egg and sperm from several prize bulls and purchase one prize breed cow. They would inject the breed cow with fertility serum so she could produce 12 to 15 eggs during ovulation. The eggs would be fertilized with the prize bull sperm, and the fertilized eggs (genetically superior) would be placed in the wombs of the other cows. When these cows calved, they would sell the cows for $5,000.00 to $8,000.00 each, and the bull calves for $50,000.00 to $80,000.00 each. The investors could purchase shares in increments of $10,000.00 (costs of egg fertilization and planting). The return on the investment was promoted at 60% to 120% per year (birthing period for cows). They offered tours of the veterinarian laboratory setup to prospective investors.

They also showed cattle on other ranches nearby, claiming that these cows were also part of their holdings. They financed the start-up expenses through a bank loan for $220,000.00. The following are the events that took place:

1. They began with 16 investors. They deposited the money and wrote phony checks for nonexistent business expenses. They reported a net profit of about 8% of gross income (the $160,000.00).
2. After 2 months, they began paying the original investors $800.00 a month.
   They continued soliciting customers and word spread on the success from the first customers.
3. The business continued for 2 more years in which they took in $2.2 million.
4. They paid out about $180,000.00 to investors; they convinced most of them to keep reinvesting their profits.

The scheme came to light when one investor, greedy for even greater profits, contacted the prize bull owner allegedly used in the business and found out that he knew nothing about the business front or the two conspirators. This investor contacted the police and an investigation began. During the police investigation, the conspirators tried to convince the police that they only needed the initial sperm from a prize bull so that they could use their own genetic bull and cows for the production of the fertile eggs. They also offered the investor his investment and profits (approximately $22,000.00). The investor declined, believing their story. A forensic accounting investigation disclosed the following:

1. The alleged veterinarian fabricated diplomas and a license to post on the business office wall.
2. The conspirators had investors in five different states.
3. The scheme netted the conspirators over $800,000.00 each during the 27 months it was in operation.
4. Both conspirators deposited most of their take in a bank in another state, probably preparing to relocate their operation.
5. Total assets for the business amounted to $32,000.00 (cows and office furniture).
6. None of the sales recorded in the company books ever occurred.
7. Two of the investors actually made a profit.

During the investigation, a search warrant was executed for the business office. The falsified license and college degrees were part of the records taken. The warrant also made the false business ledgers and records available, and identified the out-of-state bank account. The conspirators pleaded guilty and received 10-year sentences. The funds that remained were forfeited.

Another situation in which forensic accounting techniques can play an extremely important part is in the investigation of criminal enterprises. The following example demonstrates how effective the financial investigation can be in purely criminal activities. Keep in mind that the criminal enterprise is driven by the same motivation as legitimate and fraudulent enterprises—greed. The difference lies in that the criminal enterprise does not set up an elaborate front to conceal the criminal activity (except for money-laundering purposes) but attempts to conceal the criminal activity entirely.

In this next case, the criminal activity was to import and distribute marijuana. The source of the marijuana was Central and South America. It would be transported on a small barge across the Caribbean and up the eastern coast of the United States. Smaller boats would sail out to the barge and unload the shipment. The barge would carry between 1200 and 3600 pounds of marijuana on each trip. The marijuana would be put on trucks and taken to one of five rural farmhouses in the Midwest (the farm location would change for each load). At the farms, the marijuana would be packaged in 1-pound bricks and plastic wrapped (they used grocery-type wrapping machines). Some of the packages would be sold to distributors in nearby states, with the bulk of the loads being hidden in vacation vehicles (recreational vehicles and motor homes) and driven to a major distributor in the Southwest United States.

The two main couples involved in the narcotics case lived in a large city about 100 to 150 miles away from the farms used for packaging the marijuana. The police department had received anonymous reports that the four used and sold marijuana. Although their operation did almost all of its business outside the city and state where they lived, surveillance and other police investigation techniques did not uncover any illegal activity. A forensic accounting investigation was initiated. The initial investigation revealed the following information:

Each of the two couples purchased homes 4 years ago.
The homes cost about $500,000.00 each, and both couples made down
   payments of 20%.
The homes were paid off in 3 years, and substantial improvements
   were made.
The improvements were documented by building permits filed by the
   remodeling contractors and totaled $380,000.00 and $420,000.00.
The only employment that they had were part-time positions that ended
   4 years ago.
Each of the four had late-model cars that were purchased for cash. The
   two men got a new car each year, trading in their 1-year-old vehicles
   and paying the difference in cash.

A surveillance at a rock concert observed their use and sharing of marijuana with friends.

Based on the surveillance and the cursory financial investigation, search warrants were obtained for their homes.

No narcotics or drug paraphernalia were found. Financial records (included in the warrant) seized included recent bank statements, real estate closing documents, vehicle titles, credit card receipts, telephone and utility bills, and various receipts and a substantial amount of cash.

Note: It is important to include financial records in any search warrant affidavit if the officer can show that the use of the proceeds from the criminal activity is likely to be identified by the records at the location to be searched. This will be discussed further in the following chapter.

Follow-up investigation of the leads found in the records provided a wealth of information. The bank records identified the account numbers, safety deposit boxes, cash deposits and withdrawals, and businesses where major purchases were made. Real estate documents identified the agent who worked for them in finding the property, their financial qualifications to buy the properties, and witnesses to the actual transactions. Vehicle titles showed the use of cash for the purchases and what vehicles were traded in. With the exception of one small charge, the credit card receipts showed minor local charges for gas and groceries. The one other charge was for $5.00 at a five-star hotel on the West Coast. Follow-up contacts revealed that the foursome spent at least 2 to 3 weeks each year at the hotel, vacationing and entertaining friends. They spent an average of $38,000.00 in cash each year for the past 3 years. Telephone records showed repeat calls to numbers on the East Coast and Southwest. The cash tested positive for very small traces of marijuana.

Eventually, the forensic accounting investigation uncovered the source of the marijuana brought into the United States, the owner of the barge transporting the marijuana, several of the men hired to unload the barge and load the trucks, the individuals who handled the packaging, the individual who owned the five rural properties and assisted in the packaging, three of the drug mules used to transport the marijuana out west, and the major distributor who purchased most of the marijuana. More than 40,000 kilograms of marijuana were distributed by this drug conspiracy.

Eight individuals were prosecuted, and all eight plead guilty to various charges. The two couples and the farm owner pled guilty to four counts each of tax evasion, importation of marijuana, distribution of marijuana, and conspiracy to import and distribute. The mules pled guilty to filing false tax returns (they were the first to come forward and cooperate). Assets of the defendants totaling $3.2 million were seized as proceeds of the criminal activity, including the two homes, vehicles, bank accounts, farm properties, and a $1.2 million house in Hawaii.

Going back to the beginning of this case, the investigators could have settled for a misdemeanor arrest of the two couples for the possession of marijuana at the rock concert. Using forensic accounting techniques and spending almost a year on the investigation rewarded the investigators with a very large narcotics case and the satisfaction of putting an end to a major narcotics operation.

The three cases discussed in this chapter show the importance and effectiveness of following the paper trail using accepted procedures and methods of proof. Although the evidence is circumstantial, the preponderance of evidence can effectively demonstrate criminal intent to commit a crime. The cases discussed touch on what items can be part of the paper trail. The next chapter will go into more detail on what makes up the paper trail and what these items look like.

The Paper Trail

5

What Is the "Paper Trail?"

The paper trail is exactly that—a trail of paper for each financial transaction. Everyone wants the security of proof of ownership of the things they have. For tax purposes, people also keep a wide variety of records to support the claims on the returns they file. Businesses maintain still other records to promote efficiency, identify their best customers, and evaluate their operations. Even financial schemers want to know how well they are doing and who the best targets are. The documents can be as simple as a handwritten IOU to volumes of corporate ledgers. These are the documents that make up the paper trail.

In almost every financial transaction, there are multiple records prepared for what has taken place. When you buy a car, a copy of the vehicle documents goes to the lender (if it is financed), a copy goes to the purchaser for registration and licensing purposes, a copy goes to the state in which the car is registered, a copy may go to the manufacturer for warranty purposes, and a copy may go to another lender if the equity in the vehicle is used for collateral on another loan. Even something as small as buying a hamburger gets documented. A receipt goes to the customer (which can be used if the purchase is tax deductible), and a copy of the sale is recorded on the cash register to document the sale by the restaurant.

As two or more parties almost always receive documentation for each financial transaction, the paper trail can be obtained from various sources. Third parties (those people unrelated to the investigation but who are doing business with the subject of the investigation) are a valuable resource in documenting an individual's transactions. The difficulty lies in being able to identify the third parties. Often, observation of the subject during interviews or through surveillance can provide leads regarding the third parties that have had financial dealings with the subject.

The best sources of information are usually the subjects themselves if the investigator conducts a thorough interview. Because forensic accounting investigations cover an extended period of time, it is important to know the history of the subject. More details on interviewing techniques will be covered in a later chapter. If the subjects are confident in their schemes, they will often provide information and documents to persuade the investigator that no wrongdoing has occurred. Often the records provided will be the falsified ones in an attempt to conceal the financial crime. The records of the subject may also be obtained through the execution of a search warrant. For this, the investigator needs to provide a judge with proof that probable cause exists to believe that the documents are relevant to the investigation of the alleged crime and likely to be at the location for which the warrant is requested.

What Does the Paper Trail Look Like?

The following are some of the most common financial documents used in forensic accounting investigation.

Check Registers

The most common form of personal and business accounting documentation is the check register or checkbook. People log in the information about the checks they write and the deposits they make to their checking accounts. It is hoped that they will reconcile their bank accounts when they receive their monthly account statements to ensure that they have recorded the transactions accurately. The check register can provide a wealth of information depending on how diligent account holders are in recording their transactions. There are columns for the date written, payee, check number, and amount. Other columns are included for coding automatic deposits and payments, automated teller machine transactions, debit card transactions, and telephonic transfers. For individuals, this is often the personal paper trail for the majority of their financial transactions.

Although it may look different, the business check register contains similar financial transaction information. Business registers will include date, check number, payee, and amount. They may include a stub on which the business account affected by the transaction is included. The check is attached to the stub, and once the check is written, the check goes out and the stub remains as part of the business' internal record-keeping system. Many of today's business operations use electronic record-keeping and computerized accounting systems. In any case, checks are still written and recorded in business operations. Such recording provides the information necessary to accurately record business activities, verify and settle mistakes and claims, and let the business owners know the current status of the business' financial condition. These are the bank account owner's record of financial transactions.

In addition, the bank will maintain records for each account it handles. It will record daily transactions made in an account and prepare statements that summarize the account activity for each month. The bank keeps these statements, and copies are sent to account holders. The bank also maintains supporting documentation for the transactions shown in the statements, as well as for other debits and credits to the account that are made for charges against the accounts and interest paid.

In addition to keeping duplicate records of account-holder activities, banks maintain a wide variety of other customer financial transaction documentation. These would include the records of cash in and out, and account activity support for each teller's daily transactions. They would also include loan applications and their approvals and distributions; wire transfers between accounts; certificate of deposit purchases and redemptions; investment retirement accounts; and the purchase or cashing of cashier checks, money orders, and savings bonds. Banks are also required to maintain records of cash or currency transactions in excess of $10,000 by identifying the customer and completing a currency transaction report (CTR), a copy of which is filed with the U.S. Treasury Department. These provisions were implemented through the Bank Secrecy Act (31 CFR 103). For security purposes, most banks separate the responsibility for various types of transactions in different departments.

The records that are maintained by the bank on behalf of its customers are protected from public inspection. Records of the bank's internal business transactions have other legal protections that apply to personal and business records.

Stocks and Bonds

Another way money can be invested, or make the money work for you, is in the purchase of securities. The risk on the investment (the chance of losing money instead of making money) usually determines the potential for profits on the money invested. A safe investment such as U.S. savings bonds or municipal bonds will usually pay interest at a smaller percentage above the prime lending rate. Well-established companies will often pay a dividend per share owned and still offer the potential for the value of the stock to increase. Newer companies and those with lower capital asset holdings will offer the potential of greater stock price increases as the company matures and grows. Companies may also offer bonds for sale to increase their capital. Because corporate bonds are not governmentally secured or guaranteed, companies usually pay a higher interest rate to borrow funds in this way.

Publicly traded securities are usually handled through a brokerage firm. When the client orders a purchase or sale of securities, the brokerage firm will prepare a confirmation statement for the transaction. When the transaction is completed, the firm will again prepare a confirmation statement. These statements will show the amount of shares purchased or sold, the amount per share paid or received, and the commission or charge for the transaction.

Copies of these forms will be posted to the customer account and sent to the customer directly. Monthly statements (similar to bank statements) will be prepared and maintained, and a copy will be sent to the customer. These statements will show the date of the transactions, the payment of interest and dividends, amounts paid out of the accounts, and the current valuation of the securities held in the account.

Because the stockholders are the actual owners of the companies that issued the stock, the companies will also keep records of ownership to notify shareholders of matters for which they have a voting interest and will supply them with annual reports.

Stockbrokers have expanded their inventory of investments for clients to include commodities, mutual funds, over-the-counter (OTC) stocks, foreign securities, and other investments. The Securities and Exchange Commission (SEC) regulates the purchase, sale, issuance, and exchange of publicly held securities. Whenever an executive regulatory agency is involved in oversight of an industry, the paper trail increases dramatically. Oversight of the securities industry requires documentation to satisfy reporting regulations and for the purposes of auditing and review to ensure compliance with federal laws and regulations.

In addition to licensed and regulated investment opportunities, the individual may also invest in nonregulated businesses and organizations. These types of investments include part ownership in a business as a silent partner and joint ventures in business, or land development, or various product development. Private investments are not required to maintain the same type or number of records, but you can be sure that when people turn over their money to others they will require documents to show the investment and their ownership. The business receiving the investment will also want documentation to identify their patrons and to limit repayment liability. The days of doing business on your reputation and a handshake are a thing of the past.

Real Property

The term *real property* is used to differentiate tangible or physical assets that have a long life expectancy from those that only have a useful life of a few years. These assets would include items such as land, buildings, and heavy equipment and machinery. Due to the high cost of these types of assets, a large quantity of "paper" is generated for their purchase, sale, and transfer. These records are created and maintained for long periods of time by the buyers and sellers, and are also filed with several regulatory offices. Property assessors, taxing authorities, companies holding collateral interests, and investors require information on the acquisition and disposition of these types of assets. Anyone who has ever purchased a home is aware of the volume of records generated to complete the transaction.

The documents produced for the purchase of real property would begin with a purchase offer from the individual interested in buying the property to the seller listing the terms and conditions under which the buyer is willing to purchase the property. The seller can accept or decline the offer, or propose different terms in the form of a counteroffer. This is the documented version of price and terms negotiations. It is similar to the verbal negotiations that occur between a car salesman and a customer. Similar negotiations would occur between a customer and a building contractor in the form of a written contract to begin and complete the construction project. The negotiations are then finalized, and the contract would specify each party's responsibilities and obligation.

After the purchase/sale agreement is reached, other documents are prepared to complete the transaction. In a major transaction of this kind there are filing fees, tax allocations, financing costs, appraisal fees, and other costs involved in completing the sale. A closing statement is prepared to identify the related costs and to allocate these costs to the respective parties. When financing is involved, the statement will identify the lender and include the "points" paid for financing and the amount of funds borrowed. Once the closing is complete, other related documents (usually prepared in advance) are filed with the parties having an interest in the transaction and with the respective regulatory agencies.

The lender providing financing will file the mortgage against the property with the county registrar of deeds office to secure its interest in the property. Any subsequent transfer of the mortgage or satisfaction of the mortgage (acknowledging the amount being paid off) will also be filed in the registrar's office. The sale information will also be filed with the county assessor's office for valuation and tax assessment purposes. The purchasers will file a deed of record to show that they are the new owners of the property. The deed will give the legal description of the property (location determined by a grid system) and any easements, right-of-ways, or restrictions on the property use. Any outstanding liabilities for improvement to the property will also be filed in the form of liens against the property. Unpaid property tax liens are also filed in this manner.

Financial institutions involved in these transactions have other internal and regulatory rules for preparation, maintenance, and filing of documents to record all the financial aspects of the transaction. The mortgage or loan application requesting financing will include the amount of the loan, terms of repayment, interest rate, amount of down payment, and total amount of repayment (including interest) over the term or life of the loan. The bank will have the borrower complete a financial statement and will check the applicant's financial history before approving the loan. The financial statement will identify the applicant's net worth (assets and liabilities), sources and amounts of income currently being earned, and any other sources of funds to be used for the down payment or closing costs.

In these cases, the individual or business entity making the purchase and the one selling the property will have a complete "paper" history of the property. The government will have its own paper history, and other interested parties may also have records relating to the property. The paper trails created may look different because they serve different purposes, but they will all contain valuable information for the financial investigator.

The investigator must become familiar with the general record-keeping procedures, the location of the various paper trails, and the access restrictions that apply to the privacy of these records held by each interested party.

Vehicles

There are several documents prepared for the purchase and sale of vehicles. These provide proof of ownership and the amount of the transaction for taxing authorities, licensing and registration information, and a variety of other uses. The vehicle title identifies the make, model, style, and year the vehicle was manufactured; it also identifies the name and address of the buyer and seller (at the time of the transaction), the lien holders (if financing is involved), the vehicle identification number (VIN), the mileage (for cars and trucks) or engine usage (for boats and aircraft), accident damages in excess of a set amount, and the cost and taxes paid on the transfer of ownership.

Vehicles are unique in that the owner must be licensed to operate the vehicle, and the vehicle itself must be registered for use with a governmental authority. Licensing is usually required for a set period of time (one to several years). Registration is an annual requirement if the vehicle is to be used. Both licensing and registration generate another paper trail for the ownership of the vehicle. Visible proof of current registration is posted on the vehicle in the form of license plates (for cars, trucks, and motorized equipment) and by watercraft or wing numbers on boats and aircraft. The investigator needs to verify ownership through the paper trail. Access, use, and operation of a vehicle do not establish ownership.

There are different paper trails for each aspect of documentation required in the transfer of ownership of a vehicle. The buyer and seller receive copies of the sales agreement, and the state receives a copy for purposes of taxation. The purchaser and the state also receive copies of the title for the vehicle (the original is held by the lender until the financing is settled). The county in which the vehicle owner resides uses a copy of the title for registration of the vehicle to record any liens against the vehicle. Local law enforcement will also maintain records of the vehicle and owner if traffic or usage violations occur. The lending institution financing the vehicle will maintain the standard loan documents involved in the financing.

The VIN or registration number is a unique identification for the vehicle, similar to the social security numbers used to identify individuals. This

number is used by the manufacturer for warranty repair and recall information, the dealership for recording inventory and identifying the customer's
ownership, and law enforcement for recovering stolen vehicles and pursuing
forfeiture actions if the vehicle is used in the commission of a crime.

Other businesses may also maintain documentation on vehicles. Insurance companies will keep records of the cost, mileage, use, and authorized
operators of the vehicle, as well as any damages to or claims made against the
vehicle. Repair shops will keep records of the services they perform on the
vehicle, and storage and parking facilities will also keep records. Businesses
that provide usage facilities for the vehicle, such as airports, hangars, and
marinas, will also keep records of the vehicles they service. In addition, these
secondary record keepers can often provide information on the dates, times,
and frequency of usage; the operator and number of passengers or guests;
repairs and modifications made to the vehicle; and insights into the owner's
habits and lifestyle.

Other Assets

The "other assets" category covers all of the other major purchases an individual can make. As this category is so broad, only a few types of asset acquisitions will be discussed. The discussion should identify common traits in
the paper trails for a variety of other asset purchases. Taking time to identify
the parties of interest when a major purchase is made can be of help to the
investigator in finding the paper trails associated with each purchase.

Businesses will seek to satisfy the needs and wants of specific customer
bases. They will often research specific economic and demographic data, and
determine regional aspects for store locations and advertising. The customers
sought after may range from a wide base served by discount stores to a smaller
base served by department stores and specialty shops, up to the most expensive and exclusive stores that cater to a small clientele. As the motivation for
financial crimes is to gain wealth quickly, the perpetrator will want to enjoy
the fruits of the crime. They will often spend the ill-gotten gains soon after
receiving them and indulge themselves with the finer things in life.

Just as most people will spend what they can afford on a house or car, successful financial criminals will focus on purchasing more and more expensive
items to display their wealth and enhance their financial status. This does not
mean that affluence is an indicator of criminal behavior, but those who exhibit
sudden or unexplainable financial resources are often suspect. Financial investigations often begin with a report of these sudden or unexplainable increases
in wealth, sometimes out of social concern and often out of a degree of envy.

The paper trail for everyday purchases of food, clothing, and entertainment or miscellaneous items usually consists of no more than a duplicate

receipt (one for the store and one for the customer). Unless the customer is well known to the clerk as a regular customer, requests special services or items, or uses a credit card, it is difficult to document these type of purchases. If the store is more expensive or exotic in its merchandise, it will have fewer customers who will be more recognizable to the sales staff. Exclusive stores will carry items at expensive prices. To provide their customers with personal service, the stores will seek to know as much as possible about them in hopes of additional purchases and referrals. The following are a few of the most common luxury items and the variations that may occur in the paper trail.

Jewelry

The jeweler will remember the customer who comes in to purchase a three-carat diamond pendant or a handful of loose diamonds for several thousand dollars. He will make conversation, know the customer's name, and, most important, make a store record of the customer for reference so that others on the sales staff will be familiar with the customer. Expensive single stones are often microscopically marked for identification, and custom settings are often cataloged for identification and advertising purposes. The store will try to obtain information including name and address to maintain future contact with the customer, and often requests whether the customer would agree to being a reference for its goods and work. The usual business paper trail will be prepared. Other information, such as that already mentioned, will also be prepared. If insurance is provided, or if the client wants a service and cleaning contract, additional information will be prepared and maintained.

Furs and Clothing

Shops that provide expensive furs or custom clothing will also follow the sales pattern just described. Furriers will also offer and provide cleaning and storage services to their customers. Often the customer will receive appraisals on the item being purchased, and the coats will have a means of identification to certify the materials used and the quality of the product. Tailors and dressmakers will also keep contact information on their clientele for purposes of notifying the customer when the items are completed, and to let them know about new material and product availability.

Collectibles

This category is very broad and will include any item or set of items that an individual believes will increase in value over time or that holds special intrinsic value to the owner. The thought behind collectibles is that over time the number available to collectors will shrink due to breakage and wear and tear from usage. Any type of item may be collected, including autographs, bottle caps, rocks, or others with little or no initial cost, or items such as sports and celebrity memorabilia, coins, antiques, and artwork, which may have very high initial costs in acquisition. The following are a few of the more common and expensive items sought by collectors.

Antiques

This category can include a wide variety of items crafted or produced by prior generations. If the item is in good condition and rare in number, the value and costs can be enormous. These collectibles may originate from any period in history. Early Chinese, Asian, European, Greek, Roman, and Egyptian artifacts are some of the earliest collectibles. Other collectors may focus on a single culture and era in history, such as the colonial, Civil War, or World War periods in the United States. Still others may concentrate on a common category throughout history, such as military, political, books, toys, or movie posters.

Most collectors want to display their treasures as an accomplishment or an inspiration to others. Individuals who have acquired their wealth recently quickly pay the current or top price in starting their collections. It is also a way in which affluence and a large amount of disposable income can be shown off to others. The most valuable collectibles are usually well identified and categorized to ensure authenticity, and prevent fraud and deception. Many are sold through brokers or auction houses. Again, the investigator must identify all of the parties involved in the transaction and determine the extent of the paper trail required for one's own protection and peace of mind.

Philately

Philately, or stamp collecting, is a fairly common endeavor among collectors. It is estimated that there are more than 20 million stamp collectors in the United States alone. Extremely rare stamps are cataloged, and serious collectors know the number in existence. Although the average financial criminal may have no interest in stamps, their small size, the fact that these stamps are only identifiable to those who study them, and their known and constant value make this an easy way to transfer wealth in and out of the country. The paper trail on major purchases of stamps would include appraisals, authentications, sales and purchase records, and auction files if sold in that manner.

Numismatics

Numismatics, or the collecting of coins, is also a common category for collectors. Some collectors will focus on ancient coins minted during early periods of world history, and others may specialize in coins from a single country and even a specific type of coin (cent, nickel, dime, quarter, half, or dollar in U.S. denominations). Again, the rarity and condition of the coins will be the determining factor in the value of each piece. Rare coins have also been used to circumvent customs regulations. One hundred rare silver dollars can be worth several thousand dollars and easily converted to currency in a foreign country, but cannot exceed the $3000.00 reporting requirement if viewed as only $100.00.

In addition to collectible coins, there are also bullion coins, which are bought and sold at the current price of the precious metal from which they are minted. These coins may be minted by private companies or by countries around the world. They are produced using the troy system of weights and measures. The South African Krugerrand, the Canadian Maple Leaf, and the U.S. American Eagle are the better known examples of gold bullion coins, and are purchased and sold at the spot market price of gold with an additional fee per coin for the costs of handling. The coins or tokens (metals minted by private companies) may be made of any precious metal, the most common being silver, gold, and platinum. With the price of gold at about $750.00 per troy ounce, 100 coins would be worth $75,000.00. American coins minted as legal tender in the earlier years of the nation would hold as a minimum the bullion value, and if in collectible condition, far more in value.

The dealers selling the coins and bullion will often keep information on clients for the same purposes as those selling furs and jewelry. They may also want a record of major purchasers if they have the opportunity to transact additional purchases or make sales on their behalf.

Artwork

Art collections may include paintings, watercolors, lithographs, sculpture, and handcrafted items. Expensive art items are also cataloged, identified by artist, date created, title, and the medium used in the creation. Art dealers often try to keep track of ownership of items to facilitate sales and purchases between their clients. Authentication and appraisals are a standard in the industry to maintain reputations and dealer credibility.

Due to the value, and often the delicate nature of collectibles, owners will also seek assistance in the maintenance, storage, and security of these items. Dealers will keep records to protect themselves against liability and guarantee the customers' safety when the latter deal with their businesses. If the items are insured, the insurance company will keep a meticulous inventory of the items, including appraisals, photographs, and often a copy of the purchase agreement.

Although many financial criminals are clever enough to attempt to conceal the means of illegal gains by use of cash and nominees for their transactions, they cannot control the third parties they deal with in spending and enjoying their ill-gotten gains.

Liabilities

Earlier we discussed the means of increasing wealth as twofold: increasing assets and decreasing liabilities. Income, whether legally or illegally obtained, can be used for either of these purposes. The paper trail for financing purchases or obtaining cash has been touched upon in the discussions on asset acquisitions. Usually, the repayment of debts incurred is well documented by both the borrower and the lender; neither party wants to be shortchanged.

The only type of loan in which industry standards would not be required to be followed would be in the case of personal or private loans made between parties. Unless there is a close and trusting relationship between the parties in the transaction, some type of documentation will be prepared. This may be as simple as a handwritten IOU, or as formal as a land contract agreement for the purchasing, financing, and repayment of a land sale. These type of documents are not under regulatory agency filing requirements. They are, however, acknowledged by the courts in cases where a dispute arises in the fulfillment of the contract or agreement. If legal action is taken in a dispute, court records will often provide all of the details regarding the transaction.

Collecting and Preserving Evidence

6

Several methods and techniques are used to obtain evidence in all types of investigative work. These methods and their applications vary at the discretion of the investigating agent. For successful financial investigations, interviewing, documentation, and observation are three critical elements in gathering evidence.

The perpetrators of white collar crimes are often first-time offenders. Those committing financial crimes through deception and fraud are usually nonviolent, and attempt to talk their way out of responsibility. The witnesses in financial crimes are usually well educated, successful in business, and have a higher social status in the community. Friends, relatives, and associates rarely believe that the subject of the investigation is capable of committing a crime or perpetrating a fraud.

Based on these characteristics, the investigator needs to adjust the interviewing techniques to these situations. Objectivity is always required in any investigation, and this should also extend to the witnesses from whom evidence is gathered. The investigator must also realize that the business professional is apt to have much more knowledge of the regulations relating to his or her business than the investigator and also probably substantial expertise in the field. Preparation for witness contacts plays an integral part in the success of the contact and the quality of the evidence obtained. Such preparation should include knowing the background of the witnesses, their relationship to the subject of the investigation, their reputation in the community, and the frequency of their financial transactions with the subject.

A financial investigation involves the connection of a series of unrelated financial transactions that, when presented in total, provide a complete picture of an individual's financial activity over a set period of time. The evidence to support this picture is circumstantial in nature and needs to be obtained thoroughly for each transaction. It can be compared to working on a jigsaw puzzle. Sections of the puzzle are completed and joined together, and the entire picture is revealed.

The investigator needs to apply patience, diligence, and constant analysis of the pieces of evidence to be able to see and understand the financial activities of the subject, so as to determine whether a financial crime has occurred and whether others are involved.

Examples of applying these factors will be provided as we discuss the three critical elements in gathering evidence in a financial investigation.

Interviewing

Interviewing a witness involves a basic understanding of human nature. Aspects of communication, sociology, and psychology all play a part in gaining testimonial evidence and evaluating that information. The first set of interviews will be with the most likely suspects in relation to the financial discrepancies that initiated the investigation. This may encompass all the employees who could have perpetrated the embezzlement, or all the executives who could have orchestrated a securities fraud scheme, or it may be as simple as the one individual who facilitated an investment scam.

In any interview, it is important to maintain objectivity. The investigator is on a fact-finding mission and not "out to get" anyone. If the investigator fails to do this, and the witnesses feel that the results are preconceived, it can taint or ruin the case. A wrong attitude can also cause a witness to withdraw from providing complete or additional information and explanations. The investigator should conduct the interview without a personal or emotional attitude and in a professional manner. Courtesy and professional sociability with the witness can go a long way toward making the interview a success. Investigators must also keep in mind that they are conducting the interview and avoid being distracted from gaining the information they are seeking. For example:

- You meet the witness for the interview, and his or her first question to you is whether he or she is the target of your investigation. Even if the witness is currently the most likely suspect, the interviewer should state that he or she is interviewing everyone who may have information to determine who is actually responsible for the financial discrepancies. Once all of the information is obtained and analyzed, a determination will be made as to whether the discrepancies occurred due to a systemic problem, by mistake, or were intentional.

- During the interview, the witness expresses an interest in the local sports team. You respond without displaying that you are also an avid fan but for another team. The witness enters into a blow-by-blow analysis of his or her team, the individual players, and the coach. In a polite but firm manner, you have to direct him or her back to the questions you need to have answered.

Prior to arranging an interview, it is important to know your witness. The investigator should be aware of the witness' ability to provide the needed information. Was there a part-time clerk at the store? Was it the store manager or owner at the store? Who handled the transaction? The investigator may need to conduct more than one interview relating to a specific transaction if a part-time clerk made the sale, the store manager approved financing the sale, and the owner made several prior sales to the subject.

The investigator needs to know the business relationship between the witness and the subject. Is the witness in a subordinate position to the subject? If this is the case, how much influence will the subject have over the degree of cooperation from the witness? If they are partners or close associates, the discovery that a financial fraud was perpetrated could have an adverse effect on the business and reputation of the witness. Disclosure of a financial fraud can also be devastating to the business that suffers the fraud, especially if the business relies on customer confidence to make a profit. Examples include a bank in which an employee embezzles funds or a construction company that has a foreman who uses inferior materials for kickbacks.

The investigator also needs to know what the personal relationship, if any, is between the witness and the subject. If the witness is a relative of the subject, he or she often will be hesitant to provide any information. Demonstrating objectivity in this circumstance may open the witness to providing information that would tend to exonerate the subject from culpability. Relatives and associates may also have strained relationships with the subject and may provide biased information to implicate the subject. The investigator has to sort out the emotions involved and concentrate on the factual information needed. Remember that in a financial investigation the case hinges on the facts about the financial dealings of the subject and not whether the witness sees the subject as a good or bad person. A former spouse, a party in a lawsuit versus the subject, or a customer or client who believes the subject has cheated him or her is naturally going to voice complaints during the interview. To remain objective, the investigator must take care not to take sides in the dispute or be overly sympathetic to the witness:

- The witness is the ex-wife of the subject, and you discover that she and their child are dependent on the subject for support. The investigator can begin with very general questions to take the witness' focus away from her dependency or begin with questions about the divorce to remind her of former adversarial conditions between them.

- A general contractor is the witness in an investigation of faulty materials being used by a subcontractor with whom he or she has dealt with for years. The contractor may be hesitant to provide information for fear that he or she will suffer "guilt by association." The investigator could allay some of the fear by reminding the witness that the fraud appears to cover only a certain time period and that its discovery without his or her assistance may turn out to be worse for him or her than helping to remedy the situation.

The investigator should fully develop the lead information that made the interview necessary and ponder over what other information the witness may have. This gives the investigator an opportunity to consider what areas may require follow-up questions and how to prepare for those questions. Such preparation will greatly reduce interruption in the flow of the interview and the need for additional interviews with the witness to clarify information.

In a financial investigation, the investigator has to weigh and assess the information currently being obtained in the context of all the prior information gathered. The investigator also needs to be aware that witnesses and the subject will have difficulty in remembering the specifics of everyday financial activities. As such, having pertinent records ready to refresh their memory is very beneficial.

It is often helpful to limit the initial interview with the subject of an investigation to the history, background, and general financial or business practices until the investigator has had time to review and analyze the records and documents provided. In involved cases, it is not unusual to interview the subject several times to clarify issues that develop, that is, if the subject is willing to provide the investigator with the information. Individuals involved in complex schemes and conspiracies will often feign innocence and try to convince investigators that nothing illegal has occurred. Those involved in fraud conspiracies will often deny knowing the existence of or extent of the fraud scheme, or try to convince the investigator that they were told what to do without any explanation as to why. Another explanation often given is that they only made a mistake. All of these reasons are common defenses in conspiracy cases:

- In the analysis of financial records, you find a check for $2000.00 issued to a Mrs. Jane Doe. It is the only payment to an individual written on the business account. Research into her background shows that she is married to John Doe, the owner of JD's Jewelry. The business account also shows several payments made to JD's Jewelry written off as repair expenses. Upon checking the business directory, there is no listing for a JD's repair shop. During the interview, Mrs. Doe admits that the check she received and the ones written to JD's Jewelry were for jewelry purchases.

- During your interview with Mrs. Doe, she states that some pieces of the purchased jewelry were picked up by and fitted for a blonde lady in her late 20s. You met the subject's wife earlier, and she is a brunette and 47 years old. At your request, Mrs. Doe searches the records and finds the name and address of the blonde. This provides the investigator with a new lead on potential expenditures.

- The witness is a loan officer who has approved several loans that have defaulted. The loan files are complete and do not appear to be falsified. The defaulted loans are unique in that the proceeds for each were distributed in cash. The witness states that mistakes may have been made in approving the loans but he did nothing outside of the bank's regulations. All the loans defaulted were processed by the same collections officer. Analysis of the two employees' records show cash deposits of 50% of the loan proceeds to each of their accounts on the day the proceeds were disbursed. Confronting the witness with these facts will often lead to an admission and implication of the other conspirator, or the witness will fabricate a reason for the deposits. Fabrications are made off the cuff and are usually easy to disprove.

Individuals involved in white collar and organized criminal enterprises are usually intelligent and adept in their field, or have access to and use specialized legal and accounting professionals. This means that the investigator must have a basic understanding of the type of enterprise under investigation or work under a serious disadvantage. Large corporations may have thousands of employees in several locations, and utilize a large and elaborate record-keeping system. Often, there is an attempt to conceal fraud by moving the fraudulent funds through several accounts or fictitious businesses created to conceal the proceeds. In these cases, the investigator must familiarize himself or herself with the business operations. Several interviews may have to be done for this purpose before investigative interviews are conducted.

It is often necessary to employ the services of an expert as witness to explain intricate business or accounting events. This is the same as using expert testimony for medical, psychological, or other specialized areas in court proceedings. See the following case examples:

- The witness is the stockbroker to the subject of the investigation. The subject has heavily invested in a wide variety of securities, commodities, and mutual funds, and trades in these securities several times each week. The investigator may need to be walked through the transactions step by step to understand the financial ramifications of the account on the subject. The cash flow into the account could be substantial, or it may be that the investments have done well and the transactions are the result of moving the same funds around within the account. The financial investigation needs to determine the dates and amounts of money going in and out of the account. The broker will himself or herself provide assistance in analyzing the account or have someone in the office assist the investigator. Expressing an interest in the area of expertise that an individual has goes a long way in getting the help needed.

- The subject uses an elaborate fraud scheme involving alleged tax-deferring trusts. The trusts are a scam, and the subject uses the monies invested in the trusts for personal purchases. An expert in the field of trusts, living wills, and tax deferment through these types of investments can be called upon to explain how and why the trust documents are fraudulent. The same individual may be called upon for testimony in court if the case goes to trial.

Interviews of individuals and companies not related to the subject or involved in the scheme are usually referred to as third-party witnesses. These interviews involve verification of normal everyday business transactions. Courtesy and a professional attitude will help to soften the interruption of the normal business activities of these witnesses. The investigator should be prepared for questions from the witness without implying that the subject of the investigation is guilty. Remember that the subject is often a regular and good customer of the witness. As witnesses may have hundreds of customers, be ready to refresh the former's memory with the lead information that brought you to their establishment.

The next two chapters will go into more depth on documentary evidence and the evidence gained through formal observation techniques.

Gathering Documentary Evidence

7

Documents make up the bulk of evidence used in financial investigations. They are also the building blocks of discovery or the pieces of the jigsaw puzzle that result in completing the picture of the subject's financial activities. There are several rules and procedures that need to be followed in determining how and from whom documents are acquired. These rules have to be followed if the investigator hopes to use the documents as evidence.

Documentation

The purpose of the investigation is the driving force as to what documentary evidence is collected, how it is collected, and from whom. An informal investigation (consisting of internal business monitoring or systems security control for petty pilfering or theft) can determine that there is a problem and identify the process or procedural changes to correct the situation. There are no requirements for the acceptance of the results of the investigation because everything is handled internally. The documentation is reviewed, and the results are used to confront any employee involved or to correct operational procedures to close the gap on a potential problem.

Other investigations are performed to verify information provided to one party by a second party for use in making future financial transactions with the second party. Examples would include debt settlement offers and business evaluations for acquisitions or mergers. Since the records in these situations are collected primarily for information purposes and are not needed for presentation in legal actions, there is no formal procedure required in gathering the documentation.

In the majority of financial cases, there will be the anticipation of some future legal action. The documentation and the analysis of records in these cases need to be handled in the same manner as any other evidence used in civil or criminal litigation. There are specific rules on what evidence is needed, and its relevance and materiality; the competency of the witness who will introduce the documentation; and the security, handling, and preservation of the evidence to be used. These rules are contained in the rules of procedure and rules of evidence for the jurisdiction in which the case is to be heard.

Although each state may have its own version of rules for these proceedings, all will incorporate or adopt the Federal Rules of Evidence as their format. For our purposes, we will discuss the Federal Rules of Evidence keeping in mind that some jurisdictions may have variations in these rules. Under these rules, there are three general requirements that must be met for an item, document, or testimony to be accepted in the matter being heard: relevance, materiality, and competency.

Relevance

The following are Article IV, Rules 401 and 402 of the Federal Rules of Evidence:

Rule 401. Definition of "Relevant Evidence"

"Relevant evidence" means evidence having any tendency to make the existence of any fact that is of consequence to the determination of the action more probable or less probable than it would be without that evidence.

Rule 402. Relevant Evidence Generally Admissible; Irrelevant Evidence Inadmissible

All relevant evidence is admissible, except as otherwise provided by the Constitution of the United States, by Act of Congress, by these rules, or by other rules prescribed by the Supreme Court pursuant to statutory authority. Evidence which is not relevant is not admissible.

In a financial investigation, the relevancy of documents related to financial transactions for the purpose of determining the probability of a specific individual (the respondent to the charges) is broad in scope. Legal precedents have set the requirements and parameters for using indirect methods of proof based primarily on circumstantial evidence. As an example, the Supreme Court ruled that the government was required to establish the "starting point," or foundational financial condition of the defendant, to allocate the amounts of unreported income in subsequent years in a tax evasion case in *Holland v. United States*. This meant that transactions prior to the years investigated became relevant in determining the defendant's net worth before he actually began cheating on his taxes. The statute of limitations, investigative efficiency, or other factors may affect the choice of a starting point in a financial, indirect method investigation. These factors will be discussed in greater detail in the sections on indirect methods of proof. Because indirect methods of proof are based on cash flow transactions, documents reflecting a $50,000.00 increase in the value of a stock purchased in prior years would not be relevant unless the stock was sold during the years under investigation, and generated a legitimate explanation for part of the defendant's increase in wealth. Using the same reasoning, a $100.00 purchase of a painting during the years included in the investigation would be relevant. Oftentimes, financial investigations involve hundreds or even thousands of small transactions that reveal a substantial financial crime. If the financial investigation has to show the total amount of wealth gained by the defendant to establish how much was derived by fraud or theft, then all of the financial activity involving the defendant becomes relevant.

Materiality

Material evidence is defined as information relating, explaining, or having a logical connection to a fact or circumstance that would have an effect on a person's decision making relevant to that fact or circumstance. Evidence may be true and accurate, but if it does not bear on the facts or circumstances in the issue to be decided, it is not material to the case and becomes inadmissible. For example, if an individual is being tried for embezzling $1 million from a bank, it is immaterial whether the funds were in the form of transfers to his account at another bank or with a credit union. As long as the investigation shows the defendant's transfer of the funds into another account over which he has control, whether it is a bank or credit union is immaterial. In a similar way, the determination of the place from which goods were stolen would probably be considered immaterial to charges of possession of stolen property.

Competency

Competency is usually associated with the ability of witnesses to comprehend what they saw or what was done, and relate that information accurately. The competency of witnesses may be challenged on grounds of lack of mental capacity, that they are children lacking knowledge and experience, or that they are elderly, suffering from an illness such as poor eyesight or Alzheimer's disease. The introduction of documents as circumstantial evidence of a financial crime incorporates a much broader application of the rules on competency.

The easiest way to become familiar with and understand the rules for determining competency of a witness in relation to circumstantial documentary evidence is to go through the legal rules of evidence. Each judicial jurisdiction can have its own set of rules of evidence, but most will either adopt or make slight modifications to the standards set in the Federal Rules of Evidence. Following is a listing and explanation of the Federal Rules of

Evidence most often applied for competency determinations to witnesses and documentary evidence.

Rule 601. General Rule of Competency

Every person is competent to be a witness except as otherwise provided in these rules. However, in civil actions and proceedings, with respect to an element of a claim or defense as to which State law supplies the rule of decision, the competency of a witness shall be determined in accordance with State law.

Rule 601 ensures the availability of all witnesses in the adjudication of a matter before the court unless expressly denied by the rules that follow. It also acknowledges the jurisdictional rights of other courts to alter or modify these rules.

Rule 602. Lack of Personal Knowledge

A witness may not testify to a matter unless evidence is introduced sufficient to support a finding that the witness has personal knowledge of the matter. Evidence to prove personal knowledge may, but need not, consist of the witness' own testimony. This rule is subject to Rule 703, relating to opinion testimony by expert witnesses.

Rule 602 excludes witnesses who have no knowledge of or association with the matter before the court. This prohibits the introduction of speculation and prevents the delay of the proceeding and potential for confusion on the part of the jurors.

Rules 603 and 604 require an oath or affirmation be administered prior to the testimony of a witness and prior to an interpreter's presentation of testimony, should an interpreter be necessary.

Rules 605 and 606 address the exclusion of the judge from cases that he or she is hearing and the jurors from cases they have decided from testifying as to deliberations or consideration of the evidence. Exception is made in cases where extraneous prejudicial information or influences were improperly introduced to the jury.

Rules 607 through 609 provide for the limitations and processes in the impeachment of a witness or in establishing or attacking the credibility of that witness before the jury.

Rule 612. Writing Used to Refresh Memory

Except as otherwise provided in criminal proceedings by section 3500 of title 18, United States Code, if a witness uses a writing to refresh memory for the purpose of testifying, either—

(1) while testifying, or

(2) before testifying, if the court in its discretion determines it is necessary in the interests of justice,

An adverse party is entitled to have the writing produced at the hearing, to inspect it, to cross-examine the witness thereon, and to introduce in evidence those portions which relate to the testimony of the witness. If it is claimed that the writing contains matters not related to the subject matter of the testimony, the court shall examine the writing in camera, excise any portions not so related, and order delivery of the remainder to the party entitled thereto. Any portion withheld over objections shall be preserved and made available to the appellate court in the event of an appeal. If a writing is not produced or delivered pursuant to order under this rule, the court shall make any order justice requires, except that in criminal cases when the prosecution elects not to comply, the order shall be one striking the testimony or, if the court in its discretion determines that the interests of justice so require, declaring a mistrial.

Rule 612 explains the requirements involved in the use of documents and/or prior statements of the witness that have been reduced to writing (affidavits, depositions, etc.) to refresh his or her memory. Statements are often taken from witnesses in financial investigations. These statements often refer to documents reviewed by the witness in providing their statement, and copies of these records should be attached to the statement. Financial investigations may take extensive time to complete; statements of witnesses prepared at the time of interview provide an accurate representation of their anticipated testimony, and avoid delays in preparing the case for trial.

Rule 613. Prior Statements of Witnesses

(a) Examining witness concerning prior statement. In examining a witness concerning a prior statement made by the witness, whether written or not, the statement need not be shown nor its contents disclosed to the witness at that time, but on request the same shall be shown or disclosed to opposing counsel.

(b) Extrinsic evidence of prior inconsistent statement of witness. Extrinsic evidence of a prior inconsistent statement by a witness is not admissible unless the witness is afforded an opportunity to explain or deny the same, and the opposite party is afforded an opportunity to interrogate the witness thereon, or the interests of justice otherwise require. This provision does not apply to admissions of a party-opponent as defined in Rule 801(d)(2).

Rule 613 explains the circumstances and procedures for introducing prior statements made by the witness that are inconsistent with their current testimony. These statements may be used to diminish the credibility of the witness or be adequately explained by the witness.

Rule 802. Hearsay Rule

Hearsay is not admissible except as provided by these rules or by other rules prescribed by the Supreme Court pursuant to statutory authority or by Act of Congress.

Hearsay is defined in Rule 801 as a statement, other than one made by the declarant while testifying at the trial or hearing, offered in evidence to prove the truth of the matter asserted. An example would be Witness A telling what another person reported about the matter. If the information is needed by either side in the dispute, then the other person should be called upon to testify in person. Rule 803 delineates the exceptions to the hearsay rule in 23 specific situations. Many of the exceptions are used in the presentation of documentary evidence.

Rule 803. Hearsay Exceptions; Availability of Declarant Immaterial

The following are not excluded by the hearsay rule, even though the declarant is available as a witness:

(1) Present sense impression. A statement describing or explaining an event or condition made while the declarant was perceiving the event or condition, or immediately thereafter.

(2) Excited utterance. A statement relating to a startling event or condition made while the declarant was under the stress of excitement caused by the event or condition.

(3) Then existing mental, emotional, or physical condition. A statement of the declarant's then existing state of mind, emotion, sensation, or physical condition (such as intent, plan, motive, design, mental feeling, pain, and bodily health), but not including a statement of memory or belief to prove the fact remembered or believed unless it relates to the execution, revocation, identification, or terms of declarant's will.

(4) Statements for purposes of medical diagnosis or treatment. Statements made for purposes of medical diagnosis or treatment and describing medical history, or past or present symptoms, pain, or sensations, or the inception or general character of the cause or external source thereof insofar as reasonably pertinent to diagnosis or treatment.

(5) Recorded recollection. A memorandum or record concerning a matter about which a witness once had knowledge but now has insufficient recollection to enable the witness to testify fully and accurately, shown to have been made or adopted by the witness when the matter was fresh in the witness' memory and to reflect that knowledge correctly. If admitted, the memorandum or record may be read into evidence but may not itself be received as an exhibit unless offered by an adverse party.

Subsection (5) allows for the jury to hear information from a witness who is no longer able to provide that information through testimony. Contracts, agreements, logs, and other written information can be presented if it was prepared or adopted by the witness at the time.

> (6) Records of regularly conducted activity. A memorandum, report, record, or data compilation, in any form, of acts, events, conditions, opinions, or diagnoses, made at or near the time by, or from information transmitted by, a person with knowledge, if kept in the course of a regularly conducted business activity, and if it was the regular practice of that business activity to make the memorandum, report, record, or data compilation, all as shown by the testimony of the custodian or other qualified witness, or by certification that complies with Rule 902(11), Rule 902(12), or a statute permitting certification, unless the source of information or the method or circumstances of preparation indicate lack of trustworthiness. The term "business" as used in this paragraph includes business, institution, association, profession, occupation, and calling of every kind, whether or not conducted for profit.

Subsection (6) is often referred to as the "federal shop book rule." Records prepared and kept in the normal course of business for every type of business-conducting entity may be introduced by a qualified representative of that entity. This exception to the hearsay rule is used in almost all financial investigations. Representatives from banks, financial institutions, businesses, and other entities may send a representative from their business to introduce all of the financial records relating to the subject's transactions with their business. This eliminates the need to have each employee of a business having dealings with the subject testify in court.

> (7) Absence of entry in records kept in accordance with the provisions of paragraph (6). Evidence that a matter is not included in the memoranda reports, records, or data compilations, in any form, kept in accordance with the provisions of paragraph (6), to prove the nonoccurrence or nonexistence of the matter, if the matter was of a kind of which a memorandum, report, record, or data compilation was regularly made and preserved, unless the sources of information or other circumstances indicate lack of trustworthiness.

Subsection (7) allows for the use of negative proof to refute a claim of a transaction if records kept in the normal course of business do not reflect the transaction.

> (8) Public records and reports. Records, reports, statements, or data compilations, in any form, of public offices or agencies, setting forth (A) the activities of the office or agency, or (B) matters observed pursuant to duty imposed by law as to which matters there was a duty to report, excluding, however, in criminal cases matters observed by

police officers and other law enforcement personnel, or (C) in civil actions and proceedings and against the Government in criminal cases, factual findings resulting from an investigation made pursuant to authority granted by law, unless the sources of information or other circumstances indicate lack of trustworthiness.

(9) Records of vital statistics. Records or data compilations, in any form, of births, fetal deaths, deaths, or marriages, if the report thereof was made to a public office pursuant to requirements of law.

(10) Absence of public record or entry. To prove the absence of a record, report, statement, or data compilation, in any matter of which a record, report, statement, or data compilation, in any form, was regularly made and preserved by a public office or agency, evidence in the form of a certification in accordance with Rule 902, or testimony, that diligent search failed to disclose the record, report, statement, or data compilation, or entry.

(11) Records of religious organizations. Statements of births, marriages, divorces, deaths, legitimacy, ancestry, relationship by blood or marriage, or other similar facts of personal or family history, contained in a regularly kept record of a religious organization.

(12) Marriage, baptismal, and similar certificates. Statements of fact contained in a certificate that the maker performed a marriage or other ceremony or administered a sacrament, made by a clergyman, public official, or other person authorized by the rules or practices of a religious organization or by law to perform the act certified, and purporting to have been issued at the time of the act or within a reasonable time thereafter.

Subsections (8) to (12) provide exceptions for records kept by public offices and religious organizations to be introduced as evidence. Again, the rules require that the records be those kept in the normal course in the public office or religious organization. Subsection (10) allows for the use of negative proof if the existence of an act is claimed and a diligent search fails to locate the corroborating documentation.

(13) Family records. Statements of fact concerning personal or family history contained in family Bibles, genealogies, charts, engravings on rings, inscriptions on family portraits, engravings on urns, crypts, or tombstones, or the like.

Subsection (13) allows for the introduction of information recorded in or on family heirlooms to verify information on family histories.

(14) Records of documents affecting an interest in property. The record of a document purporting to establish or affect an interest in property, as proof of the content of the original recorded document and its execution and delivery by each person by whom it purports to have

been executed, if the record is a record of a public office and an applicable statute authorizes the recording of documents of that kind in that office.

(15) Statements in documents affecting an interest in property. A statement contained in a document purporting to establish or affect an interest in property if the matter stated was relevant to the purpose of the document, unless dealings with the property since the document was made have been inconsistent with the truth of the statement or the purport of the document.

Subsections (14) and (15) allow for the use of a related document indicating the terms of a transaction or the use of a property, unless subsequent actions and usage relative to the property are inconsistent with what the document states.

(16) Statements in ancient documents. Statements in a document in existence twenty years or more, the authenticity of which is established.

Subsection (16) seems to have little effect on current financial investigations but has impacted several cases in regard to the Supreme Court requirement for the determination of an accurate starting point in cases using indirect methods of proof. The need for documents to be authenticated has also generated a relatively new field in forensics. Laboratories are able to analyze documents scientifically to determine the age and manufacturer of the paper, the type and manufacturer of the inks, the age of the ink used in the document, typewriter and printer identification, and other areas used to authenticate documents.

(17) Market reports, commercial publications. Market quotations, tabulations, lists, directories, or other published compilations, generally used and relied upon by the public or by persons in particular occupations.

(18) Learned treatises. To the extent called to the attention of an expert witness upon cross-examination, statements contained in published treatises, periodicals, or pamphlets on a subject of history, medicine, or other science or art, established as a reliable authority by the testimony or admission of the witness or by other expert testimony or by judicial notice. If admitted, the statements may be read into evidence but may not be received as exhibits.

Subsections (17) and (18) allow for the introduction of information that is accepted as an accurate reflection of the truth or conditions. Historical stock market information, telephone directories, and reported events would fall into this category. Also, writings that are accepted by professionals as reference or scientifically based reports can be admitted if discussed by an expert witness for either side in the matter.

(19) Reputation concerning personal or family history. Reputation among members of a person's family by blood, adoption, or marriage, or among a person's birth, adoption, marriage, divorce, death, legitimacy, relationship by blood, adoption, or marriage, ancestry, or other similar fact of personal or family history.

(20) Reputation concerning boundaries or general history. Reputation in a community, arising before the controversy, as to boundaries of or customs affecting lands in the community, and reputation as to events of general history important to the community or State or nation in which located.

(21) Reputation as to character. Reputation of a person's character among associates or in the community.

Subsections (19) to (21) allow for items of local knowledge and acceptance to be introduced, as well as testimony as to the character and nature of the subject.

(22) Judgment of previous conviction. Evidence of a final judgment, entered after trial or upon a plea of guilty (but not upon a plea of nolo contendere), adjudging a person guilty of a crime punishable by death or imprisonment in excess of one year, to prove any fact essential to sustain the judgment, but not including, when offered by the government in a criminal prosecution for purposes other than impeachment, judgments against persons other than the accused. The pendency of an appeal may be shown but does not affect admissibility.

Subsection (22) allows for the introduction of a criminal felony record if the accused testifies (impeachment of the witness-accused).

Rule 804. Hearsay Exceptions; Declarant Unavailable

(a) Definition of unavailability. "Unavailability as a witness" includes situations in which the declarant—

(1) is exempted by ruling of the court on the ground of privilege from testifying concerning the subject matter of the declarant's statement; or

(2) persists in refusing to testify concerning the subject matter of the declarant's statement despite an order of the court to do so; or

(3) testifies to a lack of memory of the subject matter of the declarant's statement; or

(4) is unable to be present or to testify at the hearing because of death or then existing physical or mental illness or infirmity; or

(5) is absent from the hearing, and the proponent of a statement has been unable to procure the declarant's attendance (or, in the case of a hearsay exception under subdivision (b)(2), (3), or (4), the declarant's attendance or testimony) by process or other reasonable means.

>A declarant is not unavailable as a witness if exemption, refusal, claim of lack of memory, inability, or absence is due to the procurement of wrongdoing of the proponent of a statement for the purpose of preventing the witness from attending or testifying.

(b) Hearsay exceptions. The following are not excluded by the hearsay rule if the declarant is unavailable as a witness:

>(1) Former testimony. Testimony given as a witness at another hearing of the same or a different proceeding, or in a deposition taken in compliance with law in the course of the same or another proceeding, if the party against whom the testimony is now offered, or, in a civil action or proceeding, a predecessor in interest, had an opportunity and similar motive to develop the testimony by direct, cross, or redirect examination.

Subsection (1) allows the introduction of the testimony given by a witness in the current or other court proceeding, whether in person or by legal deposition, as long as the accused was afforded the opportunity to cross-examine the witness at the time the testimony was given. If the testimony is from a different proceeding but relevant to the current one, the opposing counsel in that case must have had the opportunity to cross-examine. Depositions are made and recorded verbatim, with counsel present for both sides in the dispute to afford the opportunity to question the witness.

>(2) Statement under belief of impending death. In a prosecution for homicide or in a civil action or proceeding, a statement made by a declarant while believing that the declarant's death was imminent, concerning the cause or circumstances of what the declarant believed to be impending death.

Subsection (2) is commonly referred to as the exception for "dying declarations." The statements made at the time the witness was, or believed that he or she was dying, may be introduced into evidence without the witness' presence.

>(3) Statement against interest. A statement which was at the time of its making so far contrary to the declarant's pecuniary or proprietary interest, or so far tended to subject the declarant to civil or criminal liability, or to render invalid a claim by the declarant against another, that a reasonable person in the declarant's position would not have made the statement unless believing it to be true. A statement tending to expose the declarant to criminal liability and offered to exculpate the accused is not admissible unless corroborating circumstances clearly indicate the trustworthiness of the statement.

Subsection (3) allows for the introduction of statements made that would be against the witness' own interests. The statement, if given for the sole purpose of clearing the accused in a criminal matter (such as a confession to the crime of which the defendant is accused), will not be accepted without sufficient corroboration.

Rule 901. Requirement of Authentication or Identification

(a) General provision. The requirement of authentication or identification as a condition precedent to admissibility is satisfied by evidence sufficient to support a finding that the matter in question is what its proponent claims.

(b) Illustrations. By way of illustration only, and not by way of limitation, the following are examples of authentication or identification conforming with the requirements of this rule.

(1) Testimony of witness with knowledge. Testimony that a matter is what it is claimed to be.

Subsection (1) is fairly simple in scope. An individual with knowledge of the document may introduce and testify regarding the content. A bank representative, being accepted as having knowledge of the bank's procedures and record-keeping methods, may introduce the bank's copies of records relating to transactions with the accused. The seller of a piece of property to the accused may introduce his copies of the documents relating to the sale.

(2) Nonexpert opinion on handwriting. Nonexpert opinion as to the genuineness of handwriting, based upon familiarity not acquired for purposes of the litigation.

(3) Comparison by trier or expert witness. Comparison by the trier of fact or by expert witnesses with specimens which have been authenticated.

(4) Distinctive characteristics and the like. Appearance, contents, substance, internal patterns, or other distinctive characteristics, taken in conjunction with circumstances.

Subsections (2), (3), and (4) allow for hearsay testimony in cases of identification of handwriting by an individual who can establish familiarity with the handwriting of the accused, or by a handwriting expert using other writings proven to be from the accused for comparison. They also allow for unique characteristics to be shown in the written document. Examples would include a typist who would regularly receive handwritten materials from the accused to be typed, an expert witness who has taken legally acceptable samples of the handwriting of the accused for comparison with the document in question, and introduction of any distinctive characteristic used by the accused and contained in the document, such as the dotting of i's with little hearts.

(7) Public records or reports. Evidence that a writing authorized by law to be recorded or filed and in fact recorded or filed in a public

office, or a purported public record, report, statement, or data compilation, in any form, is from the public office where items of this nature are kept.

Subsection (7) allows for the introduction of public records into evidence.

(9) Process or system. Evidence describing a process or system used to produce a result and showing that the process or system produces an accurate result.

Subsection (9) allows for the introduction of automated information into evidence as long as it can be shown that the automated system accurately computes, compiles, and presents the information.

Rule 902. Self-Authentication

Extrinsic evidence of authenticity as a condition precedent to admissibility is not required with respect to the following:

(1) Domestic public documents under seal. A document bearing a seal purporting to be that of the United States, or of any State, district, Commonwealth, territory, or insular possession thereof, or the Panama Canal Zone, or the Trust Territory of the Pacific Islands, or of a political subdivision, department, officer, or agency thereof, and a signature purporting to be an attestation or execution.

(2) Domestic public documents not under seal. A document purporting to bear the signature in the official capacity of an officer or employee of any entity included in paragraph (1) hereof, having no seal, if a public officer having a seal and having official duties in the district or political subdivision of the officer or employee certifies under seal that the signer has the official capacity and that the signature is genuine.

Subsections (1) and (2) allow the admission of documents into evidence that are under official seal of the issuing or retaining public entity and for the certification of public documents by an individual having a seal. This would cover documents signed before a notary public authorized by the state, who can witness and attest to the validity of the signature.

(3) Foreign public documents. A document purporting to be executed or attested in an official capacity by a person authorized by the laws of a foreign country to make the execution or attestation, and accompanied by a final certification as to the genuineness of the signature and official position (A) of the executing or attesting person, or (B) of any foreign official whose certificate of genuineness of signature and official position relates to the execution or attestation or is in a chain of certificates of genuineness of signature and official position relating to the execution or attestation. A final certification may

be made by a secretary of an embassy or legation, consul general, consul, vice consul, or consular agent of the United States, or a diplomatic or consular official of the foreign country assigned or accredited to the United States. If reasonable opportunity has been given to all parties to investigate the authenticity and accuracy of official documents, the court may, for good cause shown, order that they be treated as presumptively authentic without final certification or permit them to be evidenced by an attested summary with or without final certification.

Subsection (3) allows for the introduction of foreign public documents as evidence. This would allow for a marriage certificate, divorce decree, deed or other public record issued and maintained by a foreign country to be introduced into evidence.

(4) Certified copies of public records. A copy of an official record or report or entry therein, or of a document authorized by law to be recorded or filed and actually recorded or filed in a public office, including data compilations in any form, certified as correct by the custodian or other person authorized to make the certification, by certificate complying with paragraph (1), (2), or (3) of this rule or complying with any Act of Congress or rule prescribed by the Supreme Court pursuant to statutory authority.

Subsection (4) allows for the submission of certified copies of public records, both foreign and domestic, into evidence.

(5) Official publications. Books, pamphlets, or other publications purporting to be issued by public authority.
(6) Newspapers and periodicals. Printed materials purported to be newspapers or periodicals.
(7) Trade inscriptions and the like. Inscriptions, signs, tags, or labels purporting to have been affixed in the course of business and indicating ownership, control, or origin.

Subsections (5), (6), and (7) allow information contained in government publications, newspapers, and magazines, and used in business for advertising to be introduced into evidence outside the hearsay rules for exclusion.

(8) Acknowledged documents. Documents accompanied by a certificate of acknowledgment executed in the manner provided by law by a notary public or other officer authorized by law to take acknowledgments.

Subsection (8) allows duly acknowledged documents to be introduced into court by an authorized agent such as a notary public.

(11) Certified domestic records of regularly conducted activity. The original or a duplicate of a domestic record of regularly conducted

activity that would be admissible under Rule 803(6) if accompanied by a written declaration of its custodian or other qualified person, in a manner complying with any Act of Congress or rule prescribed by the Supreme Court pursuant to statutory authority, certifying that the record
  (A) was made at or near the time of the occurrence of the matters set forth by, or from information transmitted by, a person with knowledge of those matters;
  (B) was kept in the course of the regularly conducted activity; and
  (C) was made by the regularly conducted activity as a regular practice.

A party intending to offer a record into evidence under this paragraph must provide written notice of that intention to all adverse parties, and must make the record and declaration available for inspection sufficiently in advance of their offer into evidence to provide an adverse party with a fair opportunity to challenge them.

Subsection (11) allows the custodian of records to provide those records into evidence with a written declaration as to their custodial function. It also requires that the documents and custodial authorization be provided to the defense (adverse party) prior to offering the documents to the court. This ties into the trial preparation aspect of discovery and the provision of Jencks materials.

  (12) Certified foreign records of regularly conducted activity. In a civil case, the original or a duplicate of a foreign record of regularly conducted activity that would be admissible under Rule 803(6) if accompanied by a written declaration by its custodian or other qualified person certifying that the record
  (A) was made at or near the time of the occurrence of the matters set forth by, or from information transmitted by, a person with knowledge of those matters;
  (B) was kept in the course of the regularly conducted activity; and
  (C) was made by the regularly conducted activity as a regular practice.

The declaration must be signed in a manner that, if falsely made, would subject the maker to criminal penalty under the laws of the country where the declaration is signed. A party intending to offer a record into evidence under this paragraph must provide written notice of that intention to all adverse parties, and must make the record and the declaration available for inspection sufficiently in advance of their offer into evidence to provide an adverse party with a fair opportunity to challenge them.

Subsection (12) provides the same type of exception to the hearsay rule for foreign documents used in the normal course of business that subsection (11) provides for domestic documents.

Rule 1001. Definitions

For purposes of this article the following definitions are applicable:

(1) Writings and recordings. "Writings" and "recordings" consist of letters, words, or numbers, or their equivalent, set down by handwriting, typewriting, printing, photostating, photographing, magnetic impulses, mechanical or electronic recording, or other form of data compilation.
(2) Photographs. "Photographs" include still photographs, x-ray films, video tapes, and motion pictures.
(3) Original. An "original" of a writing or recording is the writing or recording itself or any counterpart intended to have the same effect by a person executing or issuing it. An "original" of a photograph includes the negative or any print therefrom. If data are stored in a computer or similar device, any printout or other output readable by sight shown to reflect the data accurately reproduces the original.

Rule 1001 provides the definitions for determining what constitutes an original in written and recorded evidence. The original is the best evidence and need not be introduced based on any of the subsequent exceptions for admission under Article X.

Rule 1002. Requirement of Original

To prove the content of a writing, recording, or photograph, the original writing, recording, or photograph is required, except as otherwise provided in these rules or by Act of Congress.

Rule 1002 states that the original of any document, recording, or photograph is required for that item to be entered into evidence. The exceptions to this requirement are contained in the following six rules.

Rule 1003. Admissibility of Duplicates

A duplicate is admissible to the same extent as an original unless (1) a genuine question is raised as to the authenticity of the original or (2) in the circumstances it would be unfair to admit the duplicate in lieu of the original.

Rule 1003 allows the same treatment of a duplicate copy as the original unless there are unique aspects relative to its authenticity (the copy or the original). An example of the need for the original would be for forensic testing (fingerprints, paper and ink analysis, or handwriting and typewriting analysis). Also, if claims are made to alterations in the duplicate that would change the intent or meaning of the original.

Rule 1004. Admissibility of Other Evidence of Contents

The original is not required, and other evidence of the contents of a writing, recording, or photograph is admissible if

(1) Originals lost, or destroyed. All originals are lost or have been destroyed, unless the proponent lost or destroyed them in bad faith; or
(2) Original not obtainable. No original can be obtained by any available judicial process or procedure; or
(3) Original in possession of opponent. At a time when an original was under the control of the party against whom offered, that party was put on notice, by the pleadings or otherwise, that the contents would be a subject of proof at the hearing, and that party does not produce the original at the hearing; or
(4) Collateral matters. The writing, recording, or photograph is not closely related to a controlling issue.

Rule 1004 allows for the use of a copy to be used in court if there is no legal means of obtaining the original, or if the document does not play a major role in the determination of the issue being litigated.

Rule 1005. Public Records

The contents of an official record, or of a document authorized to be recorded or filed and actually recorded or filed, including data compilations in any form, if otherwise admissible, may be proved by copy, certified as correct in accordance with Rule 902 or testified to be correct by a witness who has compared it with the original. If a copy which complies with the foregoing cannot be obtained by the exercise of reasonable diligence, then other evidence of the contents may be given.

Rule 1005 allows for the use of duplicates of public records. The requirement for the witness to have compared the copy with the original and to testify it as a correct copy affects the acquisition of documents during the course of the financial investigation. Because the investigation is to determine the potential for civil or criminal litigation, potential witnesses will usually retain their original records and provide the investigator with duplicates. The investigator should take the time to have the witness compare the copies with the originals and declare in their statements that the copies are true and accurate. As financial investigations often take a long time to complete, there is potential for the loss or destruction of original documents, and copies verified in this manner can be used under the Rules of Evidence.

Rule 1006. Summaries

The contents of voluminous writings, recordings, or photographs which cannot conveniently be examined in court may be presented in the form of a chart, summary, or calculation. The originals, or duplicates, shall be made available for examination or copying, or both, by other parties at reasonable time and place. The court may order that they be produced in court.

Rule 1006 plays a very important role in financial investigations. The entire financial analysis is a summary of the financial activities of the accused for set time periods and of the logical progression of comparative summaries to determine the financial gains. This rule also comes into play in the use of audio and video surveillance when the surveillance is conducted over extended periods of time. In one case, VHS recordings were made of meetings between the subject and an undercover agent. More than 200 hours of video was recorded. An expert witness in electronic monitoring viewed all of the tapes and compiled a video summary that eliminated the periods of no activity on the films. A 3-hour summary was prepared and played in court. Copies of the entire video collection were provided to the defense in discovery. The expert had to ensure that evidence of guilt as well as any exculpatory information was included in the summary.

Rule 1007. Testimony or Written Admission of Party

Contents of writings, recordings, or photographs may be proved by the testimony or deposition of the party against whom offered or by that party's written admission, without accounting for the nonproduction of the original.

Rule 1007 allows for the use of duplicates to support admissions from witnesses in cases where the documentation is against their interests.

Rule 1008. Functions of Court and Jury

When the admissibility of other evidence of contents of writings, recordings, or photographs under these rules depends upon the fulfillment of a condition of fact, the question whether the condition has been fulfilled is ordinarily for the court to determine in accordance with the provisions of Rule 104. However, when an issue is raised (a) whether the asserted writing ever existed, or (b) whether another writing, recording, or photograph produced at the trial is the original, or (c) whether other evidence of contents correctly reflects the contents, the issue is for the trier of fact to determine as in the case of other issues of fact.

Rule 1008 applies the same judicial procedures for duplicates of records as for any other evidence presented to the jury. The weight given to that evidence is a matter for the jury to assign.

With all the attention given to the procedures and requirements for the admissibility of documents in litigation contained in the Rules of Evidence, it is easy to see why the investigator in a financial case needs to keep the regulations in mind while gathering the evidence. Many of the rules apply to unique situations; however, many address requirements that are applied again and again in gathering documentary evidence. When verifying financial transactions, make sure you have the right individual. Courts require that documents be introduced as evidence by competent witnesses. Records kept in the normal course of business may be introduced by a representative of the company. It is not necessary to have the specific individual who prepared each document be called to court to introduce the documents.

Records prepared, signed, or authenticated by an individual usually require that individual for introduction in court. Also, there are times that more than one individual could be used to introduce a document. An example would be the purchase of an automobile. The salesman could introduce the sales agreement, or a representative of the dealership could introduce the sales documents. The state could introduce the registration and title information. The subject could volunteer the purchase documents and stipulate to their authenticity. The investigator should select the witness he or she thinks can best explain the transaction and is most likely to adhere to the original information provided.

Courts have recognized that the best witness to a transaction may not be available for trial and allow crucial evidence to be introduced by other means. The investigator must keep in mind that he is constitutionally prohibited from compelling records or testimony from the individual charged with the crime.

The investigator needs to be familiar with the legal restrictions placed on certain businesses that limit access to financial records. Financial institutions are prohibited from voluntarily providing account information on their customers. Banks will require that a subpoena or court order be obtained before allowing access to customer account information. Often, in the case of a good customer or a prominent individual, businesses may ask for the same type of requirement to produce records to avoid losing a customer or facing a civil damages suit.

There are special circumstances that also need to be considered. If an individual prepares records on behalf of the subject, those records may be considered records of the subject and protected under the Fourth and Fifth Amendment rights of the Constitution of the United States. An example would be the return prepared for the subject. The returns and supporting records are considered the subject's personal records.

Trying to keep in mind the rules and regulations while concentrating on obtaining the evidence can be a frustrating experience. Some simple hints can be useful. Organize the case files by similar categories and separate the completed items as they are finished. It also helps to update the summary schedules as items are completed.

Gathering Evidence through Observation

8

Evidence and leads to evidence are often gained through observation. There are several means of observation that are used in all types of investigations. The investigator must keep in mind the rules that apply to recordings of audio and visual observations in gathering this type of evidence.

Observation

Investigative observation can be viewed as going from informal to formal. Being alert and observant is a necessary skill for any type of investigation, and it is crucial in the criminal investigation of financial and business activities. Informal observations are made throughout the course of the investigation. The attitude and demeanor of witnesses, the reaction to specific questions or areas of questioning, and the nature of the relationship with the subject expressed during an interview provide the investigator with potential tips for the litigation aspect to come and potential leads to additional evidence.

Informal observations would include making note of possessions, photos, and furnishings during the course of an interview with the subject or a related entity. Such observation can provide valuable leads that may not surface by other means during the investigation. This is especially true if the interview is conducted in the home or offices of the subject, or during interviews of closely related individuals. It is also important to take a panoramic approach and good notes during the execution of search warrants. Often, the leads on financial dealings are on items that will not be taken during the execution of a search warrant. This can be extremely valuable in those cases where the investigator is confident that a warrant will not be used. Such type of investigative observation is simple to accomplish and does not require a great deal of time or resources.

An example of informal observations would be to note plaques, awards, certificates, photographs, or artwork displayed on the walls in a home or office. Patience and recording of information in note taking can often open areas for discussion during the interview and establish lead information for future contacts on the acquisition of assets or personal expenditures. In one investigation, the subject had a college degree in finance displayed on his office wall. The background check performed on the subject prior to the interview did not reveal that the subject had any higher education. During the interview, the subject acknowledged the certificate but did not expand on it beyond its acquisition. Later in the investigation it was shown that the subject was involved in an investment fraud scheme that would bilk clients out of their money. The university that supposedly issued the degree found no record of the subject's enrollment, and it was determined that the fake degree was used to help build confidence in the subject on the part of the fraud victims. Although the observation did not disclose additional financial expenditures, it went a long way with the jury in establishing the subject's intent to defraud and deceive the victims of the fraud scheme.

In another investigation, the subject had several pictures of himself with friends, apparently on skiing outings. One of the photos was taken in front of a well-known ski resort in Colorado. Further investigation revealed that the subject often purchased season passes at the resort and owned a chalet in the nearby town. The purchase of the chalet, equipment, and the passes uncovered several thousands of dollars in purchases and expenditures from funds that were obtained from illegal activities.

Formal methods of investigative observation include surveillance, undercover operations, and the execution of search warrants. In addition, the investigator may receive the observations of witnesses during interviews. In these cases, the investigator needs to focus the witness on specific information. Relative terms such as early, late, strange, and others are of little use. The investigator needs to obtain information that is as specific as possible. Colors, approximate times of day, shapes, and sizes are of much greater use to the investigation.

Surveillance

The best known method of surveillance is to physically follow and observe the subject while remaining undetected. This tool can be applied at the beginning of an investigation to establish the subject's routines and associates. Surveillance is more commonly used after the investigator has had the opportunity to identify and understand the criminal enterprise or scheme involved. It requires considerable application of investigative time and resources.

In discussing surveillance techniques, it is helpful to understand the meaning of a few terms used in executing the surveillance. The "eyeball" is the initial observation point from which the surveilling officer alerts the rest of the team as to the start of movement or activity by the subject. The "base" or "command post" is usually the station or office from which the surveillance is being conducted. In situations where the surveillance is too remote from this location, a temporary base will be established. The base monitors the surveillance activity and can be called upon for assistance in case of an emergency, or for advice if the subject acts in a manner that was completely unanticipated. The "lead" is the officer in closest proximity to the subject. To avoid suspicion on the part of the subject, officers will frequently rotate the lead position. "Cover" is a term used to identify obstructions of the view that the subject has of the surveillance vehicle or officer.

In situations where the subject is likely to monitor radio traffic or use countersurveillance measures, a code system may be prepared in advance for radio communications. Officers, vehicles, directions and anticipated stops, or destinations for the subject and their associates will all receive codes or nicknames.

With the constant breakthroughs in technology, law enforcement has been able to reduce the expense of conducting surveillance by the use of electronic equipment. Some examples are the use of time-lapse photography on stationary locations, electronic tracking and audio transmitters and receivers, telephone interceptors, and body wires. As the major criminal enterprise is extremely well funded and aware of modern technological advances, the investigator must also consider the potential for countersurveillance.

Physical surveillance can be as varied as the activities of any individual. Although it is difficult to anticipate the potential value of information to be gained through surveillance, preparation and planning become important steps in selecting the most appropriate times and places to observe the subject. Surveillance is time and resource intensive, and the potential gains need to be weighed against the resources needed. The more information the investigator has developed on the probable scheme involved in the financial crime and the probable activities and destinations of the subject, the more likely that the surveillance will be fruitful. Factors involved in preparing to conduct a surveillance include:

1. Will the subject be on foot, in a vehicle, make use of a taxi, or public transportation?
2. Do they have places they frequent, a favorite restaurant, bar, park, and so forth?
3. Do they have a set schedule, such as office hours, lunchtimes, and so on?
4. Are they a loner or do they usually have friends or a group with them?
5. Is there a need to identify people and places they may visit before or after their set routines?
6. If the initial surveillance will be by vehicle, how many different vehicles are available to the subject (full identification should be obtained in advance: make, model, year, color, license plate)?
7. If they are involved in a criminal enterprise, what are the most likely times and places they will be traveling?

8. What types of clothing will be needed if the surveillance takes you into a building, business location, or outdoor area?
9. What are the geographic characteristics of the location where the surveillance will begin, possibly take you, and end?
10. Could the subject be anticipating being followed?
11. What amount of cover will the investigators have and how far away from the subject will they need to be to avoid detection?
12. Will there be a need for specialized equipment, and how will it be concealed (handheld radios, binoculars, cameras, etc.)?

The unique aspects of the subject, investigation, and information to be gained will dictate the items most needing consideration prior to executing an investigative surveillance. The following are a few examples of situations that required interesting consideration in preparing for surveillance situations.

Example 1

Two of the main figures in a narcotics trafficking organization were to attend a music concert in a park on the Fourth of July. The investigation was trying to determine the identity of others involved in the drug conspiracy. It was antici- pated that 15,000 to 20,000 people would be in attendance. The concert would run from 2 P.M. until 8 P.M. A stationary surveillance post was used to direct the surveillance (an unmarked van). Four agents were used to mix in the crowd and try to locate the subjects. The temperature was in the low 90s, and there was a clear sky. The agents in the crowd needed radio communication with the base and each other. They also needed to carry their weapons, cameras, and identification. These items needed to be concealed so as not to draw attention to the agents or identify them as law enforcement. Some of the planning included the use of backpacks and fanny packs and beach bags to conceal equipment. All radio communications would be relayed through the base. A single beep on the radio would alert the agent to go to a concealed location and contact the base for information. Each agent used a separate radio frequency, and all com- munications between the agents would be relayed through the base. The agents dressed to fit in with the crowd (shorts, T-shirts, jeans, sandals, etc.). When the subjects were located, photos were taken of those individuals they came in con- tact with and when the concert ended they were followed to their vehicle and arrest warrants were executed.

Example 2

The subject was a loner involved in a mail fraud scheme. He lived in an isolated rural area. It was necessary to drive on 2 miles of dirt road to get to his house. He drove a four-wheel-drive pickup truck. The investigation needed to deter- mine where he was cashing the money orders he received from the scheme. Although there was no location where a parked vehicle would go unnoticed, the eyeball (direct observation point) was set up on a bluff approximately 5 miles from the suspect's home. A telescope was used to watch for his movement. Three radio-equipped vehicles were placed on the paved roads that he could use in leaving his home. The eyeball would alert the other vehicles to the subject's movement and to his direction of travel so that a moving surveillance could pick him up once he was removed from the rural setting.

Example 3

The subject in this case was selling cocaine. The investigation wanted to identify his source and potential customers. The subject lived in a condominium in a suburban area. His background indicated that he rarely became active prior to noon and was often out late. A 3-day surveillance was planned for a weekend. Three vehicles and five agents were used. The weather was cold, with mixed rain and snow. Because the eyeball vehicle could not be kept running (a running vehicle parked for an extended period of time would look suspicious to the subject as well as the entire neighborhood), hand warmers, warm clothing, and a rotation system was used to maintain the observation point. The surveillance began at 8 P.M. The subject drove to a restaurant in a strip mall at about 9:30 P.M. and had dinner and a few drinks. Two agents entered the restaurant and observed the subject from another table. While in the restaurant, the subject made four phone calls at about 15-minute intervals. The last call he made was the only one in which he spent time talking on the phone. The surveillance continued as he left the restaurant and returned to his condominium at about 10:20 P.M. At 3 A.M. the subject left his residence, returned to the strip mall, and met another man in a second vehicle. Items were transferred from the trunks of both vehicles. Two surveillance vehicles followed and identified the second individual. The other surveillance vehicle followed the subject back to his condominium and was able to identify six other vehicles that arrived between 4:30 A.M. and 6 A.M. The surveillance team had prepared with changes of clothing for a variety of potential places where the subject could have met with his contact. The information gained during the surveillance helped the team obtain search warrants that uncovered illegal narcotics trafficking, the main supplier, and 18 customers.

Moving Surveillance

There are several methods used to conduct vehicular surveillance, and often adjustments must be made immediately based on the actions of the subject. Two common approaches are the use of a lead car that is rotated periodically, whereas the other vehicles take alternate routes to checkpoints that the subject has recently passed. In cases where the subject appears to be staying on a specific road or highway, vehicles may advance beyond the subject vehicle to be available to relieve the lead vehicle. In urban or suburban areas, the lead car will still maintain direct observation, but the rotation of the lead position will be more frequent. In these situations, the backup vehicles may use parallel routes to the subject vehicle to avoid becoming familiar to the subject. Having a red car behind you for a while, then a white one, and then a blue one may not draw your attention; but the same red, white, and blue vehicles going where you are going will.

Surveillance vehicles may have modifications made to help disguise the vehicle. Panel vans are often equipped with magnetic signs and logos that can be added and changed on the sides of the vehicle. For nighttime surveillance, headlights may be connected to dashboard switches that allow the driver to turn off power to any of the headlights. For daylight surveillance, washable spray paints may be used to alter the appearance of a vehicle as being rusted or having a panel, door, or trunk or hood section being recently replaced.

Simple items should also be considered in vehicular surveillance. Dome or door light bulbs can be removed to keep the interior lights off if the door of the vehicle is opened in the dark. The number of people in each car can also be changed to make the same car appear to be different.

There are also advantages to knowing how the subject drives. If the subject regularly drives 10 to 20 miles over the speed limit, the surveillance team must try to anticipate destinations and routes to keep up with the subject and continue alternating the lead car. If the subject drives 5 to 10 miles per hour under the speed limit, the lead car may have to pass and observe from a rearview mirror until another vehicle can take over the lead. This may mean having to stop and wait for the subject to pass and get a good distance ahead before rejoining the moving surveillance.

Moving surveillance requires good communication and coordination among members of the surveillance team and a heavy dose of common sense. If the subject does something totally unexpected (makes a U-turn, runs a red light, or stops on the side of the highway), the lead car needs to react as any other driver would who was on the road. The lead car should apprise the team of the surprise move and continue on its way. One of the other vehicles can pick up the lead position or find cover for a stationary surveillance until the subject continues to move.

Surveillance may be performed by the use of electronic and photographic equipment if its goals can be reached using these tools. If it is necessary to identify the persons entering a certain building or cars entering a certain location, time-lapse photography, motion-detection switches, or pressure switches may be used to activate still photos or videotape recordings of activity. In other cases, the equipment may be manually operated from a covert location that provides a clear view of the location to be watched. It is necessary that those officers involved in the surveillance are reminded of the applicable rules of evidence and the necessity for maintaining the chain of custody on any electronic or photographic evidence obtained. Other forms of electronic devices that are used in facilitating surveillances include magnetic radio transmitters and tracking units. A magnetic transmitter is concealed on the subject vehicle. The transmitter sends out a signal to a receiver that triangulates the vehicle coordinates, allowing the surveillance team to know where the vehicle is and the route it took to get there.

Electronic Surveillance and Monitoring

The use of electronic monitoring or eavesdropping devices is strictly regulated by law and the regulations of departments and agencies in the interpretation and application of those laws. The U.S. Supreme Court has established the individual's "right to privacy," and legal precedents are used to determine the appropriate use of electronic equipment to gather evidence. There is a wide range of equipment available. Each piece of equipment is designed for a rather specific use. When contemplating this type of monitoring, the officer or agent should be able to clearly articulate the circumstances that will be involved in the monitoring, the length and scope of the monitoring, and why this type of monitoring would be the only or most efficient way to obtain the evidence needed.

Telephonic Intercepts

There are several types of telephonic intercepts. Each is geared to gather specific information from an individual's use of a telephone, and each requires a degree of probable cause to justify and obtain a court order for application. Prior to the advent of cellular telephone communications, telephone intercepts were made through individual telephone lines (landlines) connected to phones at specific locations. A trained officer or agent would tie into the line to be intercepted and divert information to a covert monitoring location through a dedicated phone line to that location. The line into the monitoring location would then be wired to the specific piece of equipment authorized in the court order. The types of equipment used include a "pen register," "trap and trace," and "wiretap." The pen register would identify the telephone numbers called from the specific telephone line in the court order. The trap and trace would identify the telephone numbers of incoming calls to the specific telephone line. The wiretap would record the actual conversations taking place on the subject telephone line. Each of these evidence-gathering actions invade the subject's right to privacy at differing levels, and the requirements needed for issuance of a court order to use these methods increase with the severity of that invasion. Time limits are set in the court order as well as the security and level of onsite supervision required. As an example, a pen register may need to be physically checked and have the evidence secured hourly, daily, or weekly, depending on the amount of telephonic usage. At the other end of the spectrum, a wiretap requires that an officer be present and listen to all conversations being recorded 24 hours a day for the term of the court order. A court order for using of a wiretap is needed when neither party to the conversation consents or is aware of the recording being made. In cases where an informant is willing to make a call to the subject and agrees to have the call recorded, administrative approval for the recording is usually all that is required.

With the development of wireless communications, technological advances are continuing to provide the same type of capabilities for the interception of wireless communications.

Undercover Operations and Body Wires

Another formal method of observation would be the infiltration of the criminal enterprise by the use of an undercover operation. This tool is the most time intensive and the most dangerous to use. If successful, an undercover operation can provide evidence, leads, and insights that would never surface through normal investigative measures. Due to the extremely invasive nature of electronic monitorings and undercover operations, Congress and the courts have strictly regulated the circumstances and methods in which they may be used.

A body wire is a means for recording a conversation with the subject. It can be worn by an undercover agent or by a consenting third party such as an informant or other witness. The recording can be made by concealing a small tape recorder and microphone on the agent or witness, or by using a voice transmitter and microphone that will transmit the conversation to a nearby location where it is recorded.

Each method provides benefits and drawbacks in its use. The concealed recorder works better in areas where there is a lot of activity or background noise. A directional microphone designed to accentuate voice-range sounds makes the recording clearer for purposes of transcription and presentation in court. The disadvantages are that the conversation to be recorded may go on longer than the tape's capacity and the need to maintain constant surveillance on the wearer for security purposes. Changing the tape can be awkward, and an explanation of gaps in the recording is difficult to justify in court.

Example

An investigation of a businessman who was involved in money laundering funds through his business utilized an undercover operation. A meeting was arranged between the subject and the undercover agent. The subject would pick up the agent at his hotel, and they would go to dinner and discuss a deal. A body recorder was concealed on the agent. The recorder had a 90-minute tape capacity. It was anticipated that the meeting would exceed the 90 minutes, so arrangements were made for the agent to excuse himself to take a phone call. The technical agent timed the taping and called the undercover agent 10 minutes before the tape ran out. The tape was changed in a storeroom. The undercover agent returned to his table, completed the meeting, and the recording was ended. With the tape being used, a surveillance team observed the meeting from across the street and from another table inside the restaurant. This maintained security for the undercover agent. The tape recording blocked most of the general noise in the restaurant, and the voices were clearly audible without enhancement.

A transmitter is beneficial in situations where the individual wearing the wire is at risk. Those monitoring and making the recording can assess the situation and provide immediate assistance if needed. The length of the monitoring and recording is only limited by the life of the battery power. This allows for extended periods to pass when no conversation is taking place. It also allows for a greater range of movement because the receiver and recorder can be used in another vehicle. The drawback is that the recording will pick up more background noise and often record sharper noises over the voices.

Example

Using an undercover agent in the investigation of a bar owner or drug dealer provides a good example of the benefits in using a transmitter-type body wire. The subject owned a bar in a town located about 120 miles from the airport. The undercover agent was introduced to the subject by an advertisement the subject listed for the sale of his bar. The subject wanted to show the undercover agent his "second set of books" that showed the bar's actual income and the potential for laundering drug money. The subject was to pick up the agent, drive to the bar, review the records, and return to the agent's hotel near the airport. The transmitter had a 2-mile range on open road, allowing the surveillance team to stay far enough away to avoid suspicion. A mobile receiver and two recorders were used in one vehicle to record any conversations that took place during the ride. The entire contact with the subject lasted approximately 11 hours, and the entire time of the contact was recorded. Dual recorders were used to avoid a gap in the recording. Each recorder had a 6-hour capacity. If the meeting would have gone over 12 hours, the first recorder was prepared to rotate back in and maintain the taping continuity. The power supply for the transmitter was good for 24 hours. Although it would have been impossible to change tapes or batteries on the undercover agent, the transmitter made the recording possible.

Recordings can be cleaned to a degree to remove some of the extraneous noises, but this requires a full explanation of methods and processes used by the technical expert introducing the recordings into evidence. They are usually transcribed for the court, and both the recordings and the transcriptions are introduced. The rules of evidence are used to determine the admissibility of recordings.

Recordings are treated as other forms of evidence. The investigator must maintain the security of the tapes, prepare duplicates of the tapes to use in developing leads, and ensure an accurate and documented log for the chain of custody of the evidence.

Search and Seizure

The laws and regulations regarding searches and seizures are constantly changing to adapt to new case law covering unique application of the rules. The onset of regulating searches and seizures began with the drafting and adoption of the Fourth and Fifth Amendments to the Constitution of the United States. The initial restrictions have been expanded, modified, and defined through the courts by judicial review and discretion. Although the courts may alter the interpretation based on changes in society, the most obvious judicial involvement comes from improper use by investigating authorities and enforcement personnel.

Amendment IV

The right of the people to be secure in their persons, houses, papers, and effects, against unreasonable searches and seizures, shall not be violated, and no Warrants shall issue, but upon probable cause, supported by Oath or affirmation, and particularly describing the place to be searched, and the persons or things to be seized.

Amendment V

No person shall be held to answer for a capital, or otherwise infamous crime, unless on a presentment or indictment of a Grand Jury, except in cases arising in the land or naval forces, or in the Militia, when in actual service in time of War or in public danger; nor shall any person be subject for the same offence to be twice put in jeopardy of life or limb; nor shall be compelled in any Criminal Case to be a witness against himself, nor be deprived of life, liberty, or property, without due process of law; nor shall private property be taken for public use, without just compensation.

A search can be defined as a close examination of an item, place, or person in an attempt to find something concealed or locate something missing. A seizure can be defined as taking possession of an item or person, legally or by force. Both the Fourth and Fifth Amendments have been expanded, defined, and modified by judicial review and discretion. The Fourth Amendment requires a warrant to be issued upon probable cause, and under oath or affirmation, and to specify the place or person to be searched and any item or person to be seized, prior to executing a search. The framers wanted to limit government and law enforcement by prohibiting "unreasonable" searches and seizures. The first question to be asked in obtaining documentary and recorded information is will the method of obtaining the evidence qualify or be considered a search.

Prior to the Supreme Court decision in *Katz v. United States* in 1967, a search was defined and applied by the courts under the "trespass doctrine." In very general terms, to be a search, the evidence-gathering method had to involve physically entering a "constitutionally protected" person, place, or thing. The Court's decision in *Katz v. United States* removed the trespass doctrine as a deciding factor in what constituted a search. In its place, the Court expanded the scope of a search to include any violation of privacy, in which it could be shown that the individual exhibited an expectation of privacy and that society would reasonably accept that expectation of privacy as valid. Terms such as *reasonable, exhibiting, and expectation* then became the test ground for further definition and interpretation by the courts. There are several court decisions that have had an effect on the interpretation as to when a warrant is required to gather evidence and what qualifies as a search. Some cases of note would include *United States v. Miller, 425 U.S. 435 (1976); Smith v. Maryland, 442 U.S. 745 (1979); United States v. White, 401 U.S. 745 (1971); and Kyllo v. United States, 533 U.S. 27 (2001).*

Technology has changed and is changing. As this happens, more ways are available for law enforcement to gather evidence. The more intrusive the means of gathering, the more regulation is applied. Even if the situation does not require an order from the court in the form of a warrant, internal procedures and regulations will address how, when, what, and where information can be gathered. In many situations, there may be multiple sources for the same information. As we discussed earlier, financial transactions are usually documented in several places, for all parties to the transaction, and in multiple copies. The investigator will be required to justify and articulate the reasons why intrusive measures such as a search warrant, wiretap, or undercover operation are necessary for a successful completion of the investigation. The use of search warrants is a valuable tool to law enforcement. The process of obtaining a warrant is also drawn from the Fourth Amendment and can be approached in four parts.

Reasonable or Unreasonable

Reasonableness is a subjective matter. However, the courts have helped to introduce objectivity in determining reasonableness in the use of search warrants by placing the decision not with the individual but basing it on societal norms. Would a reasonable person see the need to execute a search warrant based on the facts and information currently existing in the criminal investigation? Luckily, the investigator does not make the call. The information is prepared by one of the investigating officers in an affidavit requesting that the court order the search to be done. The judge becomes the objective, reasonable person who decides on the sufficiency of the evidence presented in the affidavit, as to whether a court order will be issued.

Probable Cause

In making the determination as to whether probable cause exists to order a warrant, the courts again put themselves in the place of the reasonable person. Does the evidence and information contained in the affidavit support the need for a warrant? More important, does it support the probability that the evidence sought is at the location that the officers wish to search. Probable cause is not definitive proof but rather the reasonableness of the likelihood that the evidence is there to be found. Again, the judge becomes the reasonable objective party to make that decision and to decide yes or no to the warrant requested by affidavit.

Oath or Affirmation

The oath or affirmation is the swearing in of the officer submitting the affidavit to the judge. The officer preparing the affidavit is the one who reviewed the evidence obtained thus far in the investigation, has made personal observations, has personal experience in the type of investigation being done, and believes that there is probability that additional evidence will be uncovered during the search of the location described in the affidavit. The judge will read the affidavit, question the officer requesting the warrant by affidavit, and administer the oath or affirmation. The formality and sometimes solemnity of this procedure should make it clear to the officer that this is not the time for unrealistic speculation or embellishment of the facts and circumstances involved. In almost every case in which a warrant is used to gather evidence, the defense will do everything it can to discredit the officer's affidavit in an attempt to have the evidence obtained declared inadmissible in court. If successful, it will also eliminate the leads obtained from the execution of the warrant.

Particular Description

The *particular description* requirement in the Fourth Amendment covers two distinct aspects in the drafting and execution of a search warrant. The first is the location to be searched. This constitutes the specific location to be searched, house, motel room, car, person, trunk, briefcase, and so forth. Due to errors made in identifying locations, the courts have placed additional conditions on describing the location to be searched. These include a visual description, in sufficient detail, to assure that the right location is being searched. An example is 1234 Elm St., City, State; a single family dwelling; a single-story home with gray siding and a white roof, including an attached garage and a fenced backyard that contains a white, metal storage shed. The legal description being "Lot 1 of the Elm Subdivision as shown on Plat ..."

The second aspect is the particular identification of the items to be seized during the execution of the warrant. The officer must specify the items that are anticipated to be found during the search, seized, and taken as evidence. Although there is always some uncertainty in what may be found, it is reasonable to include some general category for items that need to be taken that cannot be specifically identified in advance. In an example of a warrant on the residence of a suspected narcotics trafficker, the warrant may list marijuana, cocaine, cutting agents, scales, packaging materials, and other drug paraphernalia. The general category of other drug paraphernalia would allow the searching officers to take items such as needles, syringes, tubing, other chemicals (known to be used in the mixing or manufacture of other illegal narcotics), and any other items that the officers can justify as being in the category of other drug paraphernalia. Any contraband can also be removed during the execution of the warrant because the possession of those items is prohibited. In our example, let us say that the officers also find child pornography. The pornography would be taken, but it would be up to the courts to decide whether it could be used as evidence against the suspect for additional criminal charges because it was not anticipated and specified in the warrant. In certain cases, it may be best to suspend the search and obtain an additional warrant for items related to the new criminal activities.

Preparing an Affidavit for a Search Warrant

Before making the decision to seek a search warrant, the officer or agent needs to look objectively at the situation and be prepared to answer questions as to why the warrant is necessary. In a financial investigation, this becomes more important because there are often several paper trails that can be followed to document and prove the facts and circumstances of an individual's financial dealings. Can records other than those in the possession of the subject be obtained through third-party contacts? If so, is there a problem in specifically obtaining records of illegal or concealed financial activities? Can all of the transactions be developed through evidence outside the possession of the subject? Are a substantial number of the transactions with recalcitrant or hostile witnesses such as family, friends, close associates, or others involved in the financial crime? Is there a strong likelihood that the evidence of criminal activity will be destroyed if normal gathering methods are used? Each case will be unique in its nature and the aspects involved, but each should be scrutinized when considering the use of warrants for the purpose of gathering evidence.

The Affidavit

To avoid the "unreasonable" prohibition cited in the Fourth Amendment, there are several areas within the affidavit for a search warrant that have to be addressed and shown to be reasonable. These areas are similar to the legal requirements applied to evidence. The reasonableness would be applied to the competency of the affiant and to the relevancy of the potential in the search being productive in the investigation.

The Affiant

The judge needs assurance that the officer or agent applying for the warrant is a reasonable person, has sufficient experience in the matters contained in the affidavit, has demonstrated specialized and applicable knowledge of the criminal processes involved, and is most familiar with the specifics involved in the particular investigation. The affidavit should include the full identification of the agent or officer, the time in service, and number of similar cases the officer has investigated. The officer must also show knowledge of the location to be searched and the items to be seized. The officer must also be able to articulate the special or exigent circumstances that led to the request for the search warrant.

Probable Cause

Probable cause is just that, a reasonable probability that something is true or factual. This is the key to submitting a successful request for a search warrant. The officer must convince the judge that the subject has probably committed the crime identified in the affidavit. It must also be shown that specific, and sometimes general, evidence of the crime will probably be found in the location specified in the affidavit. To do this, the officer must put forth indications that all of these are probable and provide just cause for the warrant to be issued. Indications of guilt on the part of the subject that led to the initiation of the investigation should be provided to show that the subject is the right person to be investigated. Information should also be provided that shows the likelihood that some, if not all, of the evidence sought exists and will be located in the area to be searched. In addition, it should be shown why the officer believes that the evidence would not be available through other means of gathering.

Oath or Affirmation

The oath or affirmation aspect of the affidavit stretches or implies the aspect of probability on the part of the affiant. The affiant is sworn in and attests to the truth and accuracy of the contents of the affidavit. The oath or affirmation is not limited to the direct knowledge of the affiant but includes any other information obtained in the investigation that is included. Information obtained from witnesses, informants, experts, and inferences based on experience and service are all contained in the affidavit and, therefore, attested to by the affiant. This is a serious business in which carelessness or complacency can have a long-lasting detrimental effect on the officer's career. It may also lead to civil liability if it can be shown that the affiant altered or embellished the facts and circumstances attested to in the affidavit.

Particular Description

The last area of probability lies in the description of the location to be searched and the items to be seized. On the surface, the location would seem to be rather easy to determine and identify, but circumstances can make it difficult. In one case, an arrest warrant was issued for a vehicle used in the commission of a crime. The vehicle was identified in the affidavit by year, make, model, color, style (four-door sedan), and vehicle identification number (VIN). When the officers arrived at the subject's place of business to execute the seizure, they were confronted with 12 identical vehicles that the subject had purchased for his business under a fleet purchase agreement. The fact that the VIN number was included in the warrant made it possible for the officers to seize the correct vehicle and avoid embarrassment. Similar complications can be encountered in urban and suburban areas in locating the correct address. A physical description of the location helps ensure accuracy: Apartment 201, 123 Elm St., City, State; the apartment on the second floor, first door on the left after going up the staircase on the south entrance to the apartment building, consisting of two bedrooms, a kitchen–dining room, a living room, and one bath. This type of description makes clear which apartment is to be searched.

In the same manner, the items to be seized should be identified as accurately as possible. In financial investigations, the motive is to gain wealth through illegal means. Therefore, it is necessary to include any and all records relating to financial transactions of any kind (the officer may include a list of typical items but needs to preface the list with a phrase like "to include but not be limited to"). If the income is generated from other criminal activity, the officer should include the description of any evidence common to the commission of that type of criminal activity. As an example, the subject derives income from the sale of stolen identities. The affidavit may include birth certificates, driver's licenses, social security cards, credit cards, and other forms of identification. The officer would also want to find leads to the subject's customers. In this case, the affidavit would include address books, telephone directories, and e-mail directories in paper, digital, electronic, or other formats. Common items found in warrants involving financial crimes include currency, bank records, ownership documents, account statements, receipts, and any other documents that relate to the specific crime.

Executing the Warrant

Every government agency involved in the execution of search warrants will have standard procedures for the search methodology (grid, room, or specified area, and the double search rotation); the logging of evidence to be seized; the packaging and identification procedures; and the means for accumulating, inventorying, and removing the evidence while maintaining the chain of custody and control. These procedures will apply to any investigative unit authorized by consent or warrant in the collection of physical evidence.

The major difference encountered in a financial investigation lies in the fact that the bulk of the evidence seized will be in the form of documents and paper. Officers on the search team must be instructed on some of the nuances involved in seizing this type of evidence. If at all possible, documents to be seized should be photographed in the location where they are found (of course, this applies to all evidence seized in a search). Identification of the officer locating the documents should be noted and a summary of the documents, in sufficient detail, be made to be admissible in court. As an example, a nightstand drawer is opened and check registers for the subject's checking account are found. The check registers should be sorted into order by date or check numbers, and the evidence tag should read "Officer Smith, 07/04/00, check registers for account #12345 at Wonder Bank for the period 01/01/96 through 07/03/00 (checks 1234 through 9876)."

Special care should be taken to note any gaps in sequence and not to merge similar records found in different locations. In removing files from a desk or file cabinet, the records should be taken in the same physical order in which they were found (front to back in standing files and top to bottom on stacked files). The search should not overlook scraps of paper, papers in wastebaskets, or any other paper containing any writing or notation (check marks or notes in books, telephone directories, maps, menus, etc.). Other items to consider may include shredded and partially burned papers (document reconstruction can be done if the importance of the documents are a crucial part of the investigation). Someone trained in computer operations, security, and systems analysis should do the seizure of information in electronic format. Computer files may be protected by a self-destruct mechanism that is activated by a keystroke or simply turning off or unplugging the computer. Remember to specify the computers as well as the disks, drives, files, and any other item that may contain information in the affidavit, or request for search authority.

The following chapters will provide a basic understanding of the financial investigation and the methodology used in formulating the investigative report. We will also discuss those methods that are legally accepted as proof for use in civil and criminal litigation. Finally, we will address the case report and the preparation for presentation of the case in court.

What Is a Financial Investigation?

9

What is a white collar criminal investigation? What are the methods used to investigate and prosecute these types of crimes? What is forensic accounting? How can these tools be used to enhance other criminal investigations? These are the questions that will be addressed in the following chapters.

To begin we must understand the motivation for criminal behavior. Criminologists have struggled to find the common ground in the motivations to violate statutory rules. White collar crime, first coined by Edwin Sutherland, is a financial crime. It may involve violence and physical harm to the victims, but the root cause is greed and a lust for financial gain. Sutherland and others have strived to provide a much more specific definition to distinguish this type of crime from the myriad of "street crimes" and narrow the scope of reasons that perpetrators have for the commission of such crimes. For our purposes, it is sufficient to know that most crimes are committed for financial gain. The street mugger and the corporate executive have that much in common. The major differences are in the amount of gain, the planning required, the intricacies of the crime, and the tools needed to commit the crime.

If we use the risk–benefit approach in looking at white collar crime, it is readily seen that the potential financial benefits dwarf the risks of arrest and conviction. It is estimated that white collar crimes cost society several hundred billion dollars each year, and yet the sentences handed down in the most egregious and high-profile white collar crimes are usually no more than 5 to 10 years.

White collar crimes are usually planned and carried out by more than one individual. Often the schemes are so complex as to require several people, each with a unique position of authority or responsibility, to effect the crimes. Some of the schemes are so involved that any one of the coconspirators may not know or be aware of the others involved in the scheme, or the intricacies of how the scheme works. For the investigator to prove "beyond a reasonable doubt" each of the coconspirator's culpability, he or she must understand the scheme in its entirety. The investigator must then be able to explain the scheme accurately and in terms that a jury can understand. To accomplish this, the investigation must clearly show the financial gain to each individual involved in the illegal activity, the role played by that individual in the scheme, and his or her culpability for criminal prosecution.

However, the methodology used in these complex investigations can also be used to substantiate and corroborate the commission of other criminal acts. Just as investigators have to weave their way through reams of documents and hours upon hours of testimony to uncover illegal activities, they can use the same principles and methodology to enhance and support other crimes that are committed on a smaller scale. A criminal enterprise, no matter the size, still functions the same way as any other business operation. The difference is in the legality of the financial gain or income derived. When the investigator can prove that proceeds from illegal activities go directly into the pocket of a suspect, conviction for the illegal activity is certain to follow.

One way to describe the use of forensic accounting in a financial investigation is the compiling of all the financial transactions of a subject for consecutive time periods, and then comparing the results of the time periods in sequence to determine the income or the loss the subject incurred, period to period. In tax investigations, the time periods are set by the calendar or fiscal year of the subject. For other investigations, the time periods can be set in the manner easiest to present to a judge or jury. The increase in wealth is shown from period to period by means of spreadsheet schedules that show the financial status of the subject at the end of each period. A summary schedule is then prepared to show the increase in wealth of the subject during each period. Finally, all legal or legitimate income for the period is deducted. If a likely source for the remaining income can be shown, the remainder for each period can be accepted as being derived from that likely source. In the case of illegal income, such as from narcotics trafficking, fencing stolen goods, or fraud schemes, being able to show the gain from the illegal activity greatly improves the probability of a successful prosecution.

For example, Jim D is suspected of selling crack cocaine. He is arrested for a single sale to an undercover police officer. He has no criminal history, and he faces a minimal sentence based on the buy as his first offense. Jim has to have a source for his product, just as a retail store needs a manufacturer and a wholesaler. Jim needs a place to keep his product until it is sold, in the same way stores need storage space or a warehouse. He also needs a clientele and ways to expand his customer base, similar to the word-of-mouth expansion, advertising, and solicitation used in business.

In this case, the police officers have the discretion to charge Jim based on the buy or to extend the investigative steps. In this situation, it would be standard procedure to execute a search warrant for narcotics and narcotics paraphernalia on the residence and vehicle (if Jim has one). If the officers limit the scope of the warrant to these items, they may find additional drugs and be able to add a possession with intent to distribute charge against Jim. If the officers apply the business logic expressed earlier, they can expand the warrant to include the personal records at Jim's residence. This would include bank statements, credit card receipts, phone bills, loan statements, and any document that would show the receipt or use of illegally obtained funds.

The value of this information is not apparent on the surface and requires analysis. The officer or investigator needs to follow a few simple steps to determine whether the information obtained warrants a more extensive investigation into Jim's activities. The officer must find out as much as possible about Jim. This information can often be obtained during the interview after the arrest. Any public information available on Jim should also be obtained and reviewed, for example, traffic records, neighborhood complaints, Division of Motor Vehicle (DMV) records, National Crime Information Center (NCIC) records, and Register of Deeds. Much of the background information needed will already have been accumulated in the initial investigation of the criminal act, but any gaps in the information should be filled.

Why should the officers care about records that are months or even years old? In cases that are presented in court, the evidence put forth must be relevant to the case in chief. How can a check register from the prior year be relevant? In our case, let us say that the records we obtained show:

For the past two years, Jim has spent $25,000 to $30,000 a year on living expenses, rent, groceries, clothing, utilities, and so forth. Cash deposits to his checking account were made to cover these expenses.
Purchase of a car, $38,000 (cash), vehicle title.
Credit card purchases for 3 months at bars and restaurants; for 2 weeks the charges were out of state.
Telephone calls to 18 numbers, two to four times a week.
Long-distance telephone calls to one number twice a month.
DMV records show three moving violations in the past 6 months (same area).
Jim's personal history tells us that he was born and lived in town all his life.
He attended college for 1 year.
He worked part-time as a bartender for 2 years.
He has been unemployed for the past 2 years.

What might additional investigation reveal? What would you look into? What are potential additional sources of information you would use?

Other sources of information could include interviews with people he has been associated with: teachers, classmates, friends, relatives, the employees where he banks, the salesman that sold him his car, and his former boss and coworkers at the bar. Keep in mind that any of the people you talk to may provide leads to others who could be beneficial to the investigation. In addition, telephone subscriber information would identify the repeat calls Jim made locally and out of state. You would be wise to gather as much background information as possible on these individuals before attempting to interview them. Why would this be the case?

Here is the additional information you received by extending the investigation. The bank tells you that Jim deposits cash into his checking account every week. The amount is usually around $500.00. The deposits are usually in $20 and $50 bills. He does not have any other business with the bank (savings, loans, CDs, etc.).

The car salesman states that Jim came in and selected the car. He asked for some options to be added. He gave the salesman $13,000.00 in cash as a down payment and the balance of $25,000.00 in cash 8 days later when he picked up the vehicle. He was with a red-haired girl when he picked up the car.

Neighbors say that he must work nights because he is home during the day and gone most evenings. He has a red-haired girlfriend and does not talk to any of the neighbors.

Telephone records identified the repeat call recipients. NCIC background information shows that two of the local individuals had prior arrests for drug possession, and the out-of-state call recipient has a "call DEA" flag on the hit.

Credit card information shows that Jim paid for hotel rooms, meals, and drinks in the same town as the out-of-state call recipient.

College interviews reveal that Jim lived on the wild side and skipped a lot of classes. He received a reprimand for drinking on campus. One professor remembered seeing Jim smoking pot one evening but did not report it to the school.

What does this information indicate to you?
What will you do with this information?
Do you have any proof of further criminal activity by Jim?
Do you need further investigation?
Can you justify reasonable suspicion to your superiors to authorize a further investigation? How? What? Where? When? Who? In what order?

The potential benefits received by investigating deeper, in this example, could include any or all of the following results.

1. Jim has no legal or legitimate source of income.
2. Jim earned at least $88,000.00 in the last 2 years.
3. Jim has known illegal income from the sale of narcotics.
4. The out-of-state individual is his supplier for narcotics.
5. He was fired from bartending for having too many visits from non-customer friends at the bar.
6. Jim spent an additional $1,000.00 a month when he contacted his supplier out of town.

7. Three of the 18 customers identified by the phone records say they buy drugs from Jim.
8. Jim's minimum income from narcotics was $37,000.00 the first year and $75,000.00 the second year.
9. Jim gives up his supplier for a plea bargain, giving him a 5- to 10-year sentence.

Originally, we had Jim on a first-offense single sale of narcotics. With the additional work, we were able to break up his operation, chase his customers to other sources, identify other local addicts, possibly use some of the customers as future informants, assist law enforcement out of state in arresting the supplier, and place conspiracy charges on Jim and the supplier. Would this result be worth the extra investigative effort?

The financial evidence obtained through the investigation must be organized in a manner that demonstrates when and how much money was obtained from the illegal activity. This is the aspect of financial investigations where basic accounting principles are used. Forensic accounting involves the application of principles in a manner that works from the current financial status of the subject backward to determine when and how much money was gained. Once Jim's total income is determined year to year or time frame to time frame, we can eliminate any legitimate income received from the computation, and whatever is left must have come from another source. In our example, Jim's likely source for the other income would be from the sale of narcotics.

Organizing the evidence in a logical progression simplifies understanding how the individual financial transactions tie together to show the income. The types of transactions are sorted by category, and a schedule is prepared to show the transactions that apply to each time frame in the computation. Assets would be shown on one schedule, liabilities on another, expenditures on another, and so on. The number of transactions would dictate the number of schedules used. In our example, we believe that Jim has been selling narcotics for the past 2 years. Our time frames would be each of the 2 years. Our investigation of Jim shows a bank account and the purchase of a car as the only two assets he has. The asset schedule would show the balance in his bank account at the end of each period (year) and the purchase price of his new car.

Assets	First Year	Second Year
Bank balance	$13,000.00	$20,000.00
New car	0	$38,000.00
Totals	$13,000.00	$58,000.00

For our example, we will say that Jim had no bank account or balance prior to the first year. The next schedule prepared would identify the items

that Jim owed to other people or financial institutions. In our case, Jim has
no debts prior to or during our two time frames. A schedule is not required
for liabilities if there are none, but they will be included with zero balances
on the summary schedule to let those people seeing or reviewing the case
know that they were considered and investigated.

The next schedule prepared would identify each of the expenditures
Jim made during the 2 years under investigation. If any category of expense
(clothing, utilities, food, entertainment, travel, etc.) contains a large number
of transactions, a subschedule for that category can be made, and the balance
carried over to the expenditure schedule. For our purposes, we will assume that
the subschedules were made and show the totals in the expenditures schedule.

Expenditures	First Year	Second Year
Rent	$6,000.00	$6,600.00
Utilities	$2,000.00	$2,000.00
Traffic fines	0	$200.00
Clothing	$4,500.00	$8,500.00
Groceries	$7,200.00	$7,200.00
Travel	$5,000.00	$6,000.00
Totals	$24,700.00	$30,500.00

As there are no other categories in our example, we would then transfer
the totals to the final summary schedule. The result would look like this:

Jim's Income Years 1 and 2

Item	First Year	Second Year
Assets	$13,000.00	$58,000.00
Less: liabilities	0	0
Net worth (NW)	$13,000.00	$58,000.00
Less: prior year NW	0	13,000.00
Increase/decrease	$13,000.00	$45,000.00
Add: expenditures	24,700.00	30,500.00
Total income	$37,700.00	$75,500.00
Less: legal income	0	0
Narcotics income	$37,700.00	$75,500.00

The schedules and report for a criminal prosecution will contain only
that financial information that can be proven beyond a reasonable doubt and
as attributable to the subject of the investigation. For this reason, all evidence
used to obtain an information or an indictment must adhere to the rules of
evidence. The scope of evidence used for civil litigation is required to meet
lesser standards, and that used for internal audit and control even lesser ones.

In most criminal investigations, the unreported or illegitimate income will be a portion of the actual amounts received by the subject. Usually, a follow-up civil case will be prepared to accurately reflect the total amount of proceeds derived. Remember that the criminal case is prepared to determine the criminal culpability of the subject for the illegal activities that generated the income. As long as the criminal amounts are sufficient to warrant prosecution, the financial criminal activity is established. Keep in mind that the individual is being prosecuted for the counts of criminal activity that occur during the time frames (acts of fraud, acts of embezzlement, sales of narcotics, etc.) and not for the illegitimate income (unless tax charges are involved). Federal, state, or local tax authorities may follow the criminal investigation and add a civil tax liability, and interest and penalties to the liability of the defendant after a determination of guilt is made. In cases where the income is generated from an illegal activity (not just a failure to report legitimate income), the illegal gains are often subject to criminal or administrative forfeiture by the level of government that has jurisdiction in the case. Forfeiture statutes are designed to ensure that a criminal does not benefit from his or her criminal acts.

The Theory behind Indirect Methods of Proof

In taking on any project, it is necessary to understand the logic and purpose behind the overall construction of the project; and how and why the completed project should function. The same understanding of the logic and purpose behind the indirect methods of proof are needed for the financial criminal investigator to build and present a fully functional criminal case.

In the presentation of forensic evidence in general criminal investigations, the scientific method of analysis is used to reconstruct the factual recreation of the crime. The investigator follows the scientific procedures to arrive at an *a priori* conclusion that will satisfy the court as to proof beyond a reasonable doubt as to how, what, where, when, and why the crime was committed; and by whom. In the application of forensic accounting techniques, the same principles are applied to establish the commission of a criminal financial violation.

We will do a quick review of the scientific method and then see how each of the steps are used in the financial investigation. The first two terms that require definition are inductive and deductive reasoning. Inductive reasoning takes a specific piece of information and categorizes that item to form a general conclusion. Deductive reasoning moves in the other direction by taking a general observation and following it through to a specific conclusion that establishes a fact.

The scientific development of a theory begins with a hypothesis, or the assumption of how and why an event has occurred. The next step is the collection and classification of information or evidence pertinent to the event that is believed to have occurred. The investigator is then responsible for the synthesis of the information or evidence found. This involves relating it to the hypothesis and all the other aspects of the investigation upon which the information could have bearing. Once enough evidence or information is found to support the hypothesis, a theory of how the event occurred is formulated. Then, the investigator can determine whether further investigation will increase the accuracy of the original hypothesis and support the theory of the crime. After all of the information and evidence is obtained and worked through the scientific process, an *a priori* conclusion can be drawn to establish or disprove the event or crime.

With all of the evidence analyzed, categorized, and synthesized, the investigator can construct a logical presentation of the evidence describing the deductive reasoning employed in the process of the investigation. The case report is then prepared to show that the elements of the financial crime have been met and the evidence of intent point to the perpetrator of the financial crime.

To simplify the scientific method application in indirect methods of proof, let's look at a common item of evidence and follow it through the scientific process. Assume we are investigating a potential financial fraud committed by an individual during the years 2010 through 2011. Your suspect drives a 2011 foreign sports car. The deductive reasoning applied to this piece of information would lead the investigator to find out all of the relevant facts about the car. The dealership purchase contract would provide the date and amount of the purchase price, financing and trade-in information, and tax and licensing charges.

The vehicle would be categorized in the assets of the suspect. Analysis of the vehicle information would reveal that the cost of the vehicle was $120,000.00, it was purchased on February 14, 2011, tax and licensing fees totaled $6,832.43, a 2009 Lincoln was traded in at a value of $28,000.00 (cost basis of $38,000.00 in 2009), $42,000.00 in cash was deposited when the factory order was made (01/08/2011), and the balance of $56,832.43 was paid by cashier check from ABC Bank.

The next phase in the scientific method would be to synthesize the information obtained about the vehicle. This would include following how the information gained relates and affects all other areas of the investigation. Using the net worth method of proof, the following other categories would be impacted by the information on the suspect:

1. The asset acquisition of $120,000.00 would be included in the asset schedule for 2011.
2. The 2009 Lincoln would be removed from the asset schedule in 2011 (−$38,000.00).

3. The personal expenditures schedule would list the tax and licensing fees for 2011.
4. Bank accounts would be checked to identify the source of the down payment.
   a. If cash was withdrawn from an existing account, the reduction should be included in the year-end bank account reconciliation.
   b. If a cash hoard was claimed by the suspect and cash outside of bank accounts was used, a reduction in cash on hand should be further investigated.
5. ABC Bank should be checked to verify the suspect's purchase of the cashier's check.
   a. If ABC Bank is not used regularly by the suspect, it should be checked for any other financial activities of the suspect.
   b. Additional checks should be performed for any other sources of the funds used such as safe deposit boxes, personal loans, gifts, and inheritances.
   c. If the cashier's check was purchased by a nominee, an interview and cursory examination of the nominee's finances is necessary.

Hypothetically, if this was the only transaction that the suspect made during the periods under investigation, we could deduce that without the claim of cash on hand or the removal of cash from an existing bank account, the suspect had to have amassed $88,832.43 in 2011.

- An increase in assets of $120,000.00 for 2011 (new car)
- A decrease in assets of $38,000.00 for 2011 (trade-in)
- A personal expenditure increase of $6,832.43 (tax and licensing)

Note that the net worth method credits the suspect with a nondeductible loss (for tax purposes) on the 2009 Lincoln. This aspect of the method can be pointed out to judge or jury as to how the method shows the least amount of income the suspect had to have received during the periods under investigation.

The scientific method is applied to all indirect methods of proof. In using the scientific method for an investigation using the bank deposits and cash expenditures, our above example would be handled like this:

1. The asset acquisition (new car) and the asset disposition (trade-in) are not pertinent to the bank deposit and cash expenditure method. (This method completes the investigation by focusing on current deposited funds and the use of cash to make current expenditures.)
2. The $42,000.00 down payment would be included in the cash expenditures for 2011. This method of proof would take into account any

cash withdrawals from bank accounts to offset any possibility of cash being accumulated by the suspect for use in making part of the down payment. (Again showing that the method is designed to show the least amount of income the suspect had to have received during the periods under investigation.)

3. The purchase of the cashier's check for $56,832.43 would be shown as another cash expenditure for 2011. The same caution would be taken in analyzing the cash withdrawals for 2011 to ensure that the suspect was not being charged twice for any amount in the computation.

Under the bank deposits method, using the same scenario as in the aforementioned net worth example, we should show the same amount of income. Since the analysis of cash in and out of bank accounts would be shown in a separate schedule in the investigative report, the scientific method application to this item of information would reflect that the suspect amassed $98,832.43 in 2011. Using the same accumulation of evidence, the computations should show the same results. This is also a means for verification of the accuracy of whichever indirect method is used and to ensure that all of the relationships of each transaction have been taken into consideration.

A further look would reveal that in the net worth method, the depreciated value of the trade-in (cost of $38,000.00, trade-in value of $28,000.00) would have been reflected in the 2009 period based on the actual cost when it was acquired. This does not reflect an inconsistency in the two computations. Each method is designed to show income allocations correctly for each relevant time period.

The $10,000.00 difference is strictly based on what is being analyzed. To determine actual money flow to the individual, the bank deposits method gives the complete picture. In a determination of income from a taxing perspective, the $10,000.00 difference is adjusted back in the net worth method as a civil assessment disallowing the nondeductible loss. The bank deposits method shows the current cash and banking activity, and therefore already accounts for the nondeductible loss. Other civil adjustments would be made in the bank deposits method, and both methods would reflect the least amount of income gained by the suspect for criminal prosecution purposes.

Since the methods will balance out, either method can be used to cross-check any other method being used in the investigation. The only rationale needed is to ensure that each financial event is considered in its entirety on how it is handled or applied in the corresponding methods.

The logic and reasoning used by the courts to accept the indirect methods of proof are based on the fact that these methods employ the same level of scrutiny in presenting a financial conclusion as other sciences are used in the formulation of circumstantial evidence in other crime scene investigations.

The only difference between the two is the perspective on what is being scientifically analyzed and presented. The crime scene investigation recreates the specific time, place, and method in committing a crime. The indirect forensic financial investigation recreates the financial activities of an individual over sequential periods of time. Therefore, the accuracy and the truths uncovered from applying the scientific methods of investigation to the financial analysis carry the same weight and level of veracity in the eyes of the court.

In the early 1900s, many of the cases involving indirect methods of proof were being contested in appellate courts. The decisions varied as to guilt or acquittal. These led to the United States Supreme Court hearing and decision in *Holland v. United States* in 1954 (348 U.S. 121). In its decision, the Court set the parameters for the use, application, methodology, and reasoning behind the indirect methods and the application of forensic accounting techniques.

Requirements for Indirect Methods of Proof

10

What are the legally accepted standard methods of proof in forensic accounting investigations? There are three methods of proof that have been accepted to prove forensic accounting investigations in criminal cases. These are the specific item, the bank deposits and cash expenditures, and the net worth and expenditures methods of proof. Each method relies on a thorough investigation of the facts, deductive and inductive reasoning in the analysis of circumstantial evidence, and establishing "proof beyond a reasonable doubt" through negative proof of potential defenses.

The requirements for the use of indirect methods of proof have been established by court decisions beginning in the 1900s and continuing through to the present. Each time an innovation in indirect methodology is applied in a criminal investigation, the courts are faced with determining whether the innovation meets or violates the rules of evidence, and the requirements to prove the violation beyond a reasonable doubt. As criminal courts continue to refine the indirect methodology, civil courts and independent auditors adjust their efforts to the refinements made by the courts.

The three basic methods of proof all apply these requirements and incorporate the judicial modifications to ensure accuracy and a high level of success in their presentations. The case of *Holland v. United States* is considered a landmark decision in the use of indirect methods of proof. Although the decision specifically addresses the use of the net worth and expenditures method, the Supreme Court's explanation of its decision outlines several specific needs that have to be met for the use of forensic accounting applications to be used and deemed valid in litigation.

Holland v. United States, 348 U.S. 121 (1954)

348 U.S. 121
Holland et ux v. United States
Certiorari to the United States Court of Appeals for the Tenth Circuit
No. 37
Argued October 20–21, 1954
Decided December 6, 1954
With the Government using the "net worth" method of proof, petitioners were convicted under 145 of the Internal Revenue Code of a willful attempt to evade their income taxes for the year 1948. The Government's

computation showed an increase of $32,000 in their net worth during 1948, for which they reported only $10,211 as taxable income. Petitioners claimed that the Government failed to include in its opening net worth figure $104,000 of currency accumulated before 1933. The Government introduced no direct evidence to dispute this claim but relied on the inference that anyone who had $104,000 in cash would not have undergone the hardships and privations shown to have been endured by petitioners during the 1926–1940 period. The evidence further indicated that improvements to a hotel and other assets acquired during the 1946–1948 period were bought in installments, as if out of earnings rather than accumulated cash; and petitioner's income tax returns as far back as 1913 showed that their income was insufficient to enable them to save any appreciable amount of money. There was independent evidence of a likely source of unreported taxable income that the jury could reasonably find to be the source of the increase in the petitioner's net worth and independent evidence from which the jury could reasonably infer willfulness. Held: The judgment is affirmed. Pp. 124–129.

1. While it cannot be said that the dangers for the innocent inherent in the worth method of proof (which are summarized in the opinion) foreclose its use, they do require the exercise of great care and restraint. Pp. 125–129.

2. Trial courts should approach such cases in the full realization that the taxpayer may be ensnared in a system which, though difficult for the prosecution to utilize, is equally hard for the defendant to refute. P. 129.

3. Charges to the jury should be especially clear and should include, in addition to the formal instructions, a summary of the nature of the net worth method, the assumptions on which it rests, and the inferences available both for and against the accused. P. 129. [348 U.S. 121, 122]

4. In reviewing such cases, appellate courts should bear constantly in mind the difficulties that arise when circumstantial evidence as to guilt is the chief weapon of a method that is itself only an approximation. P. 129.

5. Section 41 of the Internal Revenue Code, expressly limiting the authority of the Government to deviate from the taxpayer's method of accounting, does not confine the net worth method of proof to situations where the taxpayer has no books or where his books are inadequate. Pp. 130–132.

6. The net worth technique used in this case was not a method of accounting different from the one employed by petitioners, and its use did not violate 41 of the Internal Revenue Code. Pp. 131–132.

7. An essential condition in such cases is the establishment, with reasonable certainty, of an opening net worth, to serve as a starting point from which to calculate future increases in the taxpayer's assets. P. 132.

8. In this case, the Government's evidence fully justified the jury's conclusion that petitioners did not have the $113,000 in currency and stocks which they claimed to have had at the beginning of 1946. Pp. 132–135.

9. When the taxpayer offers relevant explanations inconsistent with guilt, failure of the Government to investigate them might result in serious injustice; its failure to offer proof negating them would adversely affect the cogency of proof based on the circumstantial inferences of the net worth computation; and the trial judge may consider the taxpayer's explanations as true and the Government's case insufficient to go to the jury. Pp. 135–136.

10. In this case, the distant incidents relied on by petitioners and not investigated by the Government were so remote in time and in their connection with subsequent events proved by the Government that, whatever petitioner's net worth in 1933, it appeared by convincing evidence that, on January 1, 1946, they had only such assets as the Government credited to them in its opening net worth statement. P. 136.

11. A requisite to the use of the net worth method of proof is evidence supporting the inference that the increases in the defendant's net worth are attributable to currently taxable income. P. 137.

12. Where the taxpayer offers no relevant explanation of the increases in his net worth, however, the Government is not required [348 U.S. 121, 123] to negate every possible source of nontaxable income—a matter peculiarly within the knowledge of the taxpayer. P. 138.

13. In this case, there was proof of a likely source of unreported taxable income, which was adequate to support the inference that the increase in net worth was attributable to currently taxable income—even though the Government's proof did not negate all possible nontaxable sources of the alleged net worth increase, such as gifts, loans, inheritances, etc. Pp. 137–138.

14. The settled standards regarding the burden of proof in criminal cases are applicable to net worth cases. The Government must prove every element of the offense beyond a reasonable doubt, though not to a mathematical certainty. Once the Government has established its case, the defendant remains quiet at his peril. Pp. 138–139.

15. In net worth cases, willfulness is a necessary element for conviction. It must be proven by independent evidence, and it cannot be inferred from a mere understatement of income. P. 139.

16. In this case, the Government's evidence of a consistent pattern of underreporting large amounts of income, and of petitioner's failure to include all their income in their books and records, was sufficient, on proper submission, to support the jury's inference of willfulness. P. 139.

17. In this case, the instructions to the jury were not so erroneous and misleading as to constitute grounds for reversal. Pp. 139–141.

209 F.2d 516, affirmed.

Petitioners were convicted under 145 of the Internal Revenue Code of an attempt to evade their income taxes. The Court of Appeals affirmed 209 F.2d 516. This Court granted certiorari. 347 U.S. 1008. Affirmed, p. 141.

Sumner M. Redstone and Peyton Ford argued the cause for the petitioners. With them on the brief were H. D. Reed and Frank A. Bruno.

Marvin E. Frankel argued the cause for the United States. With him on the brief were Solicitor General Sobeloff, Assistant Attorney General Holland, Ellis N. Slack, and Joseph F. Goetten. [348 U.S. 121, 124]

Mr. Justice Clark delivered the opinion of the Court.

Petitioners, husband and wife, stand convicted under 145 of the Internal Revenue Code of an attempt to evade and defeat their income taxes for the year 1948. The prosecution was based on the net worth method of proof, also in issue in three companion cases, and a number of other decisions here from the Courts of Appeals of nine circuits. During the past two decades this Court has been asked to review an increasing number of criminal cases in which proof of tax evasion rested on this theory. We have denied certiorari because the cases involved only questions of evidence and, in isolation, presented no important questions of law. In 1943, the Court did have occasion to pass upon an application of the net worth theory where the taxpayer had no records. *United States v. Johnson*, 319 U.S. 503.

In recent years, however, tax-evasion convictions obtained under the net worth theory have come here with increasing frequency and left impressions beyond those of the previously unrelated petitions. We concluded that the method involved something more than the ordinary use of circumstantial evidence in the usual criminal case. Its bearing, therefore, on the safeguards traditionally [348 U.S. 121, 125] provided in the administration of criminal justice called for a consideration of the entire theory. At our last term, a number of cases arising from the Courts of Appeals brought to our attention the serious doubts of those courts regarding the implications of the net worth method. Accordingly, we granted certiorari in these four cases and have held others to await their decision.

In a typical net worth prosecution, the Government having concluded that the taxpayer's records are inadequate as a basis for determining income tax liability, attempts to establish an "opening net worth" or total net value of the taxpayer's assets at the beginning of a given year. It then proves increases in the taxpayer's net worth for each succeeding year during the period under examination and calculates the difference between the adjusted net values of the taxpayer's assets at the beginning and end of each of the years involved. The taxpayer's nondeductible expenditures, including living expenses, are added to these increases, and if the resulting figure for any year is substantially greater than the taxable income reported by the taxpayer for that year, the Government claims the excess represents unreported taxable income. In addition, it asks the jury to infer willfulness from this understatement, when taken in connection with direct evidence of "conduct, the likely effect of which would be to mislead or to conceal." *Spies v. United States*, 317 U.S. 492, 499.

Before proceeding with a discussion of these cases, we believe it important to outline the general problems implicit in this type of litigation. In this consideration we assume, as we must in view of its widespread use, that the Government deems the net worth method useful in the enforcement of the criminal sanctions of our income tax laws. Nevertheless, careful study indicates that it is so fraught with danger for the innocent that the courts must closely scrutinize its use. [348 U.S. 121, 126]

One basic assumption in establishing guilt by this method is that most assets derive from a taxable source, and that when this is not true the taxpayer is in a position to explain the discrepancy. The application of such an assumption raises serious legal problems in the administration of the criminal law. Unlike civil actions for the recovery of deficiencies, where the determinations of the Commissioner have prima facie validity, the prosecution must always prove the criminal charge beyond a reasonable doubt. This has led many of our courts to be disturbed by the use of the net worth method, particularly in its scope and the latitude which it allows prosecutors. E.g., *Demetree v. United States*, 207 F.2d 892, 894 (1953); *United States v. Caserta*, 199 F.2d 905, 907 (1952); *United States v. Fenwick*, 177 F.2d 488.

But the net worth method has not grown up overnight. It was first utilized in such cases as *Capone v. United States*, 51 F.2d 609 (1931) and *Guzik v. United States*, 54 F.2d 618 (1931), to corroborate direct proof of specific unreported income. In *United States v. Johnson*, supra, this Court approved of its use to support the inference that the taxpayer, owner of a vast and elaborately concealed network of gambling houses upon which he declared no income, had indeed received unreported income in a "substantial amount." It was a potent weapon in establishing taxable income from undisclosed sources when all other efforts failed. Since the Johnson case, however, its horizons have been widened until now it is used in run-of-the-mine cases, regardless of the amount of tax deficiency involved. In each of the four cases decided today the allegedly unreported income comes from the same disclosed sources as produced the taxpayer's reported income, and in none is the tax deficiency anything like the deficiencies in Johnson, Capone, or Guzik. The net worth method, it seems, has evolved from the final volley to the first shot in the Government's [348 U.S. 121, 127] battle for revenue, and its use in the ordinary income-bracket cases greatly increases the chances for error. This leads us to point out the dangers that must be consciously kept in mind in order to assure adequate appraisal of the specific facts in individual cases.

Effects of *Holland v. United States*

1. Among the defenses often asserted is the taxpayer's claim that the net worth increase shown by the Government's statement is in reality not an increase at all because of the existence of substantial cash on hand at the starting point. This favorite defense asserts that the cache is made up of many years' savings which for various reasons were hidden and not expended until the prosecution period. Obviously, the Government has great difficulty in refuting such a contention. However, taxpayers too encounter many obstacles in convincing the jury of the existence of such hoards. This is particularly so when the emergence of the hidden savings also uncovers a fraud on the tax-payer's creditors.

   In this connection, the taxpayer frequently gives "leads" to the Government agents indicating the specific sources from which his cash on hand has come, such as prior earnings, stock transactions, real estate profits, inheritances, gifts, etc. Sometimes these leads point back to old transactions far removed from the prosecution period. Were the Government required to run down all such leads, it would face grave investigative difficulties; still, its failure to do so might jeopardize the position of the taxpayer.

2. As we have said, the method requires assumptions, among which is the equation of unexplained increases in net worth with unreported taxable income. Obviously such an assumption has many weak-nesses. It may be that gifts, inheritances, loans, and the like account for the newly acquired wealth. There is great danger that the jury may assume that once the Government has established the figures in its worth computations, [348 U.S. 121, 128] the crime of tax eva-sion automatically follows. The possibility of this increases where the jury, without guarding instructions, is allowed to take into the jury room the various charts summarizing the computations; bare figures have a way of acquiring an existence of their own, independent of the evidence which gave rise to them.

3. Although it may sound fair to say that the taxpayer can explain the "bulge" in his net worth, he may be entirely honest and yet unable to recount his financial history. In addition, such a rule would tend to shift the burden of proof. Were the taxpayer compelled to come forward with evidence, he might risk lending support to the Government's case by showing loose business methods or losing the jury through his apparent evasiveness. Of course, in other criminal prosecutions, juries may disbelieve and convict the innocent. But the courts must minimize this danger.

4. When there are no books and records, willfulness may be inferred by the jury from that fact coupled with proof of an understatement of income. But when the Government uses the net worth method, and the books and records of the taxpayer appear correct on their face, an inference of willfulness from net worth increases alone might be unjustified, especially where the circumstances surrounding the deficiency are as consistent with innocent mistake as with willful violation. On the other hand, the very failure of the books to disclose a proved deficiency might indicate deliberate falsification.

5. In many cases of this type, the prosecution relies on the taxpayer's statements, made to revenue agents in the course of their investigation, to establish vital links in the Government's proof. But when a revenue agent confronts the taxpayer with an apparent deficiency, the latter may be more concerned with a quick settlement than an honest search for the truth. Moreover, the prosecution may pick and choose from the taxpayer's statement, [348 U.S. 121, 129] relying on the favorable portion and throwing aside that which does not bolster its position. The problem of corroboration, dealt with in the companion cases of *Smith v. United States*, post, p. 147, and *United States v. Calderon*, post, p. 160, therefore becomes crucial.

6. The statute defines the offense here involved by individual years. While the Government may be able to prove with reasonable accuracy an increase in net worth over a period of years, it often has great difficulty in relating that income sufficiently to any specific prosecution year. While a steadily increasing net worth may justify an inference of additional earnings, unless that increase can be reasonably allocated to the appropriate tax year, the taxpayer may be convicted on counts of which he is innocent.

While we cannot say that these pitfalls inherent in the net worth method foreclose its use, they do require the exercise of great care and restraint. The complexity of the problem is such that it cannot be met merely by the application of general rules. Cf. *Universal Camera Corp. v. Labor Board*, 340 U.S. 474, 489. Trial courts should approach these cases in the full realization that the taxpayer may be ensnared in a system which, though difficult for the prosecution to utilize, is equally hard for the defendant to refute. Charges should be especially clear, including, in addition to the formal instructions, a summary of the nature of the net worth method, the assumptions on which it rests, and the inferences available both for and against the accused. Appellate courts should review the cases, bearing constantly in mind the difficulties that arise when circumstantial evidence as to guilt is the chief weapon of a method that is itself only an approximation.

With these considerations as a guide, we turn to the facts. [348 U.S. 121, 130]

The indictment returned against the Hollands embraced three counts. The first two charged Marion L. Holland, the husband, with attempted evasion of his income tax for the years 1946 and 1947. He was found not guilty by the jury on both of these counts. The third count charged Holland and his wife with attempted evasion in 1948 of the tax on $19,736.74 not reported by them in their joint return. The jury found both of them guilty. Mrs. Holland was fined $5,000, while her husband was sentenced to two years' imprisonment and fined $10,000.

The Government's opening net worth computation shows defendants with a net worth of $19,152.59 at the beginning of the indictment period. Shortly thereafter, defendants purchased a hotel, bar, and restaurant, and began operating them as the Holland House. Within three years, during which they reported $31,265.92 in taxable income, their apparent net worth increased by $113,185.32. The Government's evidence indicated that, during 1948, the year for which defendants were convicted, their net worth increased by some $32,000, while the amount of taxable income reported by them totaled less than one-third that sum.

Use of Net Worth Method Where Books Are Apparently Adequate

As we have previously noted, this is not the first net worth case to reach this Court. In *United States v. Johnson,* supra, the Court affirmed a tax-evasion conviction on evidence showing that the taxpayer's expenditures had exceeded his "available declared resources." Since Johnson and his concealed establishments had destroyed [348 U.S. 121, 131] the few records they had, the Government was forced to resort to the net worth method of proof. This Court approved on the ground that "to require more ... would be tantamount to holding that skilful concealment is an invincible barrier to proof," 319 U.S., at 517–518. Petitioners ask that we restrict the Johnson case to situations where the taxpayer has kept no books. They claim that 41 of the Internal Revenue Code, 4 expressly limiting the authority of the Government to deviate from the taxpayer's method of accounting, confines the net worth method to situations where the taxpayer has no books or where his books are inadequate. Despite some support for this view among the lower courts (see *United States v. Riganto,* 121 F. Supp. 158, 161, 162; *United States v. Williams,* 208 F.2d 437,

437–438; *Remmer v. United States*, 205 F.2d 277, 286, judgment vacated on other grounds, 347 U.S. 227), we conclude that this argument must fail. The provision that the "net income shall be computed … in accordance with the method of accounting regularly employed in keeping the books of such taxpayer," refers to methods such as the cash receipts or the accrual method, which allocate income and expenses between years. *United States v. American Can Co.*, 280 U.S. 412, 419. The net worth technique as used in this case is not a method of accounting different from the one employed by defendants. It is not a method of accounting at all, except insofar as it calls upon taxpayers to account for their unexplained income. Petitioners' accounting system was appropriate [348 U.S. 121, 132] for their business purposes; and, admittedly, the Government did not detect any specific false entries therein. Nevertheless, if we believe the Government's evidence, as the jury did, we must conclude that the defendants' books were more consistent than truthful, and that many items of income had disappeared before they had even reached the recording stage. Certainly, Congress never intended to make 41 a set of blinders which prevents the Government from looking beyond the self-serving declarations in a taxpayer's books. "The United States has relied for the collection of its income tax largely upon the taxpayer's own disclosures …. This system can function successfully only if those within and near taxable income keep and render true accounts." *Spies v. United States*, 317 U.S., at 495. To protect the revenue from those who do not "render true accounts," the Government must be free to use all legal evidence available to it in determining whether the story told by the taxpayer's books accurately reflects his financial history.

Establishing a Definite Opening Net Worth

We agree with petitioners that an essential condition in cases of this type is the establishment, with reasonable certainty, of an opening net worth, to serve as a starting point from which to calculate future increases in the taxpayer's assets. The importance of accuracy in this figure is immediately apparent, as the correctness of the result depends entirely upon the inclusion in this sum of all assets on hand at the outset. The Government's net worth statement included as assets at the starting point stock costing $29,650 and $2,153.09 in cash. The Hollands claim that the Government failed to include in its opening net worth figure an accumulation of $113,000 [348 U.S. 121, 133] in currency and "hundreds and possibly thousands of shares of stock" which they owned at the beginning of the prosecution period. They asserted that the cash had been accumulated prior to the opening date, $104,000 of it before 1933, and the balance between 1933 and 1945. They had kept the money, they claimed, mostly in $100 bills and at various times in a canvas bag, a suitcase, and a metal box. They had never dipped into it until 1946, when it became the source of the apparent increase in wealth which the Government later found in the form of a home, a ranch, a hotel, and other properties. This was the main issue presented to the jury. The Government did not introduce any direct evidence to dispute this claim. Rather it relied on the inference that anyone who had had $104,000 in cash would not have undergone the hardship and privation endured by the Hollands all during the late 1920s and throughout the 1930s. During this period they lost their cafe business; accumulated $35,000 in debts which were never paid; lost their household furniture because of an unpaid balance of $92.20; suffered a default judgment for $506.66; and were forced to separate for some eight years because it was to their "economical advantage." During the latter part of this period, Mrs. Holland was obliged to support herself and their son by working at a motion picture house in Denver while her husband was in Wyoming. The evidence further indicated that improvements to the hotel, and other assets acquired during the prosecution years, were bought in installments and with bills of small denominations, as if out of earnings rather than from an accumulation of $100 bills. The Government also negatived the possibility of petitioners' accumulating such a sum by checking Mr. Holland's income tax returns as far back as 1913, showing that the income declared in previous years was insufficient to enable defendants to save any appreciable [348 U.S. 121, 134] amount of money. The jury resolved this question of the existence of a cache of cash against the Hollands, and we believe the verdict was fully supported.

As to the stock, Mr. Holland began dabbling in the stock market in a small way in 1937 and 1938. His purchases appear to have been negligible and on borrowed money. His only reported income from stocks was in his tax returns for 1944 and 1945 when he disclosed dividends of $1,600 and $1,850, respectively. While the record is unclear on this point, it appears that, during the period from 1942 to 1945, he pledged considerable stock as collateral for loans. There is no evidence, however, showing what portions of this stock Mr. Holland actually owned at any one time, since he was trading in shares from day to day. And, even if we assume that he owned all the stock, some 4,550 shares, there is evidence that Mr. Holland's stock transactions were usually in "stock selling for only a few dollars per share." In this light, the Government's figure of approximately $30,000 is not out of line. In 1946, Holland reported the sale of about $50,000 in stock, but no receipt of dividends; nor were dividends reported in subsequent years. It is reasonable to assume that he sold all of his stock in 1946. In fact, Holland stated to the revenue agents that he had not "fooled with the stock market" since the beginning of 1946; that he had not owned any stocks for two or three years prior to 1949; that he had saved about $50,000 from 1933 to 1946, and that, in 1946, he had $9,000 in cash with the balance of his savings in stocks.[*]

---

[*] From http://caselaw.lp.findlaw.com/scripts/getcase.pl?court=us&vol=348&invol=121-f6#f6

The Government's evidence, bolstered by the admissions of petitioners, provided [348 U.S. 121, 135] convincing proof that they had no stock other than the amount included in the opening net worth statement. By the same token, the petitioners' argument that the Government failed to account for the proceeds of stock sold by them before the starting date must also fail. The Government's evidence fully justified the jury's conclusion that there were no proceeds over and above the amount credited to petitioners.

The Government's Investigation of Leads

So overwhelming, indeed, was the Government's proof on the issue of cash on hand that the Government agents did not bother to check petitioners' story that some of the cash represented proceeds from the sales of two cafes in the 1920s; and that in 1933 an additional portion of this $113,000 in currency was obtained by exchanging some $12,000 in gold at a named bank. While sound administration of the criminal law requires that the net worth approach—a powerful method of proving otherwise undetectable offenses—should not be denied the Government, its failure to investigate leads furnished by the taxpayer might result in serious injustice. It is, of course, not for us to prescribe investigative procedures, but it is within the province of the courts to pass upon the sufficiency of the evidence to convict. When the Government rests its case solely on the approximations and circumstantial inferences of a net worth computation, the cogency of its proof depends upon its effective negation of reasonable explanations by the taxpayer inconsistent with guilt. Such refutation might fail when the Government does not track down relevant leads furnished by the [348 U.S. 121, 136] taxpayer—leads reasonably susceptible of being checked, which, if true, would establish the taxpayer's innocence. When the Government fails to show an investigation into the validity of such leads, the trial judge may consider them as true and the Government's case insufficient to go to the jury. This should aid in forestalling unjust prosecutions, and have the practical advantage of eliminating the dilemma, especially serious in this type of case, of the accused's being forced by the risk of an adverse verdict to come forward to substantiate leads which he had previously furnished the Government. It is a procedure entirely consistent with the position long espoused by the Government, that its duty is not to convict but to see that justice is done.

In this case, the Government's detailed investigation was a complete answer to the petitioners' explanations. Admitting that, in cases of this kind, it "would be desirable to track to its conclusion every conceivable line of inquiry," the Government centered its inquiry on the explanations of the Hollands and entered upon a detailed investigation of their lives covering several states and over a score of years. The jury could have believed that Mr. Holland had received moneys from the sale of cafes in the twenties and that he had turned in gold in 1933 and still it could reasonably have concluded that the Hollands lacked the claimed cache of currency in 1946, the crucial year. Even if these leads were assumed to be true, the Government's evidence was sufficient to convict. The distant incidents relied on by petitioners were so remote in time and in their connection with subsequent events proved by the Government that, whatever petitioners' net worth in 1933, it appears by convincing evidence that, on January 1, 1946, they had only such assets as the Government credited to them in its opening net worth statement. [348 U.S. 121, 137]

Net Worth Increases Must Be Attributable to Taxable Income

Also requisite to the use of the net worth method is evidence supporting the inference that the defendant's net worth increases are attributable to currently taxable income.

The Government introduced evidence tending to show that, although the business of the hotel apparently increased during the years in question, the reported profits fell to approximately one-quarter of the amount declared by the previous management in a comparable period; that the cash register tapes, on which the books were based, were destroyed by the petitioners; and that the books did not reflect the receipt of money later withdrawn from the hotel's cash register for the personal living expenses of the petitioners and for payments made for restaurant supplies. The unrecorded items in this latter category totaled over $12,500 for 1948. Thus there was ample evidence that not all the income from the hotel had been included in its books and records. In fact, the net worth increase claimed by the Government for 1948 could have come entirely from the unreported income of the hotel, and still the hotel's total earnings for the year would have been only 73% of the sum reported by the previous owner for the comparable period in 1945.

But petitioners claim the Government failed to adduce adequate proof because it did not negative all the possible nontaxable sources of the alleged net worth increases—gifts, loans, inheritances, etc. We cannot agree. The Government's proof, in our view, carried with it the negations the petitioners urge. Increases in net [348 U.S. 121, 138] worth, standing alone, cannot be assumed to be attributable to currently taxable income. But proof of a likely source, from which the jury could reasonably find that the net worth increases sprang, is sufficient. In the Johnson case, where there was no direct evidence of the source of the taxpayer's income, this Court's conclusion that the taxpayer "had large, unreported income was reinforced by proof … that [for certain years his] private expenditures … exceeded his available declared resources." This was sufficient to support "the finding that he had some unreported income which was properly attributable to his earnings …." *United States v. Johnson*, 319 U.S., at 517. There the taxpayer was the owner of an undisclosed business capable of producing taxable income; here the disclosed business of the petitioners was proven to be capable of producing much more income than was reported and in a quantity sufficient to account for the net worth increases. Any other rule would burden the Government with investigating the many possible nontaxable sources of income, each of which is as unlikely as it is difficult to disprove. This is not to say that the Government may disregard explanations of the defendant reasonably susceptible of being checked. But where relevant leads are not forthcoming, the Government is not required to negate every possible source of nontaxable income, a matter peculiarly within the knowledge of the defendant. See *Rossi v. United States*, 289 U.S. 89, 91–92.

The Burden of Proof Remains on the Government

Nor does this rule shift the burden of proof. The Government must still prove every element of the offense beyond a reasonable doubt though not to a mathematical certainty. The settled standards of the criminal law are applicable to net worth cases just as to prosecutions for other crimes. Once the Government has established its [348 U.S. 121, 139] case, the defendant remains quiet at his peril. Cf. *Yee Hem v. United States*, 268 U.S. 178, 185. The practical disadvantages to the taxpayer are lessened by the pressures on the Government to check and negate relevant leads.

Willfulness Must Be Present

A final element necessary for conviction is willfulness. The petitioners contend that willfulness "involves a specific intent which must be proven by independent evidence and which cannot be inferred from the mere understatement of income." This is a fair statement of the rule. Here, however, there was evidence of a consistent pattern of underreporting large amounts of income, and of the failure on petitioners' part to include all of their income in their books and records. Since, on proper submission, the jury could have found that these acts supported an inference of willfulness, their verdict must stand. *Spies v. United States*, supra, at 499–500.

The Charge to the Jury

Petitioners press upon us, finally, the contention that the instructions of the trial court were so erroneous and misleading as to constitute grounds for reversal. We have carefully reviewed the instructions and cannot agree. But some require comment. The petitioners assail the refusal of the trial judge to instruct that where the Government's evidence is circumstantial, it must be such as to exclude every reasonable hypothesis other than that of guilt. There is some support for this type of instruction in the lower court decisions, *Garst v. United States*, 180 F. 339, 343; *Anderson v. United States*, 30 F.2d 485–487; *Stutz v. United States*, 47 F.2d 1029, 1030; *Hanson v. United States*, 208 F.2d 914, 916, but the better rule is that, where the jury is properly instructed on the standards for reasonable doubt, such an additional instruction [348 U.S. 121, 140] on circumstantial evidence is confusing and incorrect, *United States v. Austin-Bagley Corp.*, 31 F.2d 229, 234, cert. denied, 279 U.S. 863; *United States v. Becker*, 62 F.2d 1007, 1010; 1 Wigmore, Evidence (3rd ed.), 25–26.

Circumstantial evidence in this respect is intrinsically no different from testimonial evidence. Admittedly, circumstantial evidence may in some cases point to a wholly incorrect result. Yet this is equally true of testimonial evidence. In both instances, a jury is asked to weigh the chances that the evidence correctly points to guilt against the possibility of inaccuracy or ambiguous inference. In both, the jury must use its experience with people and events in weighing the probabilities. If the jury is convinced beyond a reasonable doubt, we can require no more.

Even more insistent is the petitioners' attack, not made below, on the charge of the trial judge as to reasonable doubt. He defined it as "the kind of doubt ... which you folks in the more serious and important affairs of your own lives might be willing to act upon." We think this section of the charge should have been in terms of the kind of doubt that would make a person hesitate to act, see *Bishop v. United States*, 71 App. D.C. 132, 137–138, 107 F.2d 297, 303, rather than the kind on which he would be willing to act. But we believe that the instruction as given was not of the type that could mislead the jury into finding no reasonable doubt when in fact there was some. A definition of a doubt as something the jury would act upon would seem to create confusion rather than misapprehension. "Attempts to explain the term 'reasonable doubt' do not usually result in making it any clearer to the minds of the jury," *Miles v. United States*, 103 U.S. 304, 312, and we feel that, taken as a whole, the instructions correctly conveyed the concept of reasonable doubt to the jury [348 U.S. 121, 141].

Petitioners also assign as error the refusal of the trial judge to give instructions on the wording of the criminal statute under which they were indicted, even though the judge fully and correctly instructed the jury on every element of the crime. The impossibility of pointing to any way in which defendants' rights were prejudiced by this, assuming it was error, is enough to indicate that the trial judge was correct, see *United States v. Center Veal & Beef Co.*, 162 F.2d 766, 771. There is here no question of the jury's duty to apply the law to the facts. That operation implies the application of a general standard to the specific physical facts as found by the jury. The meanings of standards such as willfulness were properly explained by the trial judge in no greater particularity than necessary, and thus the jury's function was not invaded.

In the light of these considerations the judgment is Affirmed (5).

Items 1 through 4 in the Court's original decision express the Supreme Court's concern with the difficulty in preparing an indirect methods case with respect to ensuring the accuracy and completeness of the evidence used in constructing the computation. The Court realized that the presentation by the prosecution and the defense is extremely difficult when the evidence used to support criminal charges is, if not all, predominantly circumstantial in nature and requires that the judge or jury be informed well enough to see the correlation of all of the transactions that make up the computation.

Items 5 and 6 reference to standard accounting audit procedures to insure that any alleged understatement or concealment of income, determined by an indirect method of proof, shown to exist from time frame to time frame, is not the result of changing the method of accounting of the subject of the investigation. This is a primary concern in civil and criminal tax cases, but the principle would apply to any financial investigation where substantial amounts are alleged to have been secreted by the subject.

Items 7 and 8 require that the computation, to be deemed valid, must evidence a complete starting point from which to show the financial gains in the subsequent time frames. The Court would not allow a comparative computation (all indirect methods of proof present the findings comparatively) if there is not a solid point in time from which the comparisons can be made. The term "starting point" has been coined from item 7 and is used to describe the base time frame for the indirect method of proof computation.

The investigator must take care to select the time period that is most firmly established and closest to the time the alleged fraud or financial crimes occurred. Ideally, it is the time just prior to the alleged criminal activity. This makes the evidence needed most current and easier to obtain. Although this is the optimum situation, the starting point in some criminal tax cases has been established as far back in time as the first year an individual filed a return.

Items 9 and 10 require that the investigator, using an indirect method of proof, follow all of the leads uncovered during the investigation that may explain the increase in wealth. This is stressed by the Court in those instances where the subject has provided explanations that would nullify illegal activity. The Court did address the need for the leads to have at least a probability of being found to be true. As an example, the subject of an indirect method case claimed to have saved money in a cigar box over 17 years by taking the bills from his wallet each evening and placing them in the cigar box. He claimed the savings equaled the $547,000.00 understatement of income. During his explanation, he stated that the bills would be $1s, $5s, $10s, and, once in a while, $20s. The investigator obtained an identical cigar box and, with the cooperation of a local bank, filled the box with new $100 bills. Tightly packed, the box could only hold $85,000.00. This amount was credited to the subject's cash on hand in the starting point base year. The subject was convicted on all three counts of tax fraud.

Items 11 and 12 state that the indirect method of proof used must show that the alleged income be proven to have been gained during the time frames in the computation in which they appear. They also require that the investigating agency (in following all leads) negate all possible nontaxable sources of income (legal sources in other financial cases). This is a logical approach for the investigator to ensure that the amounts charged are, in fact, from the sources alleged.

Negative proof may sound like a contradiction in terms, but it represents a substantial part of financial crimes investigations. In the same way that a suspect may be cleared of a crime by having a verifiable alibi for when the crime occurred, the investigator must prove "beyond a reasonable doubt" that legitimate sources of income were not available. As stated by Sir Arthur Conan Doyle in his Sherlock Holmes stories, "If all things are proven impossible, then whatever is left, no matter how improbable, must be true."

In white collar criminal investigation, all legitimate sources of income must be eliminated or credited back to the subject in the financial computation. The subject may have participated in activities that were improper, immoral, and/or unscrupulous; but this does not prove him or her culpable of a criminal act. He or she is not guilty until the investigator can prove that these actions cannot account for the financial gains received.

Items 13 and 14 require the investigator to establish a likely source for the income revealed in the indirect method computation. Without a likely source for the understatements shown in the computation, the defense has a ready-made argument for the evidence not meeting the standards of proof beyond a reasonable doubt. Item 14 also reminds the investigator of the legal necessity to prove all of the statutory provisions of the laws that the subject is charged with, in addition to ensuring the mathematical accuracy of the computations. To expand the subject's illegal activities by use of indirect methods, the corresponding illegal activity must be proven and shown to be a likely source for the unreported or concealed income.

Items 15 and 16 stress the need for the investigator to also show that the alleged unreported or concealed income was the result of an intentional act, rather than mere oversight or honest mistake. Showing a large amount of income through computation does not, in and of itself, show the subject's intention to conceal the income. The nature of the subject's record-keeping practices in this case is deemed sufficient to infer willfulness. Other items that can infer willfulness would include the acquisition and ownership of assets using a false name or in the names of nominees, destruction of personal records when made aware of the investigation, predominant or exclusive use of cash in financial transactions to reduce the paper trail, and traveling outside one's usual area to acquire assets or make expenditures (e.g., living in the Midwest and traveling to New York to buy jewelry or furs).

In the next several paragraphs, the Court cites other decisions regarding the use of indirect methods of proof and explains the thought process it went through in deciding to affirm the conviction. Each of the prior cases cited has modified and explained variations in the presentation of indirect methods of proof. In addition, the Court takes time to reiterate the concerns with indirect methodology. The voluminous use of circumstantial evidence, the need for a solid starting point, and the need to establish intent are all restated. The Court then addresses the specific defenses presented in the case, and how it viewed the potential viability of the defenses. It also discusses the prosecution's means for overcoming the proposed defenses and why it felt the prosecution case sufficiently covered the defenses. We will review some of the specific concerns in greater detail.

The first defense presented in the *Holland* case was the existence of a cash hoard prior to the time frames in the computation. As the Court noted, this defense is common in financial investigations using indirect methods of proof. The cash hoard is then said to be used during the time frames of the investigation and therefore explains the increases in wealth. Often, the subject using this defense has to admit to a prior fraud to have acquired the wealth. That is usually enough to cause judge or jury to ignore the cash hoard defense. Circumstantial evidence can be obtained during the investigation to help in refuting this type of defense. The fact that loans or credit purchases were made in prior time periods would indicate that the subject did not have sufficient means to make those purchases. Net worth information presented to banks for loan applications that do not show the cash hoard as an asset would be another indication. Each case will present unique evidence in helping to refute the existence of a cash hoard on behalf of the subject.

The second defense is the implication that the computation may not consider the existence of possible nontaxable sources (legitimate sources for other financial investigations) that could explain the increase in wealth shown in the indirect method computation. As stated earlier, the investigation must show an attempt to verify any proposed defense, and in cases where the subject decides to apply his constitutional rights, any potential defense in regard to the taxability or legitimacy of the increases allocated by the investigative computation. Remember that, in criminal cases, the subject has the right to refuse to talk to the investigator without the fear of having the silence held against him or her. This is also expressed in the third section of defense addressed by the Court.

The fourth defense is that of an "honest mistake" being made to appear as a willful criminal act. The Court restates that the investigation must address willfulness distinctly in the evidence presented by the prosecution. The fact that inadequate or no records exist on the part of the subject does not by itself infer willful culpability.

The fifth defense addressed by the Supreme Court is related to the requirement that all leads are developed in the case. The investigator may not pick and choose which of the statements made by the subject, or any of the witnesses, to use in the court presentation. The subsequent ruling in *Brady v. Maryland*, 373 U.S. 83, 83 S.Ct. 1194 (1963), requires the prosecution to provide to the defense counsel all materials and information obtained during the investigation that are favorable to the defendant.

The sixth potential defense addressed by the Court was in regard to the need for the evidence to allocate increases in wealth accurately to each time frame used in the computation. This is of the utmost importance in criminal tax cases, but would also be of concern in any financial investigation that needs to specify amounts relative to different time frames.

The *Holland v. United States* decision closes with the Court explaining its decision, in light of the concerns it raised with the net worth method, in relation to the specific facts and circumstances existing in the case.

The Standard Methods of Proof

11

Specific Items

The specific item method of proof is the simplest way to conduct a forensic accounting investigation and the easiest to present to a prosecutor and a jury. The investigation focuses on specific illegal or unreported transactions and shows the financial gain received by the perpetrator from the alleged illegal activity. The specific item method is used primarily in cases where the financial crime involves a single type of fraud or when the evidence of financial gains from the crime is sufficiently complete for presentation to a jury.

The following is an example in which a single fraud is repeated over a period of time.

Example 1

A medical transportation company provides transportation to and from the hospital for patients who require regular treatments or therapy. The company is paid in part by insurance companies, Medicare, or Medicaid. The company bills the providers for services on a mileage basis. The company continues regular round-trip billings even if the patient is only riding one way or makes other arrangements for transportation. The company also bills the insurance providers for an additional weekly trip for patients who were traveling several times a week, but have improved and do not require as many visits.

A comparative analysis of the patient appointment records and the transportation company's billing records would show the inconsistencies and identify the patients who were being used by the company. The investigator would be able to follow the leads obtained and receive the necessary testimony from the patients to show that the company was overbilling the insurance providers. The providers would gladly cooperate in providing investigators their records of payment to the transportation company. The scheme would be reasonably simple to present to a jury because the same falsification was made over and over again by the company.

Specific items are just that, specific documentary evidence that proves financial gain from a pattern of illegal acts. When a thief is found selling a stolen item, the transaction corroborates his commission of the crime. Similarly, when a white collar criminal builds a criminal enterprise to gain financially from a series of illegal acts, the profits he receives can be attributed to the specific illegal acts committed.

The specific item method shows the profit from each fraudulent transaction in the financial criminal activity. In most cases, the perpetrator will attempt to conceal the ill-gotten gains. This may take the form of using false names or corporate shells to disassociate the criminal proceeds from the individual committing the fraud or funneling the proceeds to a different location that would be undisclosed in normal financial activities. Offshore or out-of-state bank accounts or investments are often used in the attempt to conceal the proceeds. The perpetrators may construct a scheme to falsify the illegality of the funds received by altering the books and records of their business, or fail to record the proceeds altogether.

In the example of the medical transportation company, the investigator would compare the payment records of the insurance providers with the medical facilities' patient logs and identify those patients who were used for the purpose of filing false claims. If the transportation company records are made available (by waiver of the company, by subpoena, or through the execution of a search warrant), they could be used in the same manner of comparison to identify the false claims.

Once the patients (used in the scheme) are identified, they would be interviewed to corroborate the information gained through the records comparison. Patients who are unable to remember the specifics of their transportation use or medical treatment schedule, or are no longer available for interview (deceased) should be separated for other attempts to obtain corroboration. Financial investigations rely on circumstantial evidence and, therefore, the more the evidence obtained to establish the motive and means of the crime, the more certain is the success of the investigation. Employees of the transportation company would also be interviewed. It is unlikely that all of them would be included in a conspiracy because it would dilute the criminal gains from the scheme. The investigator would obtain as much information as possible as to the work schedules, driving logs, mileage records for the transporting vehicles, and patients served by the drivers. Just as deceased patients can no longer receive treatments, a vehicle cannot make 30 round-trips if the mileage on that vehicle can only support 15. If treatments are only provided on Mondays through Saturdays, any charges for Sunday transportation would need to be specifically addressed. In the same manner, any trips that are shown in the records that could not be possible (five vehicles available, and seven trips logged at the same time and on the same day) also require further scrutiny.

Always be aware that a circumstantial case often relies heavily on the investigator's use of negative proof as well as multiple means of corroboration. The characteristics involved in financial crime investigations require that all potential evidence be explored, and that different avenues of logic be used to refute the possible defenses of "innocent error" or "shoddy record keeping." In cases where an indirect method of proof is used, the investigation must present sufficient evidence to overcome any anticipated or potential defenses and to establish the intent to defraud to the jury.

The second phase in the investigation will be to follow the money trail. Once the evidence obtained shows the fraudulent activity, the investigator must focus on identifying all of the people involved in the scheme, the illegal benefits that each received, and the location or use that was made of the illegal proceeds. Two possible scenarios were presented that the company could use to conceal the funds derived from the scheme. One was to conceal the false charges within the books and records of the business. The other would be to fail to record the fictitious claim payments altogether and to divert the illegal proceeds. In either case, the investigator can trace the funds from their source: the insurance providers paying the claims. Once the false claims have been identified, the investigator can follow the flow of the payment for these claims to the transportation company. The checks issued for the claims will provide a lot of information. The canceled checks will show the identification of the bank where the check was cashed or deposited. If the check was transferred to a third party, it will show the signatures of both the transportation company officer issuing the check and the individual to whom the check was given. In this day of electronic transfers, the same information can still be obtained by the bank authorizing the transfer and the receiving financial institution.

If the funds go through the company records as legitimate receipts, the investigator must determine whether the false claims (recorded as legitimate income) are offset by false expenses so that the illegal funds can be directed to and used by the perpetrator. If the money generated by the false claims is diverted prior to being received by the business (before entry into the books and records), the paper trail should help identify the recipient of the funds. Never presume the guilt or innocence of a suspect before obtaining and analyzing all the records available. Any individual who has the ability to file claims on behalf of the transportation company could make the false claims. The perpetrator may be the president of the company, the head of billing, an account manager, a receivable and payable officer at the medical facility, someone in the mail department, patients or families of patients in collusion with any of these other individuals, or anyone who could gain access to and use the business practices and policies of the company to perpetrate the fraud. Following the money to its final destination provides the circumstantial evidence necessary to identify all of the people involved and convince a jury of their culpability in the crime. The money trail also provides evidence toward motive, knowledge, and intent, which are inclusive in the elements of criminal financial investigations.

Example 2

We have Jane, of Jane's Auto Sales. Other used car dealers have made complaints that she "must be doing something illegal" to sell her cars so cheap. At this point, the officer receiving the complaints has to apply his or her enforcement discretion; let the complaints be shelved as "too vague" or look into the matter. For our example, we will make a cursory review of the records most readily available.

Department of Motor Vehicle (DMV) records show that Jane sold 50 to 60 cars a year for the past 2 years. The car sales are of medium to high-end vehicles, and she consistently sells them for $3,000.00 to $5,000.00 below National Automobile Dealer's Association (NADA) wholesale prices. The vehicles are all 1 to 2 years old. County records show that Jane moved into town and opened the business 2 years ago. She moved here from out of state and purchased a home in a nice neighborhood. She is 34 years old, divorced, and has no children. What conclusions do you draw? What are your next steps?

Is she a better salesperson than the other dealers in town? Is she falsifying information to DMV? What information and why? Is she receiving cash payments that are unreported? Is she misrepresenting the vehicles to customers?

Further investigation shows that Jane sold her prior house for $150,000.00 and purchased her new home for $285,000, with a down payment of $85,000.00. Jane's mortgage application states that she earns $150,000.00 per year. She purchases all of her vehicles from S & F brokers, a business located three states away. Her cousin is a one-third partner in S & F. Law enforcement records show that S & F is under investigation for dealing in stolen and chopped vehicles. Customer interviews and vehicle inspections reveal altered or missing vehicle identification numbers and block tags. Three of the initial vehicles inspected match national stolen vehicle reports.

It appears that Jane is selling stolen vehicles. What evidence do you need to support prosecution? How can you get it? If Jane agrees to an interview, what questions will you ask?

Bank Deposits and Cash Expenditures

The theory behind the bank deposits and cash expenditures method of proof is to identify other income through an analysis of the individual's banking activity. It is geared toward the individual who has both legitimate and illegal income commingled in one or more bank accounts. This method requires that the investigator identify and obtain the records for all of the bank accounts that the suspect has signatory authority over. It is usually applied when the suspect makes regular and routine deposits to his or her accounts. The legal assumption is that the individual deposits funds as they are received. The investigative analysis accounts for the regular deposits, transfers between banks, and the cash expenditures made by the individual.

This method identifies and calculates income by determining the changes in bank account activity during specific time frames. As in other indirect methods of proof, the time frames run consecutively. The total deposits reflect the current income of the individual. Adjustments are made to correct the computation for consideration of nonincome items, cash, and funds that do not enter into the bank accounts. The method uses the legal assumption that regular deposits to accounts reflect current income. The method also considers the potential defenses of cash hoard and undocumented personal loans. Although it sounds simple in theory, the bank deposits method requires that all financial activities be analyzed and considered in finalizing the computation to ensure accuracy and provide the necessary proof beyond a reasonable doubt.

The investigator must be able to prove that all of the deposits made and the checks written on each account in the computation were made during the alleged time period. This requires that each account be reconciled to consider any checks outstanding and any deposits in transit. Banks post the time frame for recording personal transactions. We have all seen the signs that state, "Transactions made after 4:00 P.M. will be posted on the following day." In addition to personal transactions, there may be delays in postings for telephonic, mailed, or other bank transaction methods, as well as delays for unexpected events (weather, disaster) and holidays.

The process for reconciling a bank account is simple. It is the same procedure that is recommended for balancing a personal checking account, which is usually included in the monthly statement. The reconciliations reduce the account activity to the actual transaction dates for the desired time period. The starting point is the balance shown on the bank statement. Checks written but not clearing the bank account are subtracted from the account balance. Deposits made but not as yet recorded are added to the balance. Interest received on the account is added to the check register balance. If all of the items are considered and the mathematical computations are done correctly, the statement and checkbook balances will be the same, and the account is reconciled.

If the bank statement time period does not coincide with the time periods used in the investigation, the account reconciliations must be adjusted to conform to the investigative periods. As an example, the bank issues its statements for the time periods from the 15th of the month through the 14th of the subsequent month. If the investigation uses the end of the month for presenting the evidence, the investigator needs to complete the reconciliation in mid-month. The bank balance for the end of the month would be used instead of the closing balance of the statement period (most bank statements provide daily balance information on the statement). Outstanding checks and deposits in transit would be used to complete the reconciliation for the time period needed.

Although the deposits are a crucial part of the circumstantial evidence presented in this method, each deposit for the time frames in the investigation should be identified and explained in summary schedules. The schedules will list all of the deposits for the time period and identify the date of the deposit, the amount of the deposit, and an explanation of the deposit. The following is a short example:

John Doe
ABC Bank; Account #123456
Deposits Analysis—01/01/2007 through 12/31/2007

Date	Amount	Explanation
01/08	641.24	Paycheck—Carl's Grocery
01/12	2,000.00	Cash deposit, source unknown
01/15	641.24	Paycheck—Carl's Grocery
01/20	6,000.00	Loan proceeds—ABC Bank, loan #6543

The analysis of the bank accounts must ensure that the funds deposited are not counted twice. What steps would you need to take to ensure that this did not happen?

The accuracy of the computation determines whether a successful prosecution is possible. If the defense can find any mistake in the identification of the deposits or in the calculations made by the investigator, they will use it to plant doubt in the minds of the jury. This can cause the rest of the computation to lose credibility and lead to a dismissal of the charges. The investigator must ensure that the numerical transpositions from the evidence to the summary schedules are correct and that all of the mathematical computations are accurate. In addition, the investigator must show that the computation is complete (all leads were followed) and accurate in presenting all of the financial activities of the subject of the investigation. To ensure accuracy, the bank deposits method of proof requires that all adjustments are made to the computation to reflect real and potential benefits to the subject. The investigation is to show the least amount of unreported or illegal income that the subject had to have received during the investigative time frames. If financial transactions cannot be firmly established, they must not be included in the amounts charged against the subject. If items cannot be proven, and they could have a potential benefit to the subject, the computation must allow for the potential benefit to the subject.

Common adjustments to the bank deposits method of proof computation are

1. Providing a credit to the subject for any redeposited items. This ensures that the income represented by the deposit is not charged as income more than once in the computation.
2. Providing an adjustment for any cash withdrawals or checks written to cash. As cash expenditures are added to the income computation,

it is necessary to credit the subject with any cash that is taken from the bank accounts. This allows for the possibility that the cash taken from the account could be used for the cash expenditure.

3. Following the same logic, deposits made to an account from non-income sources are also subtracted from the criminal computation. Items such as proceeds from the sale of an asset, refunds, rebates, gifts, and loan proceeds are examples of nonincome-type items that may be deposited.

4. If any deposited items are found that thorough investigation cannot identify as to the source, they must be shown in the computation. These items can be included in the computation if they establish the pattern of depositing illegal or unreported proceeds. Establishing this relationship is a key factor in presenting the means and operation of the scheme used to defraud or generate the illegal income. If not, they must be credited to the subject of the investigation.

Cash expenditures are added to the criminal computation to account for income that was received but never deposited to a bank account. Individuals involved in criminal activities often believe that if they use cash, there is less likelihood of leaving a paper trail to their financial activities. Another method of concealing income is the use of a secreted bank account in another jurisdiction. An account is established in another state or country, and illegal or unreported income is deposited exclusively to that account. Often this account will be in the name of a fictitious company or under a false or nominee name to distance the subject from the funds. The bank deposits method of proof is ideal in situations where the subject attempts to conceal the ill-gotten funds in this manner.

To demonstrate the accuracy of the criminal computation to the jury, the investigator must make sure that cash expenditures are not counted twice. What can you do to show that this did not happen? As mentioned earlier, cash withdrawals and checks written to cash are subtracted from the criminal computation. It is equally important to follow the flow of cash in the subject's financial activities as it is to ensure that all deposits are accounted for properly. Cash expenditures are the second major dollar item in the computation reflecting the income of the subject. An in-depth analysis of the cash flow can assist the investigator in demonstrating the accuracy of the computation and can be used to refute some potential defenses that may be presented by the defense. As an example, let us assume that the subject made a cash purchase of a boat for $32,000.00 in April of one of the years in the investigation, withdrew $30,000.00 cash from the bank in December, and made a $30,000.00 down payment on a chalet in the mountains in the following February. If our time frames in the investigation are set on calendar years, the following argument can be made to a jury.

1. The $30,000.00 withdrawal in December could not have been used for the April purchase because it was taken out after the April purchase was made.
2. If no cash purchases are included in the computation after the December withdrawal, the subject must have had an increase of $30,000.00 in cash on hand for the year.
3. The $30,000.00 could have been used in the subsequent year for cash purchases included in the computation that occurred in January or February (including the chalet down payment) and are credited to the benefit of the subject in the computation.

The investigator also has to show that all potential bank accounts are considered. How could a person hide a bank account?

If the investigator fails to follow all leads as to accounts under the control of the subject of the investigation, and an additional account (or accounts) is presented at trial, the entire bank deposits presentation becomes useless even if further analysis of the account could reveal even more income than originally charged. In the term "all accounts," the investigator must include nontraditional accounts that can be used in the same way that a standard checking or savings account can be used. Individual retirement accounts, certificates of deposit, lines of credit, brokerage accounts, and credit cards are examples of nontraditional banking tools that can be used by the subject of the investigation. To ensure a complete computation of income, each individual bank record must be analyzed for lead information into other accounts, expenditures, or nonincome sources of funds available to the subject of the investigation. The following are a few examples of how investigative leads can be found in the records obtained. They are provided from actual cases.

- In an investigation in Ohio, a check was found that was written for two drinks at an expensive hotel in Arizona. Follow-up investigation revealed several thousand dollars in expenses paid in cash at the resort hotel during the periods under investigation.

- In an investigation in New Mexico, the subject provided 12 boxes of business records for inspection, confident that he had concealed his income from discovery. In the bottom of one box was an envelope from a bank in another city in New Mexico. Follow-up investigation revealed another account in the name of his daughter that he opened as custodian of the account. More than $100,000.00 of unreported income was funneled through this account in each year of the investigation.

- In an investigation in Michigan, a money order was purchased from a bank for approximately $140.00, payable to an exclusive furrier. Follow-up investigation found that the payment was for storage of three fur coats purchased for cash by the wife of the subject during the time periods under investigation.

Following is a simple example of a bank deposits and cash expenditures summary schedule. The first step is to record the deposits, make the adjustments, and determine the net deposits for the specific time frame.

Item	2004	2005	2006
Deposits			
Bank 1 Acct# XXXXX		$82,000.00	
Bank 2 Acct# XXXXXXX		$20,000.00	
Total deposits		$102,000.00	
Less: Loan proceeds		$3,500.00	
Transfers		$8,500.00	
Vehicle rebate		$2,000.00	
Sale of stock		$6,000.00	
Checks to cash		$2,000.00	
Net deposits		$80,000.00	

The next step would be to add the cash expenditures (the purchases made with funds that were never deposited to the bank accounts). If the individual operates a business, the business records will show total expenditures, the bank statements and business check registers will show the portion of the total expenditures paid by check, and the difference will be the portion that had to be paid by cash. An example:

Total business expenses	$42,000.00
Total expenses by check	$32,000.00
Cash expenses	$10,000.00

Next, we would add any personal expenditures made using cash. For our example, we will say that the documented cash expenditures for 2005 total $10,000.00. The result of our computation would show that this individual had to have earned at least $100,000 in 2005. A total of $80,000.00 deposited to his bank accounts, $10,000.00 in business expenses paid by cash, and $10,000.00 in personal expenses paid by cash provide the $100,000.00 total. If his or her business records show that he or she earned $50,000.00 from normal and legitimate business dealings, the remaining $50,000.00 had to have come from another source, or he or she is lying about how much was earned. If we have established an illegal activity as a likely source, we can attribute the additional income to this source.

The need to identify deposits, withdrawals, and checks drawn on bank accounts is required to ensure that the money, used or controlled by the individual, has been charged against him or her correctly for the purposes of establishing criminal culpability. This includes both the legitimate funds and the illegal funds received.

The following is an example of the use of the bank deposits and cash expenditures method of proof as it was used in an investigation in New Mexico.

Example

A vehicle dealer reinvested the majority of his income each year to improve and expand his business operations. He had a personal checking account, a personal savings account, and two business checking accounts. He deposited the proceeds from his new vehicle sales into the business accounts and transferred money from those accounts to his personal accounts as his personal income from running the business. The growth of his business enterprise did not correspond to the number of new vehicles he was selling. Vehicle registrations were obtained from the Department of Motor Vehicles, indicating the title transfer to the dealer's customers. The new vehicle sales matched the reported income for the dealership. The company books and records showed a substantial increase in inventory from year to year. This increase was attributed to used vehicles taken in as trades on new vehicles. The dealer failed to record most of the used (trade-in vehicle) sales. Analysis of his banking records showed one transfer to an account in another state. Further investigation showed that the dealer had accounts in the states and was depositing the used vehicle sales proceeds into those accounts. The investigation resulted in a plea of guilty to four counts of tax evasion, and the dealer faced a prison term of 5 to 20 years, criminal fines, and civil liability for the corrected tax due, penalties, and interest.

What information can be obtained from bank records? The obvious information includes amounts deposited, transferred, and spent. What other information can be found? Review the sample canceled check, deposit slip, and statement (Figure 11.1, Figure 11.2, and Figure 11.3, respectively). List the information you find, and state what you would do with that information.

Review your own bank records (in detail). What could someone find out about you from these records? Remember that financial habits or patterns say a lot about an individual.

The bank deposits and cash expenditures method of proof is most appropriate to use when regular deposits of income are made to the accounts, and the bank records are complete and readily available to the investigator. All financial transactions must be analyzed and investigated to ensure that the investigator has considered all the accounts over which the subject has control.

This method allows for the determination of illegal or (in tax cases) unreported income commingled with licit or legitimate earnings. It can be used to

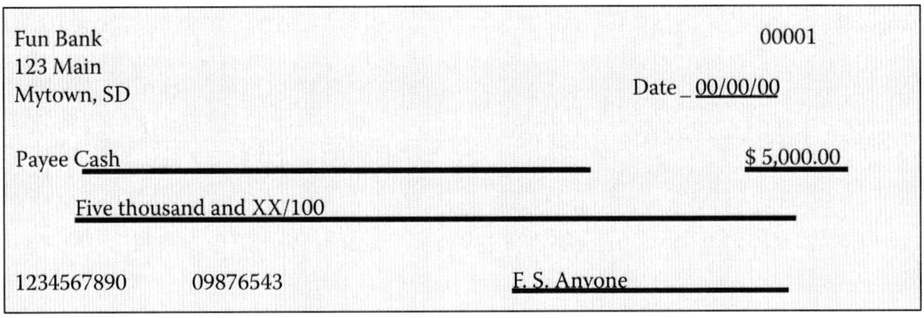

Fun Bank
123 Main
Mytown, SD
00001
Date 00/00/00
Payee Cash
$ 5,000.00
Five thousand and XX/100
1234567890
09876543
F. S. Anyone

Figure 11.1 Front of a check.

H. A. Always
S. O. Never
Endorse Above Line
Last Bank
of
Other Town
GG

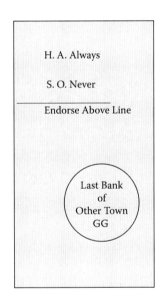

Figure 11.2 Back of a check.

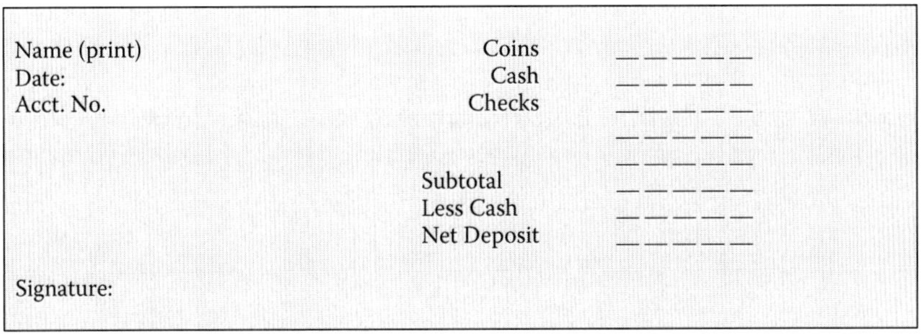

Name (print)
Date:
Acct. No.
Coins
Cash
Checks
Subtotal
Less Cash
Net Deposit
Signature:

Figure 11.3 A deposit slip.

establish a greater extent of illegal activity than can be determined through specific illegal acts based on greater receipts of income that were generated by the illegal activity but could not be supported beyond a reasonable doubt for prosecution purposes.

Net Worth and Personal Expenditures

The net worth and personal expenditures method of proof is the most comprehensive and, therefore, the most difficult to present for the prosecution and to prove to a judge or jury. This method began early in the criminal prosecutions of federal tax violations. One of the landmark U.S. Supreme Court decisions to weigh the accuracy and use of the net worth method was *Holland v. United States*, which was discussed in detail in Chapter 10. In its decision, the Supreme Court found that the method was acceptable for criminal prosecution if the prosecution was able to negate all other possible sources of income. This decision opened the door to indirect methods of proof and for a wider scope of investigative innovation in dealing with a broad variety of criminal activities. The trial and prosecution of gangster Al Capone for tax evasion led law enforcement to pursue any and all avenues of criminal prosecution to break up and disburse organized criminal activities.

Today, aspects of financial investigative techniques are used to maintain internal security and control, corroborate other criminal activities, and verify statements and assertions made in civil litigation. Comprehensive financial investigations provide a much more thorough investigation into organized criminal enterprises. They are often used to complete the extent of the criminal enterprise and to identify all of the individuals involved in the criminal operation. Investigations into ethnic organized crime groups, drug rings and cartels, major corporate fraud schemes, and regulatory criminal activities employ financial investigative techniques to prosecute the violators and to help ensure that the criminal problems are eliminated.

The net worth and personal expenditures method documents, analyzes, and interprets all of the financial activity of an individual, group of individuals, organization, or corporation for a set period of time. It computes the total amount of wealth in the possession of the subject at a specific time (the end of the time periods used in the investigation). These amounts are sequentially compared to determine the financial gain or loss incurred by the subject from one period to the next. In simpler terms, it is comparable to completing a financial statement for a loan application. If you completed one at the beginning of the month and another at the end of the month, the difference would show how much money you earned for that month.

To make the financial analysis complete, certain adjustments must be made to ensure the accuracy of the computation. Personal expenditures made during the respective time periods are added to the net worth increases or decreases computed in the net worth summary schedule. Based on the complexities or variations in the subject's financial activity, other adjustments may be necessary. If the subject owns and operates a business, and depreciation is taken on equipment, then an adjustment is made for the income offset by the depreciation deduction. Each case is different and requires the application of logic and intuitiveness on the part of the investigator. As the method title indicates, the bulk of the analysis is contained in the net worth and personal expenditures.

The net worth is a complete listing of assets less liabilities, or what you own less what you owe. Because it tries to determine monies earned, all assets are listed at cost (value appreciation cannot be included) and all liabilities at net received (loan fees and costs, and interest expenses are treated in the expenditures analysis). These items are included at the full amount regardless of when during the time period (usually the calendar year) they were acquired. They remain in the computation until they are sold or disposed of by the subject. The liabilities are handled in a similar fashion. This accounts for financial activity regarding tangible assets and liabilities. Next is the documentation of personal expenditures. There is a cost to every item an individual buys. To complete the computation, these expenditures must be added to the net worth increases to accurately reflect earnings. Because some expenditures are impossible to document historically, the net worth and expenditures method reflects the least amount of income the entity acquired during the specified time period. Indirect methods of proof can be viewed as an analytical comparison of "financial snapshots" of the subject's financial condition. The following is a simple example of a net worth and personal expenditures summary schedule:

	12/31/2005	12/31/2006	Change
Assets			
Cash in bank	$5,000.00	$8,000.00	$3,000.00
House	$100,000.00	$100,000.00	$0
Vehicle	$12,000.00	$24,000.00	$12,000.00
Total assets	$117,000.00	$132,000.00	$15,000.00
Liabilities			
Mortgage	$80,000.00	$70,000.00	$10,000.00
Car loan	$10,000.00	$6,000.00	$4,000.00
Total liabilities	$90,000.00	$76,000.00	$14,000.00
Net worth	$27,000.00	$56,000.00	$29,000.00
Add: Personal exp. 2006			$22,000.00
2006 Net worth and expenditures			$51,000.00

There are several safeguards that must be followed to ensure the accuracy of the computation. Expenditures that represent assets or a reduction in liabilities cannot be included in the computation of personal expenses. In this case, the starting point is 12/31/2005. The starting point must be accurate and fully documented. This is clearly required in the *Holland v. United States* decision. Without a solid starting point, the entire case becomes useless and unfit for prosecutorial purposes.

Exercise 1

Consider the nature of assets and liabilities, then list as many other assets and liabilities (at least five of each) that could be found in a net worth computation. What items would be included as personal expenditures? What potential defenses can you anticipate to this type of computation?

If you were given the opportunity to interview the subject, what questions would you ask? If not given an opportunity to interview the subject, what steps would you take regarding the potential defenses you identified?

The net worth and expenditures method is most often used when the investigator is faced with an uncooperative subject. The subject asserts his constitutional right to deny an interview and to provide any documents during the investigation. In these situations, the investigator must rely on third-party witnesses to construct the financial history of the entity under investigation. The following is an example of a case that utilized the net worth and personal expenditures method. The case was completed and prosecuted in the Lower Peninsula of Michigan.

Example

The subject of the investigation was self-employed as a real estate salesman in a rural area approximately 70 miles outside Detroit. He reported little or no income for several years. He decided not to speak to the investigator but did provide his real estate business records. He conducted his financial transactions predominately with cash and lived in a modest home that he inherited. He was married and had one child. During the investigation, one of the customers interviewed provided information that he had made two purchases through the subject's business. The business records showed only one transaction. The witness explained that he purchased his home with the subject as the broker and another directly from the subject on a land contract. In Michigan, land contracts were not required to be filed with the county of records until the contract was fulfilled and the deed was to be transferred. Further investigation showed that the subject had made several purchases and sales of property using land contracts personally and for clients. None of these sales was reported in his business records. The subject also placed properties in the name of a very elderly relative (this relative was incapable of making decisions, and the subject had a power of attorney to handle all of her affairs). Again, these transactions were not reported as income or recorded in the books and records of the business. The results of the net worth and personal expenditures investigation showed that the subject had earned more than $40,000 a year for the past 4 years. He was convicted in a jury trial, fined, and sentenced in federal district court.

Interesting aspects of the case included the subject's claim of a cash hoard (refuted in establishing the starting point of the case), the attempted coercion of clients not to talk to the investigator, the identification and interview of the notary publics that witnessed the land contracts, and the subject's purchase of several expensive items (new vehicles for himself and his wife, a fishing boat, and jewelry). All of these would contribute to establishing the fraud and the subject's intent to commit the fraud.

Hybrid Methods

Hybrid methods of proof are used in unique situations.[*] They are a combination of the indirect methods discussed. Combining the methods poses several problems in presenting the case for prosecution. An example in which a hybrid method could be employed is if the subject of investigation owns a bar, runs an illegal bookmaking operation, skims cash receipts to reduce his sales taxes, and finances a narcotics trafficking operation in another nearby town. Each operation may afford a different method of proof to establish the income generated. Combining indirect methods requires the investigator to prove the independence of each method so that no funds are considered twice in the overall computations.

We will not go into examples of this type of investigation or exercises due to complexities involved and their rare occurrence. It is sufficient to know that the forensic accounting investigator can adjust and be as innovative as necessary to complete the investigation.

There are also methods that are used to provide initial indications of the existence of fraud or other illegal activity. These are cursory financial investigative techniques that can be used to help determine if further financial investigation is warranted. They are usually applied when records and information are provided, and do not require the in-depth documentation and corroboration needed in the formal indirect methods of proof.

Percentage Markup

The percentage markup method is used by auditors to check whether a business is in line with the industry averages in the area. It is most appropriate when the business is a retail activity selling a limited type of product.

---

[*] This type of investigation is being included for informational purposes.

An example would be a bar or tavern. If the neighborhood bars in the area make a 15% to 20% profit on liquor sales, the auditor can determine where in this range the specific bar fits in.

The auditor would check the liquor inventory figures at the beginning and end of the year. The difference would then be added to the wholesale liquor purchases, and that total would be multiplied by the industry percentages. A large discrepancy in either direction would direct the auditor to dig deeper to explain the discrepancy. Here is an example:

John's Friendly Bar	
Beginning inventory	$2,800.00
Ending inventory	$2,400.00
Difference (Beginning − Ending)	$400.00
Purchases (add)	$210,000.00
Total sales	$210,400.00

$.15 \times 210,400.00 = \$31,560.00$
$.20 \times 210,400.00 = \$42,080.00$

What would you look for if the bar owner reports earning $15,200.00?
What would you look for if the bar owner reports earning $150,000.00?
If a major discrepancy is found, the auditor should try to identify reasons that could affect the particular bar's operation.
What legitimate reasons could affect the earnings being lower?
What legitimate reasons could affect the earnings being higher?

The Cash-T

The Cash-T is no more than a balancing of specific business accounts for a set period of time. As explained in Chapter 2, a double-entry set of books and records relies on debiting one account and crediting the related account for each transaction so that the books will balance. The Cash-T makes a cursory computation of transactions to an account, over the specific period of time being analyzed, to see if the books and records for that account balance. Remember that a business account, such as the cash account, may have offsetting entries from a wide variety of other business accounts. Any expense paid would result in a debit to the expense account and a credit to the cash account, and any income account (sales, rebates, etc.) would result in a credit to those accounts and a debit to the cash account. In auditing, the Cash-T is often used to determine whether financial discrepancies exist that require further investigation. It is also used to isolate certain transactions that affect the specific concerns of the auditor. (See Figure 11.4.)

The Cash-T Is Set Up as Follows:

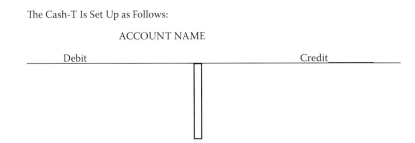

Figure 11.4 Cash-T format.

The Cash-T name is derived from the appearance of the schedule and its predominant use in analyzing the cash account. This type of analysis would identify all of the transactions that impact on the cash account. If the account is accurate (at least from the standpoint of the books and records), both sides of the "T" will equal each other or "balance."

What Processes Are Common to All Indirect Methods of Proof?

12

Certain factors are common to all indirect methods of proof. The logic behind each of the methods we discussed is to determine what must have occurred during our time frames to cause the change in financial condition and then compare the changes sequentially to the following time frames. To do this, the investigator has to comply with the rules set by the courts for the use and admissibility of evidence in an indirect method of proof.

Indirect methods of proof get their name from the fact that each puts forward, almost exclusively, circumstantial evidence to prove a criminal violation of law. The judiciary was quite skeptical of these methods when they were first put forward in the 1920s and 1930s. In 1954, the U.S. Supreme Court finally addressed the use of the net worth method of proof in *Holland v. United States*. The Court delineated the pitfalls in using this method (the same pitfalls that would be found in any indirect method) and identified the precautions necessary for a prosecution under these methods to stand.

The rules of evidence are the regulations under which law enforcement and the criminal justice system must operate in their duty to serve and protect the public. A loose comparison would be found in the game of Monopoly. If the investigator breaks the rules, the subject gets a "get out of jail free" card. If the rules are severely broken and the investigator found willful in the breakage, the investigator may get the "go directly to jail" card.

This is where the investigating officer must establish due diligence in his or her compilation and analysis of the evidence and circumstances of the case. The evidence must put forth the inference of guilt when presented logically to the judge or jury. The preponderance of the circumstantial evidence and the elimination of all potential defenses must convince the jury that the explanation of events presented is the only logical one for the results found in the computation.

The investigator must apply both deductive and inductive reasoning to the facts he or she has uncovered. To prove this beyond a reasonable doubt, the investigator has to prove a valid starting point, a likely source for the unreported or hidden income, identify the participants in the criminal enterprise, show that all leads in the investigation were followed and addressed, that the computation is mathematically accurate, and that all potential defenses identified in the investigation have been considered and addressed.

Criminal Financial Investigations

These requirements apply to each of the indirect methods of proof and have to be explained in the final report prepared by the investigator recommending prosecution.

Starting Point

The term *starting point* refers to the base time period used to start the indirect method comparisons. It is the initial snapshot of the subject's financial condition. It is the foundation or cornerstone upon which all of the investigator's assertions are based. Just as the Bible states that "the wise man builds his house on the rock," the wise investigator builds his case on a solid starting point.

The ideal situation for establishing the starting point in an indirect method of proof case is the period just prior to the first period under investigation. In a tax case, where fiscal or calendar years are used as the time frames, the ideal starting point is the year before the first year in which fraud occurs. Keep in mind that each type of crime carries a specific statute of limitations that restricts the investigation to prosecutable periods. If the fraud has been perpetrated for a long time, only the periods in which the statute is still open can be prosecuted. The investigator must review the statutes recommended for prosecution to know what periods to investigate. The evidence used in the financial investigation will be more current and easier to obtain if the starting point is closer to the first period under investigation. Records are usually still in existence and in better condition the more recent they are. Also, it is more likely that the custodian of the records (witness) will still be available for testimony and an explanation of the records. Recent financial transactions are also more easily recollected by the witnesses needed to introduce and explain the transactions. Although this is the optimum situation, the starting point in financial investigations has been established by tracking the financial activity of the subject as far back in time as the first year that the individual had a job. One net worth investigation in Michigan went back more than 30 years to the subject's first year after graduating from high school to build the financial starting point for the case. The ability to create a solid and complete starting point will always take precedence over a close proximity to the periods under investigation.

Various factors need to be considered in selecting the proper starting point for an investigation. If the subject recently relocated to your jurisdiction, you may want to consider the time period just prior to his or her move. If it is discovered that the fraud or financial crime was taking place in the prior jurisdiction, you may want to consider the feasibility of a joint investigation with the authorities in the other jurisdiction or the possibility of gaining the venue for the criminal activities outside your jurisdiction. If the subject made a substantial purchase, such as a house or business, that required filing financial information with a bank or other lending institution, you may choose that time period to utilize the subject's admissions as to the financial condition on loan or mortgage applications. If the subject has been divorced or filed for bankruptcy in the past, you may want to use the civil court filings on property and support settlements, or the final disposition from bankruptcy. Any major event in the subject's past may be a key in determining what time period is used for the starting point. In any case, the investigator will have to bring the comparative computations made up to the period prior to the periods under investigation. Let us look at a potential scenario:

Exercise 1

An individual moved to your town 5 years ago. He was employed at a fast-food restaurant for the first 2 years and has been unemployed for the last 3 years. He has been identified, through surveillance on another case, as associating with a group of suspected drug addicts and street distributors 3 years ago. He was arrested for theft and received a sentence of probation, again, 3 years ago. He purchased a 2-year-old Mercedes and moved into an exclusive apartment complex last year. You have suspicion that he has worked his way into an organized drug ring.

What time periods could be used as the starting point? Which would you use and why?

Likely Source of Income

To attribute the financial gains to a specific illegal activity (or in tax cases, legal income that is unreported), the investigator must provide the evidence as to the illegal activity being the likely source of the receipts. Courts have accepted reasonable suspicion as the benchmark of proof necessary. If there are multiple sources of income, the investigator needs to eliminate those sources that are not derived from the alleged criminal activity.

Based on this requirement, the income determined by the indirect method of proof will most likely be a lesser amount than that actually gained by the subject from the criminal activity. This is due to the fact that the investigation will not be able to find every dollar of illegal income or be able to obtain adequate proof for all of the income generated through the criminal activity. Even in specific items cases, the investigator is likely to find only the majority of the illegal or secreted income. In a criminal prosecution, it is not necessary to prove all the income by using an indirect method of proof, but it is necessary to prove all of the income charged in the case. Substantiality must be considered to show the prosecutor, judge, and jury that the amount of the financial crime warrants criminal prosecution. This aspect of indirect methods of proof and financial investigations overall must be clearly explained in the presentation to the court. It must be understood that the amounts being presented are the least amounts the subject derived from the illegal activity. Establishing the likely source of income is one of the several common factors in a financial investigation that requires making use of negative proof.

Negative proof may sound like a contradiction in terms, but it represents a substantial part of financial investigations. In the same way that a suspect may be cleared of committing a crime by having a verifiable alibi for the time the crime occurred, the investigator can prove beyond a reasonable doubt that certain financial transactions, sources of income, and potential defenses could not be true reflections of the subject's financial activities. As stated by Sherlock Holmes in the film versions of Sir Arthur Conan Doyle's famed detective stories, "If all things are proven impossible, then whatever is left, no matter how improbable, must be true." It becomes "Elementary, my dear Watson" when inductive and deductive reasoning are applied to a thorough and complete financial investigation. This is the goal of the investigator—to present a vast amount of independent financial activities in an extensive set of financial schedules and summaries to 12 diverse members on a jury so that they see the result as an obvious truth, or as being "elementary."

In a white collar criminal investigation, all legitimate sources of income (if reported correctly) must be credited back to the subject in the financial computation. The subject may have participated in activities that were improper, immoral, or unscrupulous; but this does not prove that he or she is culpable of a crime. The subject is not going to face trial until the investigator can prove that the financial gains shown in the computation are the result of criminal activities that the subject performed willfully.

If specific amounts of unreported income can be traced to criminal activity, including the result of fraud schemes, other income proven by the indirect method of computation can be attributed to that same "likely source" once all other sources have already been accounted for in the computation. Determining the likely source for the investigation relies heavily on the use of negative proof. Evidence showing that something did not occur goes far in circumstantially providing the reasonable suspicion needed for the jury to accept the likely source. As an example, the defendant in a case in New Mexico claimed that the unreported income shown in the case was really his own private savings that were used to make the purchases and pay the expenditures. When he needed money, he would go to the private stash and take out what he needed. He stated that the cash in his home was accumulated over the 30 years prior to the years under investigation. The subject claimed that he had saved more than $350,000.00 that he used during the 4 years being charged against him. During an interview, the investigator was able to get the subject to go into great detail about the prior year's savings and the $350,000.00 cash hoard. The subject stated that he kept a cigar box in the wall behind his medicine cabinet in the bathroom. Each evening he would take a bill out of his pocket and slide it through the slot inside the medicine cabinet and into the cigar box. It would usually be a $5, $10, or $20 bill. He stated, positively, that it was never a bill larger than a $20. He never needed the money until the 4 years under investigation and that was the first time he removed money from the cigar box. Because he used up all of the savings, he threw away the cigar box and has since remodeled the bathroom. After the interview, the investigator obtained an identical cigar box to the one described by the subject. He took the cigar box to a local bank and asked them to fill the box with as many $20 bills as possible. The bank used new bills wrapped in $1,000 bundles. The box held less than $20,000.00 when full. In the bank deposits computation, the investigator gave the subject credit for $20,000 cash on hand in the opening year of the 4-year case. The credit reduced the first year understatement of income, but it still left the subject liable for more than $100,000.00 in unreported income for that year. Although the subject's story would be difficult for a judge or jury to believe, accepting the story to its maximum ($20,000.00) left no doubt in the mind of the subject's attorney that the investigator followed all leads, was not padding the amounts in the computation and, most important, had established credibility in the computation. The defense attorney realized that a jury could not possibly have reasonable doubt about the case or the amounts charged. Counsel advised and convinced his client to plead guilty to all four felony charges, and accept the fines and penalties that would be assessed by the court.

Although the courts only require a likely source of income, seemingly unrelated circumstantial evidence may be used to provide the necessary proof to meet this requirement.

In a case of overcharging the county government for legal services as a public defender, an attorney was found to be charging 1-hour increments for any contact with clients assigned by the court. He would regularly telephone his clients and bill the county for 1 hour on each case. Most of the calls would last less than 5 minutes each. This scheme would add an additional 4 to 6 hours a day being charged to the county. The payment records of the county were destroyed in a flood of the basement storage area. Only the records prepared and maintained after the flooding were available (the last 6 months). These records were not a part of the time period being investigated, but an analysis of these records was made. The analysis showed days for which the attorney charged the county for 10 to 14 hours of legal services. The attorney's bank records for this time period were also reviewed, and other payments (from other clients) were identified. Interviews of the other clients disclosed the time spent by the attorney on their cases.

A compilation and comparison of all of the information showed days on which the attorney claimed more than 24 hours being billed to clients and the county. The county bank records were analyzed, and the amounts paid to the attorney during the periods under investigation showed the same pattern. Further investigation revealed billings for days when the attorney was out of the country on vacations, weekend and holiday time being charged, and even charges for days he was in the hospital. The indirect method of proof investigation showed substantial amounts of unreported income, and the overcharging scheme was used and accepted by the court as the likely source of income.

Another scenario would be a situation in which the subject was found to have a substantial income through the use of an indirect method of proof. The subject is a single female who has been receiving welfare and food stamp assistance during the period under investigation. A background check shows two convictions for minor narcotics violations: one prior to the period under investigation and one during the period. The likely source of the income she received could be attributed to trafficking in narcotics.

Identify All of the Players

Most of the financial crimes investigated are complex and involve more than one individual. Caution must be taken in an indirect method of proof case not to focus solely on the main subject behind the scheme but to include analyses of any and all of the coconspirators who may be involved. This includes those individuals who may play only a small part in the scheme and those who may have only participated during a portion of the time that the scheme was in operation.

This is not a court-defined requirement for indirect methods of proof but rather a precautionary requirement developed through investigative experience. If the conspirators are close enough to be sharing in the proceeds of a criminal fraud, they are most likely willing to provide false defenses for one another in the court. At the least, they will probably attempt to continue the concealment and deception in the fraud scheme. This may be the result of self-preservation instincts in hopes of keeping the coconspirators from divulging their part in the scheme, or an attempt to overcome prosecution and conviction of any of the coconspirators that would also shelter the conspirators from prosecution.

Examples of ways in which failing to identify one or more of the coconspirators can destroy an investigation follow: The subject has been shown to have received more than $100,000.00 per year over the last 3 years, which cannot be accounted for from legitimate sources. The likely source of income is from his involvement in an insurance fraud scheme. He insured paintings worth more than a million dollars over this period of time. He filed claims of

$700,000.00 the first year and $350,000.00 the third year. The first claim was from the theft of the paintings, and the second from a fire.

The case goes to trial, and the indirect method of proof establishes the monetary gains beyond a reasonable doubt. Because all of the funds were not traced, it is likely that others were involved in the fraud scheme. The defense calls a witness that states he gave the defendant the $300,000 over the 3 years in a protracted attempt to purchase Chinese art pieces. The money was, in essence, a surety put up to show that the buyer was sincere in the negotiations. The witness provides three cashier's checks issued by him to the defendant.

There is no time for a further investigation into the veracity of the witness' statements once the trial has begun. It is unlikely that the court would grant a continuance sufficient in length to allow the investigator to check out the story. The jury will have to consider the witness testimony as reasonable doubt, and all the effort that went into the case will disappear with an acquittal. The witness may have been involved with the defendant in the scheme, and the payments represent the defendant's share of the illegally obtained proceeds.

Following All Available Leads

Leads are the information that points the investigator to relevant evidence needed to complete the financial investigation and to ensure that the indirect method computation is as comprehensive as possible. Leads are found in every aspect of the investigative endeavor. They are found in the development of the subject's history and background. They surface during interviews of the subject, friends, relatives, and associates. They are also uncovered in the analysis of documentary evidence. Throughout the course of the investigation, leads will come to light, and the investigator is obligated to follow those leads through to fruition. It is only after all of the leads have been examined, evaluated, and explained that the investigator can be assured that the case is ready to be recommended for prosecution.

Following all of the leads is an investigative requirement imposed by the courts, within the scope of feasibility. It ensures that all evidence, in favor of and against the subject, has been considered and addressed in the criminal prosecution case. Because financial investigations rely on the use of circumstantial evidence, this requirement supports the fact that the logic applied to the facts is, in fact, the total picture of the subject's financial activities, and ensures that the rights and protections afforded the accused have not been violated. When the investigator has demonstrated to the judge or jury that all leads, no matter how great an effect they have on the case, have been followed, it is extremely difficult for the defense to challenge the quality of the investigation or infer bias on the part of the investigator. Evidence obtained during the investigation that is favorable to the subject is required to be given to the defense by the Supreme Court decision in *Brady v. Maryland*, 373 U.S. 83, 83 S.Ct. 1194 (1963).

Leads may come at any time and from any aspect of the investigation. The investigator must be thorough in recording testimony, analyzing records, and applying logic to the information that is obtained. In one investigation in South Dakota, the subject was under investigation for theft by fraud from the company where he was employed as a salesman. He would complete false orders from customers for items that were being specially priced and store the goods in a warehouse. When the special pricing event was over, he would sell those items to his customers at the regular price and keep the difference. He used the warehouse owner to provide capital for the purchases and storage of the goods. The warehouse owner died before the investigation started, and his widow sold the business. This information led the investigator to contact the widow and request an interview. The widow had moved out of state to a retirement community in the Southwest. During the interview, the investigator found out that all of the warehouse records were in the widow's possession. She provided the records for inspection and stated that her late husband had personal transactions with the subject as well as a business relationship. The records showed the receipt and shipping out of the goods used in the fraud scheme. Personal notes were also found in the records that showed the split of the fraud scheme profits with the deceased warehouse owner. During the interview of the widow, the investigator asked if she had any contacts with the subject since she moved. Although this seems like an insignificant thing to ask, the results helped to make the case by establishing the subject's knowledge and intent to defraud through the scheme. She replied that the subject called her about 2 months ago and asked her to destroy any records she may have and not to talk to any authorities about her late husband's affairs.

Another example of how apparently insignificant leads can enhance and complete a financial investigation occurred in a case in Ohio. The investigation was of a group of individuals involved in a conspiracy to import and distribute narcotics. The four people under investigation went to great lengths to conceal their activities. They made their financial transactions using cash, used special nicknames in their communications about the conspiracy, and used nominees and false names to acquire remote farm locations to conduct their drug activities. Analysis of the personal records of the subjects included a look at their credit card purchases for a 6-month period. The charges were minimal and made at various convenience stores in the area. The investigator noticed one charge for $120.00 for the rent of a storage garage in another state. A telephone call to the rental company revealed that a garage was rented in the name of one of the coconspirators for temporary storage. The payment was for 2 months when the coconspirator was in Hawaii. Further investigation revealed that the subjects used the garage to store marijuana until it could be shipped to Ohio. Interviews of the rental staff and an analysis of the rental records identified other coconspirators who visited the garage at different times. The results of following the lead were the identification of five other individuals involved in the conspiracy, identification of the code names assigned to each of the coconspirators, identification of a home purchased in Hawaii for $1.2 million and personal expenditures exceeding $100,000.00 in the area of the rented garage.

Following the leads can provide the evidence needed to make a case a great case; failure to follow the leads can kill a case that has the potential to be a great case. The fact that courts require this in indirect methods cases to protect individual rights ensures that the investigator completes the best investigation possible.

Mathematical Accuracy

As stated earlier, in a criminal financial investigation, the computation of income is a determination of the least amount of income the subject had to have earned during the periods under investigation. It may seem obvious to state that the investigator needs to be sure of the figures presented in the computation, but the repercussions may not be as obvious. It is not unusual for the summary schedules, appendices, and prosecution reports to contain thousands of numbers. Inversion, incorrect transposition, and misreading from hard-to-read documentary evidence are all possible in compiling the final computations. Modern technology eliminates most of the risk in the adding and subtracting of numbers, but human error still plays a part in the inputting and formulating of the schedules and summaries. Incorrect numbers and mathematical mistakes, found by the defense and presented during trial, can cause the entire case to become questionable in the eyes of the jury. It can also play a role in how the jury sees the efficiency and professionalism of the lead investigator.

The natural flow of the numbers in the computation will be from the evidence to summary schedules, and then to the final summary or appendix. Just as a double-entry set of books allows for cross-checking and referencing entries, the investigator can run certain comparisons to verify the accuracy of the computation. Evidentiary numbers can be referenced to related records such as bank records and witness testimony. Bank records can also be used to verify the accuracy of amounts listed in purchase and expenditure schedules. Totals for the computation can be computed directly from evidence and compared to the totals in the final report. If inconsistencies arise, it is the investigator's responsibility to find the inconsistency and correct the errors.

Nothing is as embarrassing to an investigator as having professional charts and graphs presented to a jury, only to have the defense highlight errors to the jury and blot out numbers from the charts and graphs. The jury will remember the theatrics that the defense will be allowed to use and lose sight of the meaning of the computation. Even if the errors are minimal, it takes a great effort on the part of the prosecution to save credibility on behalf of the investigator and the computation if it can be saved or restored at all.

Addressing Potential Defenses

During any investigation, potential defenses will be brought to the attention of the investigator. They may come directly from the subject during interviews, from witnesses who have a close association with the subject, or from the investigative steps taken in general. Identifying these defenses and being able to refute or explain them in the prosecution report, and subsequently to judge and jury, is necessary to having success in the case. In addition to the defenses that are provided to the investigator, any other possible defenses that are plausible should at least be considered. Indirect methods of proof rely on the believability of the investigator's logical analysis of circumstantial evidence. Any potential doubts that could be planted in a jury's mind need to be anticipated and a plan of action prepared if they are used.

Certain defenses have been regarded as being most successful in the indirect method of proof investigations. Due to the frequency of their use, reports recommending prosecution using these methods address these defenses as a matter of course. Cash hoard, personal loans, and denial of true ownership are three of the most frequent defenses given to refute a financial criminal investigation.

The Cash Hoard

The cash hoard defense alleges that the unreported or illegal income charged in the indirect method of computation was really derived from cash the subject had accumulated in time periods prior to the periods in the computation and was used during the time periods of the investigative computation. The purported result of this argument is that the entire computation is erroneous and the case should be dismissed. If the money was available to the subject from this source (the cash hoard), then it was not earned, as alleged in the investigation, during the periods charged. To use this defense, the subject must provide the judge and jury with a convincing story as to how the money was accumulated; where and how it was kept; and when, why, and how it was used during the time periods of the investigation. If the defense is presented early in the investigation, the investigator is required to determine the plausibility of the story and be able to refute the defense by following the leads given by the subject or close the investigation. Addressing a cash hoard defense in indirect methods cases is necessary even if it is not presented during the investigation. Because it stems solely from the subject, it can be presented at any time, and the investigator, and especially the prosecutor, does not want to be surprised by its assertion in court.

Many variations on the cash hoard defense can be found in court records of financial cases. Those that have worked are still adapted in financial cases, and those that have failed consistently have been abandoned. An admission to gaining illegal or unreported income in earlier time periods and using it during the periods of the investigation as a defense has been tried but has not been successful. Courts have not accepted the credibility of an admitted violator to be truthful about when they were crooks. The standard story given to support a cash hoard is the accumulation of savings over a lifetime, kept in cash, and maintained in a hiding place that is kept secret. The stories range from hiding the cash in wall panels or floorboards to filling glass jars with cash and burying them in the yard. This defense had greater believability in the 1930s and 1940s following the bank failures of the Great Depression. Deposit insurance and banking regulation have made the argument of lack of trust in banks fade away after time. However, the defense is still used with an unlimited supply of reasons being presented by defendants.

Following all of the procedures needed in preparing an indirect method of proof case provides many avenues for the investigator to take to refute a cash hoard defense. Establishing the starting point by conducting a complete analysis of financial transactions prior to the periods under investigation can show that little or no cash from legitimate sources could be available for savings prior to the periods under investigation. Analysis of the financial records can show financial activities that are inconsistent with having a substantial amount of cash prior to this period. Taking out loans, making minimum payments on time or credit purchases, selling of personal items or assets to make purchases, and late or missed payments would all indicate that the subject did not have a mattress full of money at home. Testimony of witnesses who were with the subject when purchases or expenditures were made would indicate the subject's financial status and use of cash. Loan applications and financing statements would provide the subject's statements as to the amount of cash he had available at the time the documents were prepared. Another form of investigative analysis more commonly used in bank deposit and cash expenditures cases is to analyze the flow of cash in the subject's transactions. This can show that the alleged amounts were not conducted using cash. In this case, the cash hoard may be listed in each time period in the investigation as the asset, cash on hand. Any or all of these items can be used as circumstantial evidence as to whether the subject had or could have had a cash hoard available.

Personal Loans

Another common defense to indirect methods of proof is to have another individual who is under their control or has blind allegiance to the subject testify that he or she loaned money to the subject without any documents being prepared to record the transaction. If this defense is put forth during the investigation, the investigator has the opportunity to interview the person making the loan and to investigate their ability to make a substantial cash loan. To preempt this defense in case it is only presented in court, the investigator has to be completely familiar with the means and methods used in the financial transactions made by the subject. It is unlikely that the subject will remember his or her own financial dealings in as great a detail as the investigator has in recreating the transactions. Dates of purchases, deposits, and income charged can be compared to the alleged loans to determine if the alleged funds were available or could have been used to account for the items in the criminal computation.

If all of the interviews (with the subject and the witnesses) are complete and include questions about loaning money or extending credit to the subject, inconsistencies in the testimony will tend to discredit the witness' testimony in court. It is crucial that the investigator keeps this potential defense in mind when interviewing and obtaining evidence, especially from witnesses related to and openly sympathetic to the subject. If a personal loan is claimed to be made by a witness, it is necessary to expand the questioning to all of the details about the loan, and the actions of the witness and the subject at the time it was made. Because the investigation is historical in nature, witnesses may not realize that getting the money or giving it to the subject would be impossible. Cash withdrawals cannot be made on Sundays or bank holidays, and the money could not be given to the subject if they were in a location different from that of the witness. If the subject was on a 2-week cruise vacation in Hawaii, and the witness in an office in Chicago, it would be impossible for the witness to give the subject the money.

Denial of True Ownership

The denial of being the true owner of assets held in one's name is another defense presented in indirect methods cases. The subject will state that the assets were purchased by him or her, but the money used to purchase the asset came from another person. This defense requires the cooperation of the individual named as the true owner. The exclusive use of the asset, the listing of the asset on financial statements filed by the subject, and the subsequent sale of the asset and retaining the proceeds are all means by which the investigator can refute this type of defense. If time is available, the financial condition of the alleged true owner may be analyzed to show whether he or she had the resources to provide the necessary funds.

This defense can also be presented in reverse when the subject uses fictitious names or entities to register assets or make expenditures. If the subject has sufficient influence over others, he or she may use them to purchase assets and make expenditures as nominees. In one case, the head of an organized crime family used underlings to make stock purchases, purchase real property, and buy cashier checks from various banks to make purchases on his behalf.

If this difficulty is encountered in the investigation, the investigator must go through the painstaking process of analyzing each and every financial transaction with extreme scrutiny.

The next three chapters will provide simple examples of how the schedules appear in each of the three indirect methods of proof computations that have been discussed. These examples are suggested as ways to organize and present the investigative findings. Each case will lend itself to presentation in a variety of ways, and each investigator will develop a method that works best for him or her in preparing the final presentation.

The Specific Items Case

13

The format for a specific items presentation can be approached in several ways. Following is an example of a generic computation. Notice that common items are separated into schedules that are referenced on the main schedule, often referred to as an appendix (in this example, Appendix A).

The large column on the left side of the schedule contains a description of the items that are used in the computation. The first smaller column to the right will reference the witness number and the specific exhibits that prove the amount of the item. After this column, the others are used chronologically to display the amounts being used in the computation. In a formal computation, a wide column on the far right is used to fully describe the documentary evidence exhibited.

The last page of the sample computation is referred to as the list of witnesses and gives the relevant witness information with a description of each item of evidence they will introduce. The rules of evidence dictates which witness is competent to introduce which items into evidence. The list of witnesses will include any witness referred to in the narrative prosecution report, in addition to the criminal computation. The witnesses are usually numbered in the order they appear in the report to simplify the case presentation. An example of the list of witnesses is contained in Chapter 15 in the net worth and expenditures computation.

The investigative report follows the investigative steps taken in the case. Draft or cursory schedules are prepared to identify the evidence found, the witness providing the evidence, and the financial effect the evidence has on the case. Separate schedules for each category should be made to identify and correlate similar financial transactions, and to separate the evidence, as it is obtained, to facilitate preparation of the final report.

The following example will provide a summary of the case, the evidence found during the investigation, and samples of how the evidence would be reduced to schedules. In addition, the discretionary decisions made in the case will be discussed. This example is based on the investigator's decision to use the specific items method of proof.

Case Summary

John Doe is a loan officer at the City Bank. He began working at the bank after getting an associate degree in finance in 2001. The position at the bank was his first full-time job. In 2005, he was promoted to the position of loan officer. As loan officer, he was responsible for issuing loans and determining when they were no longer collectible. An anonymous call is received that John Doe's spending and lifestyle have increased dramatically in the past 3 years, and he is still at the same job.

Evidence Developed

The records from the bank show:

1. Doe is single and has worked for the bank since January 10, 2001. He was promoted on February 1, 2005, to loan officer. He has earned the following amounts from his salary at the bank: 2001, $17,000.00; 2002, $18,000.00; 2003, $18,700.00; 2004, $19,200.00; 2005, $32,500.00; 2006, $35,700.00; and 2007, $39,200.00.
2. As the bank's loan officer, Doe is responsible for all of the loans made and the determination of which loans should be written off as uncollectible.
3. The number of loans written off increased between 2004 and 2005, but has remained constant from 2005 through 2007.
4. The bank wrote off an average of 10 loans per year from 2005 through 2007.
5. The dollar amount of loans written off during these years increased in each of the last 3 years.

An analysis of Doe's personal financial records shows:

1. He has had his salary directly deposited into a checking account at the bank since he began his employment.
2. Checks written on the account use up most of the funds deposited. He has an average balance in the account of $400.00.
3. In 2005, he began making minimum payments on his credit card balances (prior to this, he used to pay the balances due in full).
4. In 2006, he stops making rent payments and begins making mortgage payments. He also pays off the outstanding balance on his credit card.

5. In 2007, he transfers $18,000.00 from his checking account into a new high-yield savings account.

Other information obtained during the investigation shows:

1. In 2005, Doe's rent went up from $500.00 to $650.00 per month.
2. Also in 2005, he begins having substantially more charges on his credit card for entertainment expenses.
3. In 2006, he purchases a condominium for $160,000.00, with a down payment of $8,000.00 and closing costs of $1,750.00. The mortgage payments are $850.00 per month.
4. In 2007, he talked to the other employees about his great vacation to Myrtle Beach, South Carolina.
5. Also in 2007, he purchases a 2008 sport utility vehicle for $32,800.00.

Further analysis of the bank loan records reveals:

1. Borrowers for the defaulted loans from 2005 through 2007 were identified.
2. The first loan that Doe wrote off in 2005 was a loan his brother-in-law made with the bank 2 years earlier. The loan balance was $27,000.00 in his brother-in-law's business.
3. Several of the written-off loans were made to recently started businesses.

Other Information

The investigator decided to contact the borrowers who had loans written off between 2005 and the end of 2007. All but nine of the loans were to businesses that had operated in a six-county area. The businesses had since closed. Interviews of the former business owners revealed that they obtained business loans for various legitimate reasons, but their plans did not work out, and they defaulted on the loans and subsequently went out of business.

Doe's brother-in-law was also interviewed. He stated that he obtained a loan from the bank to open a small diner. The diner broke even or lost a little each month for the first year it was open. In 2005, the bank wrote off the loan. There were no assets owned by the business (location and equipment were leased). The business had a few hundred dollars that was applied to the loan, and a balance of $27,000.00 was written off. He stated that he did not know that his brother-in-law was responsible for the write-off. He also stated that he has never loaned or gifted any money to Doe. He states that the check for $5,000.00 that he gave to Doe was the repayment of money Doe loaned him when he was starting the diner. He paid Doe rather than give it back to the bank.

The remaining nine loans that were written off (two in 2005, three in 2006, and four in 2007) went to recently registered businesses that could not be located in telephone books or business directories. A search of the state business registration office provided the names and addresses of the owners and registered agents. None of the individuals named could be located, and several of the addresses listed did not exist or were those of people who had never heard of the business.

The investigator went back to the loan records obtained from the bank and followed the loan proceeds on the nine suspect loans. The loan proceeds were wire transferred to nine different business accounts at nine different banks in bordering states.

The nine out-of-state accounts were opened under the nine business names used for the defaulted loans. Each account was opened between September 2005 and February 2006, with an initial deposit of $200.00. The accounts were all opened by the same individual, a John Poe, residing in the city where the loans were issued. The only transactions in each of the accounts were a single wire deposit from City Bank and periodic cash withdrawals ($8,000.00 to $9,000.00 each) until the balance was zeroed out and the accounts were closed. An enlargement of the driver license photograph of John Doe was shown to the out-of-state bankers, and seven of the nine identified the photo as that of John Poe. The identification for opening each of the accounts was checked, and the information was shown to be false, including name, address, date of birth, and Social Security number.

The bank records for the nine accounts were obtained and taken as evidence, as well as statements from the bankers identifying the records and the contacts with the individual claiming to be John Poe. A schedule was prepared chronologically following the financial activity in the nine accounts. Another schedule was prepared showing the chronology of the defaulted loans from City Bank records. The two schedules were compared, and they revealed that the dates when the proceeds were wired from City Bank as loan proceeds on the defaulted loans coincided with the wire deposits received in the nine accounts. The schedule of cash expenditures made by John Doe (including the condominium and SUV purchases) occurred within a few days of sufficient funds being withdrawn from the nine accounts.

Several factors were considered by the investigator in making the decision to use the specific items method of proof for presenting this case. The investigator felt that the loan fraud scheme was the only fraud being perpetrated by John Doe. The illegal gains from the fraud scheme could be traced directly to each of the nine fraudulent loans. The proceeds from the scheme could be shown to be going to John Doe exclusively. The use of false identification and out-of-state banks to conceal the proceeds was strong circumstantial evidence relating to Doe's knowledge of wrongdoing and intent to defraud the bank.

Other factors were involved in attempting to understand the flow of Doe's financial situation. With his promotion in 2005, his spending habits show an increase in "partying" type expenses (based on checks drawn on his account and the increase in his credit card charges). It also indicates that he was getting into debt and feeling a financial crunch as indicated by the transition to minimum payments on his credit card. This was probably aggravated by the increase in his rent. The write-off of his brother-in-law's note early in 2005 could have given him the idea for the loan fraud scheme. The $5,000.00 he received from his brother-in-law was probably a kickback for writing off the loan, as Doe did not have the means to loan anyone $5,000.00, and his bank records do not show a check or withdrawal for that amount. The scheme was to file false loan documents with the bank, distribute the loan proceeds to out-of-state banks, collect the money through cash withdrawals (under the currency reporting requirements of $10,000.00), close the accounts, write off the loans, and keep the cash.

Following are examples of how the evidence would be reflected in work schedules, report schedules, and the overall case summary schedule for working this case using the specific items method of proof.

The first task is to make sense of the information obtained and contained in the evidence. Work schedules are prepared to place all similar information into categories so that the investigator can analyze the data. In our example, we would analyze the written-off loans done by Doe.

The records from City Bank would contain all of the data for the schedule. All of the loans written off by Doe would be placed on the schedule in chronological order, identifying the loan number, date of the loan and amount, date and amount written off, and the corresponding witness and exhibit number. Because we know that Doe wrote off 10 loans per year, the schedule would have 30 entries for the time period January 1, 2005, through December 31, 2007.

To make the schedule more manageable, the loans would be totaled for each year. This work schedule then becomes the general information from which any specific irregularity would be identified. The items requiring further investigation in our example have been highlighted.

The next step would be to further document the loans that were written off. Each of the borrowers who had a loan written off would be interviewed. In the preceding schedule, the loans for borrowers who could not be located (highlighted) would direct the investigation to review the loan disbursement files. Our example shows that the loan proceeds for the "suspicious" loans were all wire transferred to out-of-state banks. Our investigation further disclosed that Doe opened the accounts and subsequently withdrew the proceeds using sham business names and a false name for himself.

The receipt of illegal income is usually assessed when the individual has possession and control of the funds. In a situation where the defense presents

City Bank
Write-Off Summary

Date	Loan Number	Amount	Write-Off Date	Amount	W/E#
12/12/03	1214	$28,000.00	01/06/05	$27,000.00	W1-1
12/28/03	1242	$25,000.00	01/10/05	$22,000.00	W1-2
01/06/04	1255	$20,000.00	02/10/05	$19,000.00	W1-3
05/15/04	1501	$30,000.00	02/16/05	$29,000.00	W1-4
06/08/04	1633	$18,000.00	03/12/05	$17,500.00	W1-5
09/06/04	1776	$32,000.00	04/04/05	$31,100.00	W1-6
11/21/04	1850	$30,000.00	05/01/05	$30,000.00	W1-7
01/04/05	1929	$35,000.00	06/15/05	$35,000.00	W1-8
02/20/05	2004	$35,000.00	07/15/05	$35,000.00	W1-9
03/03/05	2062	$17,000.00	12/10/05	$15,500.00	W1-10
Total 2005		$270,000.00		$261,100.00	
03/13/05	2077	$138,000.00	01/10/06	$135,000.00	W1-11
03/30/05	2091	$22,000.00	01/20/06	$21,000.00	W1-12
01/21/06	2140	$35,000.00	05/05/06	$35,000.00	W1-13
04/26/06	2297	$35,000.00	09/01/06	$35,000.00	W1-14
05/05/06	2313	$25,000.00	10/01/06	$25,000.00	W1-15
05/27/06	2351	$22,000.00	10/30/06	$21,000.00	W1-16
06/03/06	2366	$90,000.00	11/01/06	$89,500.00	W1-17
06/16/06	2381	$35,000.00	11/01/06	$35,000.00	W1-18
07/01/06	2404	$29,000.00	12/07/06	$28,000.00	W1-19
09/15/06	2511	$55,000.00	12/15/06	$50,500.00	W1-20
Total 2006		$486,000.00		$475,000.00	
10/10/06	2555	$47,000.00	01/15/07	$46,000.00	W1-21
10/29/06	2575	$33,000.00	01/21/07	$32,000.00	W1-22
11/09/06	2600	$118,000.00	03/04/07	$115,000.00	W1-23
01/04/07	2717	$45,000.00	05/05/07	$45,000.00	W1-24
01/18/07	2732	$45,000.00	05/20/07	$45,000.00	W1-25
01/28/07	2744	$32,000.00	05/30/07	$32,000.00	W1-26
02/09/07	2800	$100,000.00	06/15/07	$98,000.00	W1-27
04/08/07	3011	$17,000.00	10/10/07	$17,000.00	W1-28
04/11/07	3026	$45,000.00	10/15/07	$45,000.00	W1-29
04/17/07	3051	$45,000.00	10/22/07	$45,000.00	W1-30
Total 2007		$527,000.00		$520,000.00	

that the individual had full intention to repay the loans, the income would be charged when the note was written off as uncollectible (forgiveness of indebtedness constitutes the waiver of the liability by the lender, and the amounts become income to the forgiven borrower). For the sake of simplicity, our case has both the issuance of the loans and the write off of the loans occurring in the same year.

Other schedules and computations would also be prepared. An analysis of Doe's checking account activity would be made for all of the years he had been employed. This analysis serves a twofold purpose: It reviews prior financial activities to identify if other irregularities are present, and it is used to support the starting point for the indirect method of proof. In our example, all of the money that Doe defrauded from the bank is accounted for, and the starting point becomes a useful tool in painting a picture of Doe's financial activities and potential financial events, which may indicate motive, means, and intent (all are needed for a criminal conviction). As we are not concerned with expenditures, the checks drawn on his account do not require in-depth analysis. The deposits to the account should be given in a separate schedule to show that none of the fraudulent loan proceeds were placed in his regular account (all deposits from employment at bank) and that the major cash purchases did not come from his checking account. This, again, becomes a piece of circumstantial evidence pointing to Doe's attempt to conceal the fraudulent gains.

Although expenditures do not figure in the specific items method of computation of income, unusual or "luxury"-type expenditures are fully documented and used to prove other elements of the crime. The use of cash for major purchases, such as the condominium and the SUV, can be used to infer the attempt to conceal receipt of the fraudulent funds and to show the direct benefit of the criminal activity to the subject. The same would be true on the additional asset acquired (the savings account), and these show earnings far in excess of his legitimate income.

If we add the cash expenditures and the cash asset acquisition discovered during the investigation thus far, we would only account for $58,000.00 of the $355,000.00 fraudulent loan proceeds. The investigation requires that further steps be taken to find out where the rest of the money went. We would want to determine if Doe had coconspirators in the scheme who also shared in the illegal proceeds. The bank would want to know where to go to try to recoup the monies it lost through the fraud scheme. The investigator wants to make sure that all violations that Doe may have committed are uncovered and documented for prosecution.

Following all of the leads would direct the investigation to the out-of-state banks to determine where the rest of the fraudulent proceeds went. The same general investigative procedures would be applied to the new locations. For our case example, three of the out-of-state banks are located in the Myrtle Beach area, and these accounts were opened and closed out after the vacation that Doe talked so much about to his coworkers. Property records, vehicle registrations, and other public record searches would reveal whether the fraudulent income was used for major purchases in the vicinity of the banks. For the purpose of our example, the searches reveal the following information:

Doe purchased a two-bedroom beach house near Myrtle Beach in January 2007 for $192,000.00.
Doe purchased a boat in May 2007 for $74,000.00.

Interviews of the real estate agent and the boat broker revealed that Doe made both purchases with cashier checks drawn on the three banks he used for wire transferring the false loan proceeds. Each of the cashier checks was in the amount of $9,000.00; 21 checks were used for the house, and 8 checks for the boat. He purchased cashier checks from different branches of the banks on consecutive days, acquiring the total amount needed in about a week for the house purchase, and in 2 days for the boat purchase. This evidence would act as proof for additional charges of money laundering against Doe for trying to avoid the currency transaction reporting requirements (statue requires a currency transaction report be filed for cash transactions in excess of $10,000.00) by making multiple cash transactions below the dollar requirement when the intent is to exceed the amount (smurfing).

The false identity used by Doe to open the out-of-state accounts is another action that has potential for additional criminal charges. The use of a false Social Security number is a felony under federal law. The investigator should provide the evidence and allow the prosecution to decide what additional charges to include.

With the follow-up completed in our example, we can now account for Doe's personal use of an additional $266,000 of the $355,000 defrauded from City Bank. Combined with the $58,000 we documented in his hometown, we have accounted for $324,000 of the illegal income. As the use of the funds is circumstantial evidence used to negate the potential defense of others being involved in the scheme, it is not necessary to trace the small amount remaining. It is likely that Doe used the funds on his new lifestyle expenditures. The specific items case will still be the primary source of evidence to charge the total amount taken by fraud from the bank.

If the investigator believes that the $5000 that Doe received from his brother-in-law was, in fact, a kickback to get his loan written off, a case may be developed against the brother-in-law. Completion of that investigation would not be necessary to move forward to prosecution of Doe for the bank fraud and/or the money laundering or false Social Security Number, because there is no indication that the brother-in-law was involved in those activities as a coconspirator. Again, the investigator needs to make sense of the new evidence acquired for presentation to the prosecutor and eventual use in court proceedings. A schedule should be prepared to show the investigator's analysis of Doe's legitimate income (deposit analysis of Doe's checking account), an expenditures schedule made for the use of the fraudulent loan proceeds, and the final specific items schedule prepared to establish the starting point and allocate the fraudulent acts to the respective time periods (calendar-year time periods for 2005 through 2007). The following are examples of the schedules.

Deposits Schedule First Bank Acct. #3241
John Doe – 2005

DATE	DESCRIPTION	AMOUNT	2005	2006	2007	W/E #
01/14/05	Direct Deposit Payroll	$938.00	$938.00			W1-35
01/28/05	Direct Deposit Payroll	$938.00	$938.00			W1-35
02/14/05	Direct Deposit Payroll	$938.00	$938.00			W1-35
02/28/05	Direct Deposit Payroll	$938.00	$938.00			W1-35
03/14/05	Direct Deposit Payroll	$938.00	$938.00			W1-35
03/28/05	Direct Deposit Payroll	$938.00	$938.00			W1-35
04/14/05	Direct Deposit Payroll	$938.00	$938.00			W1-35
04/28/05	Direct Deposit Payroll	$938.00	$938.00			W1-35
05/14/05	Direct Deposit Payroll	$938.00	$938.00			W1-35
05/28/05	Direct Deposit Payroll	$938.00	$938.00			W1-35
06/14/05	Direct Deposit Payroll	$938.00	$938.00			W1-35
06/28/05	Direct Deposit Payroll	$938.00	$938.00			W1-35
07/14/05	Direct Deposit Payroll	$938.00	$938.00			W1-35
07/28/05	Direct Deposit Payroll	$938.00	$938.00			W1-35
08/14/05	Direct Deposit Payroll	$938.00	$938.00			W1-35
08/28/05	Direct Deposit Payroll	$938.00	$938.00			W1-35
09/14/05	Direct Deposit Payroll	$938.00	$938.00			W1-35
09/28/05	Direct Deposit Payroll	$938.00	$938.00			W1-35
10/14/05	Direct Deposit Payroll	$938.00	$938.00			W1-35
10/28/05	Direct Deposit Payroll	$938.00	$938.00			W1-35
11/14/05	Direct Deposit Payroll	$938.00	$938.00			W1-35
11/28/05	Direct Deposit Payroll	$938.00	$938.00			W1-35
12/14/05	Direct Deposit Payroll	$938.00	$938.00			W1-35
12/28/05	Direct Deposit Payroll	$938.00	$938.00			W1-35

Deposits Schedule First Bank Acct. #3241
John Doe – 2006

DATE	DESCRIPTION	AMOUNT	2005	2006	2007	W/E #
01/14/06	Direct Deposit Payroll	$1,043.00		$1,043.00		W1-36
01/28/06	Direct Deposit Payroll	$1,043.00		$1,043.00		W1-36
02/14/06	Direct Deposit Payroll	$1,043.00		$1,043.00		W1-36
02/28/06	Direct Deposit Payroll	$1,043.00		$1,043.00		W1-36
03/14/06	Direct Deposit Payroll	$1,043.00		$1,043.00		W1-36
03/28/06	Direct Deposit Payroll	$1,043.00		$1,043.00		W1-36
04/14/06	Direct Deposit Payroll	$1,043.00		$1,043.00		W1-36
04/28/06	Direct Deposit Payroll	$1,043.00		$1,043.00		W1-36
05/14/06	Direct Deposit Payroll	$1,043.00		$1,043.00		W1-36
05/28/06	Direct Deposit Payroll	$1,043.00		$1,043.00		W1-36
06/14/06	Direct Deposit Payroll	$1,043.00		$1,043.00		W1-36
06/28/06	Direct Deposit Payroll	$1,043.00		$1,043.00		W1-36
07/14/06	Direct Deposit Payroll	$1,043.00		$1,043.00		W1-36
07/28/06	Direct Deposit Payroll	$1,043.00		$1,043.00		W1-36
08/14/06	Direct Deposit Payroll	$1,043.00		$1,043.00		W1-36
08/28/06	Direct Deposit Payroll	$1,043.00		$1,043.00		W1-36
09/14/06	Direct Deposit Payroll	$1,043.00		$1,043.00		W1-36
09/28/06	Direct Deposit Payroll	$1,043.00		$1,043.00		W1-36
10/14/06	Direct Deposit Payroll	$1,043.00		$1,043.00		W1-36
10/28/06	Direct Deposit Payroll	$1,043.00		$1,043.00		W1-36
11/14/06	Direct Deposit Payroll	$1,043.00		$1,043.00		W1-36
11/28/06	Direct Deposit Payroll	$1,043.00		$1,043.00		W1-36
12/14/06	Direct Deposit Payroll	$1,043.00		$1,043.00		W1-36
12/28/06	Direct Deposit Payroll	$1,043.00		$1,043.00		W1-36

Deposits Schedule First Bank Acct. #3241
John Doe – 2007

DATE	DESCRIPTION	AMOUNT	2005	2006	2007	W/E #
01/14/07	Direct Deposit Payroll	$1,120.00			$1,120.00	W1-37
01/28/07	Direct Deposit Payroll	$1,120.00			$1,120.00	W1-37
02/14/07	Direct Deposit Payroll	$1,120.00			$1,120.00	W1-37
02/28/07	Direct Deposit Payroll	$1,120.00			$1,120.00	W1-37
03/14/07	Direct Deposit Payroll	$1,120.00			$1,120.00	W1-37
03/28/07	Direct Deposit Payroll	$1,120.00			$1,120.00	W1-37
04/14/07	Direct Deposit Payroll	$1,120.00			$1,120.00	W1-37
04/28/07	Direct Deposit Payroll	$1,120.00			$1,120.00	W1-37
05/14/07	Direct Deposit Payroll	$1,120.00			$1,120.00	W1-37
05/28/07	Direct Deposit Payroll	$1,120.00			$1,120.00	W1-37
06/14/07	Direct Deposit Payroll	$1,120.00			$1,120.00	W1-37
06/28/07	Direct Deposit Payroll	$1,120.00			$1,120.00	W1-37
07/14/07	Direct Deposit Payroll	$1,120.00			$1,120.00	W1-37
07/28/07	Direct Deposit Payroll	$1,120.00			$1,120.00	W1-37
08/14/07	Direct Deposit Payroll	$1,120.00			$1,120.00	W1-37
08/28/07	Direct Deposit Payroll	$1,120.00			$1,120.00	W1-37
09/14/07	Direct Deposit Payroll	$1,120.00			$1,120.00	W1-37
09/28/07	Direct Deposit Payroll	$1,120.00			$1,120.00	W1-37
10/14/07	Direct Deposit Payroll	$1,120.00			$1,120.00	W1-37
10/28/07	Direct Deposit Payroll	$1,120.00			$1,120.00	W1-37
11/14/07	Direct Deposit Payroll	$1,120.00			$1,120.00	W1-37
11/28/07	Direct Deposit Payroll	$1,120.00			$1,120.00	W1-37
12/14/07	Direct Deposit Payroll	$1,120.00			$1,120.00	W1-37
12/28/07	Direct Deposit Payroll	$1,120.00			$1,120.00	W1-37
Totals			**$22,512.00**	**$25,032.00**	**$26,880.00**	

The deposits schedule illustrated only reflects the 3 years under investigation. In reality, all the 7 years of the account activity would be scheduled out for the case report. In addition, bank account reconciliations would be made to reflect accurate year-end balances, and the expenditures from the account (checks written) would also be analyzed. The purpose for the extensive bank analyses is to establish a firm and accurate starting point, and to provide circumstantial evidence relating to the subject's state of mind leading up to the commission of the fraud, and the financial patterns and conditions that existed prior to the periods under investigation.

The other schedules used in our example are the summaries of the actual fraudulent loans and the cash expenditures that Doe made with the fraudulent loan proceeds. The use of schedules in a financial investigation is an easy and important means for gathering similar financial activities in groups so that the type of activity can be seen in a total picture. Changes, inconsistencies, and irregularities can provide the plausible reasons the subject had that led to the commission of the crime. In our case, it is easy to imagine that Doe began spending heavier than his promotion could afford. The write-off of his brother-in-law's loan (made in 2003) could easily have given Doe the idea for the fraud scheme. The use of schedules and the development of a complete financial history of the subject allows the people evaluating the case report for prosecution the potential to see the aggregate amounts of financial activity in all areas and gain an understanding of the subject's state of mind in committing the crime. The following is an example of the schedule of specific items of fraudulent income for John Doe.

Fraudulent Loans, John Doe
2005 through 2007

| Date Issued | Date of Write-Off | Loan Number | Amount Written Off | | | W/E# |
			2005	2006	2007	
01/04/05	06/15/05	1929	$35,000.00	0	0	W1-8
02/20/05	07/15/05	2004	$35,000.00	0	0	W1-9
01/21/06	05/05/06	2140	0	$35,000.00	0	W1-13
04/26/06	09/01/06	2297	0	$35,000.00	0	W1-14
06/16/06	11/01/06	2361	0	$35,000.00	0	W1-18
01/04/07	05/05/07	2717	0	0	$45,000.00	W1-24
01/18/07	05/20/07	2732	0	0	$45,000.00	W1-25
04/11/07	10/15/07	3026	0	0	$45,000.00	W1-29
04/17/07	10/22/07	3051	0	0	$45,000.00	W1-30
Totals			$70,000.00	$105,000.00	$180,000.00	

To eliminate any doubt that Doe was the recipient of the fraudulent loan proceeds, a schedule of his use of these funds would also be included. This would be a schedule of his cash expenditures over the 3-year period.

John Doe Cash Expenditures
2005 through 2007

Date	Item	2005	2006	2007	W/E#
01/07/06	Down payment, Condo	0	$8,000.00	0	W16-1,2
01/18/07	Savings account	0	0	$18,000.00	W1-5
01/30/07	Beach house	0	0	$192,000.00	W17-1,2
05/17/07	Boat	0	0	$74,000.00	W18-1,2
09/28/07	SUV	0	0	$32,000.00	W15-1,2
Totals		0	$8,000.00	$316,000.00	

Analysis of the cash expenditures in relation to the dates of the false loans being issued shows that Doe delayed in spending the proceeds he received from the false loan scheme for almost a year. We can speculate that he was unsure that the scheme would work and kept the cash until he felt confident that he would not get caught. If discovered early on, he would probably have made an attempt to return the funds and hope that he would not be prosecuted. In an indirect methods case, the use of illegally obtained funds does not have to correspond to the times that the funds were obtained. The investigator does, however, need to show a relationship between the receipt of the alleged illegal funds to the amounts generated from the fraud scheme.

In a simple specific items case like our example, a summary schedule or appendix showing all of the categories covered in the other schedules may not be necessary. The scope of the financial activities and the number of individual transactions will be the deciding factor for the investigator on whether to use a summary schedule. Following is how the summary schedule would look in our case example.

Appendix A, Specific Items Computation of Fraudulent Income
Doe, John: Case #12345
321 Main
Anytown, Anystate 54321

Item	2004	2005	2006	2007	Ref.
		Income			
Net income (bank)	$13,440.00	$22,512.00	$25,032.00	$26,880.00	Sch 1
Fraudulent loans	0	$70,000.00	$105,000.00	$180,000.00	Sch 2
Total income	$13,440.00	$92,512.00	$130,032.00	$206,880.00	
		Expenditures			
By check	$13,102.00	$22,488.00	$25,008.00	$26,990.00	Sch 3
By cash	0	0	$8,000.00	$316,000.00	Sch 4
Totals	$13,102.00	$22,488.00	$33,008.00	$342,990.00	
Income	$13,440.00	$92,512.00	$130,032.00	$206,880.00	
Less expenditures	$13,102.00	$22,488.00	$33,008.00	$342,990.00	
Totals	$338.00	$70,024.00	$97,024.00	($136,110.00)	
Total income (all years)	$442,864.00				
Expenditures (all years)	$411,588.00				
Cash unaccounted for	$31,276.00				

As you can see from the given appendix, the evidence in the case is not complicated enough to require the appendix for purposes of clarity and understanding. The appendix can be included as a ready reference and guide to the supporting schedules, and it does identify the amount of fraudulent income that was not specifically identified with a specific purchase during the investigation. The narrative portion of the report will walk the prosecution through the financial history of the subject and refer the reader to the appropriate schedules that delineate the common financial transactions.

The specific items method of proof is the easiest form of forensic accounting to employ in a financial investigation. The fraudulent items can stand alone, but when placed in a historical perspective, they can clearly show a judge or jury the overall plans of the violator and the total harm or injury caused to the victims.

The purpose in providing examples of schedules that show how similar transactions can be consolidated within respective time periods is to give the investigator a means of combining transactions so that the prosecution and the triers of fact are not overwhelmed by hundreds or thousands of individual transactions. In addition, the appendix acts as the thumbnail presentation of the case in its entirety.

From the investigative standpoint, the work schedules help to organize and consolidate the evidence as it is obtained over the course of the investigation. To help ensure the accuracy of the case presentation, it is beneficial to have the final summary schedules prepared early in the investigation and to transfer items to those schedules as the evidence is completed for each transaction.

The schedules in this example have been prepared based on a simple scheme. The witness and exhibit references are equally simplified. The witness and exhibit references identify the qualified witness to introduce a document or multiple documents into evidence. It will also reference other witnesses that may have additional information about the document but not be qualified to introduce it. As an example, a subject's check is introduced by the bank (a qualified custodian of the record) and the recipient called as a witness to its purpose. Investigations will often uncover several witnesses for a single transaction to be fully documented or proven. Therefore, the witness and evidence references may include several different witnesses and numerous documentary exhibits.

The next two chapters will show the structure of the bank deposits and cash expenditures, and the net worth and personal expenditures methods of proof. These methods are much more complex to present, and the preparation of concise and accurate schedules becomes mandatory if the investigator is to be successful in completing the case.

The specific item method is employed when the subject has a single or very few sources of illegal income, or a single or limited method of fraud or other illegal activity. Embezzlement, a Ponzi scheme, and money laundering (as a smurf) would fall under the single-source situation. Skimming receipts, fencing stolen property, and price fixing would fall under the single-method situation.

List three crimes in which you could apply this method. Explain your reasons why, and what leads and witnesses would make this method work in your cases.

This method is an easy and accepted way to present the financial results of a criminal activity. It requires that the investigator has sufficient evidence to support the individual items. This method is limited in its presentation compared to the indirect methods of proof that are discussed in the next two chapters. This method takes a snapshot of each instance of the criminal activity rather than inferring the financial gains from the illegal activity by presenting a complete financial history of the subject under investigation.

Specific items can be used to support almost any other criminal charge. Tracking the proceeds of the crime to the alleged perpetrator, and showing what he or she used the proceeds for, corroborates the commission of the crime that was originally charged.

Exercises

1. You are investigating the operator of a telemarketing scam. He received $1000 investments each from several people and did not provide the promised return on the investments. Five of the investors came forward and filed criminal complaints. You executed a search warrant, and obtained the operator's bank records and the documents used to entice investors.
   - List the steps you would take to continue your investigation.
   - What information do you need from the investment victims?
   - What records do you need from the investors?
   - What information may be available in the records obtained from the search?
   - What additional information could be found in the bank's records of the operator's accounts?
   - The operator claims that he sells the investment for an offshore corporation and only receives a commission for the sales. How do you verify or refute (negative proof) this claim?
   - Be prepared to discuss and defend your decisions.
2. Ralph is a known bookmaker. He spent $400,000.00 last year. During your interview, he states that he won the money in Las Vegas in January. What follow-up questions do you ask? What investigative steps do you take?
3. Karl is being investigated as a pimp. He has accumulated more than $250,000.00 per year in assets during the last 2 years. He states that he received the money in gifts and personal loans, as he was diagnosed with cancer. What follow-up questions do you ask? What investigative steps do you take?

The Bank Deposits and Cash Expenditures Case

14

The bank deposits and cash expenditures method of proof is used in many criminal financial investigations, most often when the investigators believe that they have obtained all of the bank records of the subject, and when the subject makes regular and periodic deposits to those accounts.

The theory behind this method is quite simple. A person is limited in what they can do with money they receive. They can put it in a bank, or they can spend it in the form of cash. It also presumes that regular periodic deposits made to bank accounts would come from a current source of income. This method traces and analyzes all the deposits made to bank accounts, and the flow and usage of cash by the subject of the investigation. In this type of investigation, it is crucial that the investigator establish an accurate starting point for the investigation. Although deposits made and cash used for expenditures could be alleged to come from monies previously earned, selecting a starting point that obviates this excuse is the only means to overcome this type of defense and convince the judge and jury that the alleged amounts of income represent only the income gained during the periods under investigation.

This is a much more complicated method of proof for the investigator to present. It requires that all income from any source be determined, and then all legitimate sources are removed to leave only the illegal or unreported income designated to each of the periods used to charge the subject. The entire financial history of the subject is investigated and presented for prosecution. If we think of the specific items case as snapshots of illegal activity, we can view the bank deposits and cash expenditures method as a "documentary film" of the subject's financial dealings.

Again, the presentation uses appendices and schedules to separate like items and to facilitate the explanation of the overall financial activities of the subject. The following are examples of a simple bank deposits and cash expenditures analysis. Appendix A is the overall summary, and schedules 1 through 5 show the like items that make up the summary.

Appendix A, in our example, is the summary schedule of the entire financial investigation. The analysis of deposits for each of the subject's bank accounts are referenced to the corresponding subschedules (schedules 1–3). An additional deposits schedule is included as schedule 4. The expenditures by check schedules, one for each checking account, are schedules 5 through 7. The adjustments to the gross deposits are contained in schedule 8 and the additional cash expenditures are included in Appendix A.

Case Summary

Joe Buck owns and operates a small tattoo parlor in the downtown area of Mayberry. The shop and a small apartment over the shop are rented by Buck and his girlfriend Jane Doe. Buck is 40 years old, and Doe is 26 years old; they have no children. Joe has operated the tattoo parlor for the last 2 years and pays rent of $550.00 per month for both the shop and the apartment. Buck drives a Harley motorcycle that he keeps in a shed behind the shop.

Complaint calls have been received against the parlor and the clientele, and the noise from motorcycle and car traffic, occurring mostly on Friday and Saturday nights. Other complaints have been made about loud and vulgar language and public drunkenness at the location during the 2 years he has been in business. Notice of the complaints was made to Buck, and the drinking and loud language stops for a while. He states that many of his customers drive motorcycles or older (and louder) cars. They also schedule tattoo sessions in the evening hours. He says he cannot turn away business unless he wants to close the shop and collect welfare. There are no statutory or regulatory provisions being violated by Joe that would allow action on the complaints. The residential area from which the complaints are coming is behind the shop, one block from the business area downtown.

An anonymous complaint comes in from an angry woman who says she thinks her son (16 years old) got marijuana from the tattoo parlor. A background check is run on Joe Buck and Jane Doe, and a surveillance is run on the tattoo parlor for four consecutive weekends to see if there is any suspicious activity taking place. The backgrounds show:

1. Buck's rap sheet shows four arrests for possession of a controlled substance and one conviction. It also shows one possession charge with the intent to distribute, which also resulted in a conviction. He served 3 years in jail on the latter conviction.
2. He moved to Mayberry 2 years ago and opened the tattoo parlor.
3. He has no military service record and has never been married.
4. Department of Motor Vehicles records show that he owned a 1998 Honda motorcycle when he moved to town. In 2006 (2 years ago), he traded in the Honda and purchased a classic Harley motorcycle.
5. He lives in the apartment above the shop.

The surveillance runs from sundown (about 7 P.M.) until 2 A.M. The results of the surveillance indicate the following information on the activities at the tattoo parlor:

1. Activity at the parlor is heaviest between 10 P.M. and 1 A.M.
2. License plate logs are made of the customer vehicles visiting the parlor. Analysis of the logs shows that 10 motorcycles and 7 cars visit the parlor repeatedly. These customers only stay for 8 to 10 minutes on each visit. Other customers stay between 30 and 45 minutes on a visit.
3. On the third weekend of the surveillance, an older green van arrived at the parlor. The vehicle pulled into the alley behind the parlor, and two packages were taken into the parlor's rear door.
4. Vehicle registrations identified the owners of the repeat customers and the van.
5. A trash pickup was made on the garbage abandoned from the tattoo parlor. There were several sketches of tattoos, empty and used tattoo supplies, junk mail, an envelope from State Bank with some numbers written on the back, fast-food wrappers, and other normal trash contents. A hit was made on the contents by a drug-detection dog.

Warrants were obtained to search Buck's tattoo parlor, apartment, and shed, and were also issued to obtain his bank records. The search of the location revealed cigarette wrappers, pipes, and about a quarter pound of marijuana. The warrant included business and personal records. Bank statements, utility bills and statements, vendor receipts, $5,200.00 in cash, and other documents were taken. The bank statements seized showed that Buck had a business and a personal checking account, and a savings account at State Bank. The cash was found in two locations: $5,000.00 in $20 and $50 bills wrapped with a rubber band and a note with an address written on it, and $200.00 in change, $1s and $5s in a coffee can on the dresser. The following is the information obtained from the records taken during the execution of the search warrant:

1. Analysis of the business records showed that Buck had a gross income of $38,000.00 in 2006 and $40,000.00 in 2007. Business expenses were $14,000.00 in 2006 and $16,000.00 in 2007, resulting in a net income of $24,000 for each year. He paid himself $2,000.00 a month from the business.
2. These records also showed that he paid $10,000.00 and $9,000.00, respectively, of his business expenses by check from the business account. His calendar of clients and appointments showed him doing tattoos on Mondays through Saturdays between 10 A.M. and 6 P.M.

3. Analysis of the utility bills and statements showed that he was timely in his payments. Vendor receipts showed that he purchased his inks and needles from a single supplier in California.
4. The bank records showed that Buck made weekly deposits to his business checking account in amounts between $700.00 and $1,000.00. At the end of each month he would transfer $2,000.00 from the business checking account to his personal checking account. He would also deposit $250.00 to $500.00 into his personal savings account monthly, during each of the years.
5. The bank records did not show any other regular payments for loans or credit cards. There were no payments to credit card companies, and no credit card statements were found during the search. The business checking account was opened with a deposit of $1,200.00.
6. One receipt was found for the purchase of a $580.00 dress from an exclusive shop in town. The check number listed on the receipt did not correspond with the check registers or checking account statements for either of Buck's accounts.
7. A marriage certificate from a Las Vegas marriage parlor shows that Buck and Doe were married 2 weeks before moving to town. Apparently, Doe is still using her maiden name for her bank account and as identification on the rent application.

Because the subject made regular and periodic deposits of his reported income to his bank accounts and the records of his bank transactions were available, the investigator chose the bank deposits and cash expenditures method of proof to investigate Buck's financial activities. In following all of the leads available through the information obtained, the following additional information was obtained:

1. Doe's background check showed that she was never employed after graduating from high school. She had one arrest for being drunk and disorderly (the charges were dropped), and she had one conviction for shoplifting.
2. The rent application for the shop and apartment showed that Buck was self-employed, and he listed his earnings as approximately $45,000.00 per year. The two checking accounts with State Bank were listed, as well as his 1998 motorcycle and $2,000.00 in cash. There were no liabilities listed on his application. Doe was also a tenant on the application. The only item listed for her was a checking account at a bank in an adjoining state (her hometown and former residence location). It showed a balance of $212.00.

3. Interviews at the dress shop where the dress was purchased by Doe using the out of sequence check revealed the account number for her out-of-state checking account and several cash purchases at the shop during the past 2 years.
4. Contacts with the vendors that Buck dealt with verified the expenses that were recorded in his business records. The vendor information corroborated the records for the amounts paid by check and the amounts paid by cash.
5. The bank records showed only one deposit that was made by a transfer of funds from Doe's account to Buck's business account. The transfer was for $2,200.00 on April 12, 2006. Buck issued a check on April 14, 2006, for $2,800.00 to pay his taxes. The records obtained by the warrant would include the opening documents for the accounts, the signature cards, monthly statements, deposit slips, canceled checks, and any other debits or credits made to the accounts.
6. The motorcycle shop was contacted and the owner stated that Buck purchased the Harley for $32,000.00 with the Honda as a trade-in. He said that Buck paid the $32,000.00 in cash.

The next step in the financial investigation is to prepare the schedules of the like items for the analysis to determine whether an additional source of income exists. In the bank deposits and cash expenditures method, the like items will be the deposits to the bank accounts and the expenditures made in cash.

Because Buck has three accounts and Doe has one account, four separate analyses will be prepared for the deposits into each account and four others for the expenditures and withdrawals made out of each account. The summary schedule, or appendix, will be used to tie the supporting schedules together and to make the necessary adjustments to ensure the accuracy of the computation.

For our examples, we will simplify the financial activities of Buck and Doe. This will provide an accurate example of the schedules used for the bank deposits and cash expenditures method but in a much more abbreviated form than usually encountered in this type of investigation.

In cases where the subject is self-employed, it is often a good idea to begin the account analyses with the business accounts because there are often adjustments that need to be made that will be identified through the analysis. The investigator should make notes on the potential adjustment items (and any new leads that are discovered) as the schedule is being prepared and the analysis is being performed.

Remember the earlier suggestion to initially prepare folders for the separate items of interest in the investigation and add folders for additional items as they are uncovered during the investigation.

The following are the example schedules that will show the categories of like items that require analysis and presentation when using the bank deposits and cash expenditures method of proof. The first four schedules are used to analyze the deposits made to each of the bank accounts for which Buck and Doe have signatory authority. The next three schedules are used to identify and analyze the checks drawn on the three checking accounts. Because there were no withdrawals made from the savings account, there is no need to prepare a schedule to analyze and trace withdrawals from the account.

Schedule 8 is used to identify the categories and amounts of adjustments needed to make the bank deposits and cash expenditures method of proof an accurate reflection of the actual income received by Buck and Doe for the time periods of the investigation. The last schedule is the summary schedule (appendix) that ties all of the financial information together to show how much income Buck and Doe had to have received during the periods under investigation (2006 and 2007) to have conducted the financial activities that they did during these 2 years. An explanation of the items contained on the schedules and their importance in determining income will follow the schedules.

Joe Buck, Business Checking Account 2006 through 2007		Deposits Analysis		Schedule 1, page 1	
Date	Description	2006	2007	Reference	
01/02/06	Opening deposit in cash	$1,200.00		W1-1,2,3	
01/07/06	Business receipts	$650.00		W1-1,2,3	
01/14/06	Business receipts	$750.00		W1-1,2,3	
01/21/06	Business receipts	$750.00		W1-1,2,3	
01/28/06	Business receipts	$750.00		W1-1,2,3	
02/04/06	Business receipts	$750.00		W1-1,2,4	
02/11/06	Business receipts	$750.00		W1-1,2,4	
02/18/06	Business receipts	$950.00		W1-1,2,4	
02/25/06	Business receipts	$950.00		W1-1,2,4	
03/04/06	Business receipts	$950.00		W1-1,2,5	
03/11/06	Business receipts	$950.00		W1-1,2,5	
03/18/06	Business receipts	$950.00		W1-1,2,5	
03/25/06	Business receipts	$800.00		W1-1,2,5	
04/01/06	Business receipts	$800.00		W1-1,2,6	
04/08/06	Business receipts	$800.00		W1-1,2,6	
04/12/06	Transfer from Jane Doe account	$2,200.00		W13-1,2	
04/15/06	Business receipts	$800.00		W1-1,2,6	
04/22/06	Business receipts	$800.00		W1-1,2,6	
04/29/06	Business receipts	$800.00		W1-1,2,6	
05/06/06	Business receipts	$800.00		W1-1,2,7	
06/10/06	Business receipts	$950.00		W1-1,2,8	
06/17/06	Business receipts	$750.00		W1-1,2,8	

Joe Buck, Business Checking Account (continued)   **Schedule 1, page 1**
2006 through 2007   **Deposits Analysis**

Date	Description	2006	2007	Reference
06/24/06	Business receipts	$950.00		W1-1,2,8
07/01/06	Business receipts	$950.00		W1-1,2,9
07/08/06	Business receipts	$800.00		W1-1,2,9
07/15/06	Business receipts	$950.00		W1-1,2,9
07/22/06	Business receipts	$800.00		W1-1,2,9
07/29/06	Business receipts	$950.00		W1-1,2,9
08/05/06	Business receipts	$800.00		W1-1,2,10
08/12/06	Business receipts	$950.00		W1-1,2,10
08/19/06	Business receipts	$800.00		W1-1,2,10
08/26/06	Business receipts	$950.00		W1-1,2,10
	Subtotals page 1	$28,750.00		

Joe Buck, Business Checking Account   **Schedule 1, page 2**
2006 through 2007   **Deposits Analysis**

Date	Description	2006	2007	Reference
	Subtotal from page 1	$28,750.00		
09/02/06	Business receipts	$970.00		W1-1,2,11
09/09/06	Business receipts	$970.00		W1-1,2,11
09/16/06	Business receipts	$970.00		W1-1,2,11
09/23/06	Business receipts	$970.00		W1-1,2,11
09/30/06	Business receipts	$970.00		W1-1,2,11
10/07/06	Business receipts	$970.00		W1-1,2,12
10/14/06	Business receipts	$890.00		W1-1,2,12
10/21/06	Business receipts	$990.00		W1-1,2,12
10/28/06	Business receipts	$990.00		W1-1,2,12
11/04/06	Business receipts	$990.00		W1-1,2,13
11/11/06	Business receipts	$990.00		W1-1,2,13
11/18/06	Business receipts	$990.00		W1-1,2,13
11/25/06	Business receipts	$990.00		W1-1,2,13
01/07/07	Business receipts		$900.00	W1-1,2,14
01/14/07	Business receipts		$940.00	W1-1,2,14
01/21/07	Business receipts		$960.00	W1-1,2,14
01/28/07	Business receipts		$900.00	W1-1,2,14
02/04/07	Business receipts		$960.00	W1-1,2,15
02/11/07	Business receipts		$900.00	W1-1,2,15
02/18/07	Business receipts		$960.00	W1-1,2,15
02/25/07	Business receipts		$900.00	W1-1,2,15
03/04/07	Business receipts		$960.00	W1-1,2,16
03/11/07	Business receipts		$900.00	W1-1,2,16

continued

Joe Buck, Business Checking Account (continued)   **Schedule 1, page 2**
2006 through 2007   **Deposits Analysis**

Date	Description	2006	2007	Reference
03/18/07	Business receipts		$960.00	W1-1,2,16
03/25/07	Business receipts		$900.00	W1-1,2,16
04/01/07	Business receipts		$960.00	W1-1,2,17
04/08/07	Business receipts		$900.00	W1-1,2,17
04/15/07	Business receipts		$960.00	W1-1,2,17
04/22/07	Business receipts		$900.00	W1-1,2,17
04/29/07	Business receipts		$960.00	W1-1,2,17
	Subtotals page 2	$41,400.00	$15,820.00	

Joe Buck, Business Checking Account   **Schedule 1, page 3**
2006 through 2007   **Deposits Analysis**

Date	Description	2006	2007	Reference
	Subtotals from page 2	$41,400.00	$15,820.00	
05/06/07	Business receipts		$900.00	W1-1,2,18
06/10/07	Business receipts		$960.00	W1-1,2,19
06/17/07	Business receipts		$900.00	W1-1,2,19
06/24/07	Business receipts		$960.00	W1-1,2,19
07/01/07	Business receipts		$900.00	W1-1,2,20
07/08/07	Business receipts		$960.00	W1-1,2,20
07/15/07	Business receipts		$900.00	W1-1,2,20
07/22/07	Business receipts		$960.00	W1-1,2,20
07/29/07	Business receipts		$900.00	W1-1,2,20
08/05/07	Business receipts		$960.00	W1-1,2,21
08/12/07	Business receipts		$900.00	W1-1,2,21
08/19/07	Business receipts		$960.00	W1-1,2,21
08/26/07	Business receipts		$900.00	W1-1,2,21
09/02/07	Business receipts		$960.00	W1-1,2,22
09/09/07	Business receipts		$900.00	W1-1,2,22
09/16/07	Business receipts		$960.00	W1-1,2,22
09/23/07	Business receipts		$900.00	W1-1,2,22
09/30/07	Business receipts		$960.00	W1-1,2,22
10/07/07	Business receipts		$900.00	W1-1,2,23
10/14/07	Business receipts		$960.00	W1-1,2,23
10/21/07	Business receipts		$900.00	W1-1,2,23
10/28/07	Business receipts		$960.00	W1-1,2,23
11/04/07	Business receipts		$900.00	W1-1,2,24
11/11/07	Business receipts		$960.00	W1-1,2,24
11/18/07	Business receipts		$900.00	W1-1,2,24
11/25/07	Business receipts		$960.00	W1-1,2,24
	Totals	$41,400.00	$40,000.00	

Schedule 1 is a listing of all the deposits made to the business account. It shows the date, description of the deposit, and the amount allocated to the proper time period (2006 or 2007). It also identifies the witness and documents used to prove the items.

Joe Buck, Personal Savings Account   Schedule 2, page 1
2006 through 2007   **Deposits Analysis**

Date	Description	Transfer/CWD	2006	2007	Reference
01/30/06	Transfer	$2,000.00	$2,000.00		W1-25,26,27
02/28/06	Transfer	$2,000.00	$2,000.00		W1-25,26,28
03/30/06	Transfer	$2,000.00	$2,000.00		W1-25,26,29
04/30/06	Transfer	$2,000.00	$2,000.00		W1-25,26,30
05/05/06	Transfer	$2,000.00	$2,000.00		W1-25,26,31
06/30/06	Transfer	$2,000.00	$2,000.00		W1-25,26,32
07/30/06	Transfer	$2,000.00	$2,000.00		W1-25,26,33
08/30/06	Transfer	$2,000.00	$2,000.00		W1-25,26,34
09/30/06	Transfer	$2,000.00	$2,000.00		W1-25,26,35
10/30/06	Transfer	$2,000.00	$2,000.00		W1-25,26,36
11/30/06	Transfer	$2,000.00	$2,000.00		W1-25,26,37
12/10/06	Transfer	$2,000.00	$2,000.00		W1-25,26,38
01/25/07	Transfer	$2,000.00		$2,000.00	W1-25,26,39
02/25/07	Transfer	$2,000.00		$2,000.00	W1-25,26,40
03/25/07	Transfer	$2,000.00		$2,000.00	W1-25,26,41
04/25/07	Transfer	$2,000.00		$2,000.00	W1-25,26,42
05/05/07	Transfer	$2,000.00		$2,000.00	W1-25,26,43
06/30/07	Transfer	$2,000.00		$2,000.00	W1-25,26,44
07/30/07	Transfer	$2,000.00		$2,000.00	W1-25,26,45
08/30/07	Transfer	$2,000.00		$2,000.00	W1-25,26,46
09/30/07	Transfer	$2,000.00		$2,000.00	W1-25,26,47
10/30/07	Transfer	$2,000.00		$2,000.00	W1-25,26,48
11/25/07	Transfer	$2,000.00		$2,000.00	W1-25,26,49
12/12/07	Transfer	$2,000.00		$2,000.00	W1-25,26,50
Totals			$24,000.00	$24,000.00	

Schedule 2 identifies the deposits to the personal checking account. These deposits represent the profit from Buck's tattoo parlor. All of the items are transferred from the business checking account made by automatic banking transfers. Cash withdrawals would also be identified but none occurred. Transfers and cash withdrawals are two categories that are considered in the adjustments shown in schedule 8.

Joe Buck, Personal Savings Account   **Schedule 3, page 1**
2006 through 2007   **Deposits Analysis**

Date	Description	Transfer/CWD	2006	2007	Reference
01/10/06	Cash deposit		$250.00		W1-51,52
02/05/06	Cash deposit		$450.00		W1-51,52
03/01/06	Cash deposit		$500.00		W1-51,52
03/25/06	Cash deposit		$500.00		W1-51,52
04/14/06	Cash deposit		$500.00		W1-51,52
05/01/06	Cash deposit		$500.00		W1-51,52
06/30/06	Cash deposit		$500.00		W1-51,52
07/08/06	Cash deposit		$500.00		W1-51,52
07/28/06	Cash deposit		$500.00		W1-51,52
08/09/06	Cash deposit		$500.00		W1-51,52
09/01/06	Cash deposit		$500.00		W1-51,52
09/20/06	Cash deposit		$500.00		W1-51,52
10/05/06	Cash deposit		$500.00		W1-51,52
10/22/06	Cash deposit		$500.00		W1-51,52
11/09/06	Cash deposit		$500.00		W1-51,52
11/20/06	Cash deposit		$500.00		W1-51,52
12/02/06	Cash deposit		$500.00		W1-51,52
01/04/07	Cash deposit			$500.00	W1-51,53
01/25/07	Cash deposit			$500.00	W1-51,53
02/09/07	Cash deposit			$500.00	W1-51,53
03/03/07	Cash deposit			$500.00	W1-51,53
03/18/07	Cash deposit			$500.00	W1-51,53
04/08/07	Cash deposit			$500.00	W1-51,53
05/04/07	Cash deposit			$500.00	W1-51,53
06/06/07	Cash deposit			$500.00	W1-51,53
07/09/07	Cash deposit			$500.00	W1-51,53
08/18/07	Cash deposit			$500.00	W1-51,53
09/26/07	Cash deposit			$500.00	W1-51,53
10/10/07	Cash deposit			$500.00	W1-51,53
11/04/07	Cash deposit			$500.00	W1-51,53
12/01/07	Cash deposit			$500.00	W1-51,53
Totals			$8,200.00	$7,000.00	

Schedule 3 identifies all of the deposits to Joe Buck's personal savings account for the periods under investigation.

Jane Doe—Second Bank Checking Account   **Schedule 4, page 1**
2006 through 2007   **Deposits Analysis**

Date	Description	Transfer/CWD	2006	2007	Reference
01/18/06	Cash deposit		$2,400.00		W2-1,2,3

Jane Doe—Second Bank Checking Account (continued)   **Schedule 4, page 1**
2006 through 2007   **Deposits Analysis**

Date	Description	Transfer/CWD	2006	2007	Reference
02/24/06	Cash deposit		$5,800.00		W2-1,2,4
03/31/06	Cash deposit		$6,500.00		W2-1,2,5
04/28/06	Cash deposit		$7,200.00		W2-1,2,6
07/15/06	Cash deposit		$36,500.00		W2-1,2,9
08/22/06	Cash deposit		$6,800.00		W2-1,2,10
09/29/06	Cash deposit		$7,600.00		W2-1,2,11
10/15/06	Cash deposit		$8,400.00		W2-1,2,12
11/20/06	Cash deposit		$9,000.00		W2-1,2,13
01/04/07	Cash deposit			$29,500.00	W2-1,2,15
02/06/07	Cash deposit			$8,700.00	W2-1,2,16
03/09/07	Cash deposit			$6,400.00	W2-1,2,17
04/16/07	Cash deposit			$6,700.00	W2-1,2,18
05/04/07	Cash deposit			$6,300.00	W2-1,2,19
07/28/07	Cash deposit			$54,000.00	W2-1,2,21
08/18/07	Cash deposit			$7,700.00	W2-1,2,22
09/06/07	Cash deposit			$6,500.00	W2-1,2,23
10/01/07	Cash deposit			$8,200.00	W2-1,2,24
10/29/07	Cash deposit			$5,800.00	W2-1,2,24
11/30/07	Cash deposit			$8,000.00	W2-1,2,25
Totals			$90,200.00	$147,800.00	

The preceding schedule is a listing of the deposits in Jane Doe's account. This account could have been identified by following either of the leads: the transfer to Buck's account or the receipt from the dress shop.

The account is in Jane's maiden name, and the bank records for the account would show that she added Joe Buck as a signator (allowed to access the account) after they were married. It appears that the account is used to conceal the income from a source other than the tattoo parlor. Based on our guess that the likely source of income is narcotics trafficking, this is the probable hiding place for the illegal income.

Joe Buck, Business Checking Account   **Schedule 5, page 1**
2006 through 2007   **Check Analysis**

Check #	Payee	Date	Amount	2006	2007	Reference
1001	Vendor	01/15/06	$400.00	$400.00		W1-1,3
1002	Supplies	01/15/06	$40.00	$40.00		W1-1,3
1003	Voided	01/18/06	$0.00	$0.00		W1-1,3
1004	Utilities	01/25/06	$60.00	$60.00		W1-1,3

continued

Joe Buck, Business Checking Account (continued)   **Schedule 5, page 1**
2006 through 2007   **Check Analysis**

Check #	Payee	Date	Amount	2006	2007	Reference
1005	Rent	01/31/06	$550.00	$550.00		W1-1,3
1006	Vendor	02/12/06	$400.00	$400.00		W1-1,4
1007	Supplies	02/14/06	$40.00	$40.00		W1-1,4
1008	Utilities	02/25/06	$60.00	$60.00		W1-1,4
1009	Rent	02/28/06	$550.00	$550.00		W1-1,4
1010	Supplies	03/07/06	$40.00	$40.00		W1-1,5
1011	Utilities	03/25/06	$60.00	$60.00		W1-1,5
1012	Rent	03/31/06	$550.00	$550.00		W1-1,5
1013	Vendor	04/18/06	$400.00	$400.00		W1-1,6
1014	Utilities	04/25/06	$60.00	$60.00		W1-1,6
1015	Rent	04/30/06	$550.00	$550.00		W1-1,6
1016	Vendor	05/15/06	$400.00	$400.00		W1-1,7
1017	Utilities	05/25/06	$60.00	$60.00		W1-1,7
1018	Rent	05/30/06	$550.00	$550.00		W1-1,7
1019	Utilities	06/25/06	$60.00	$60.00		W1-1,8
1020	Rent	06/30/06	$550.00	$550.00		W1-1,8
1021	Utilities	07/25/06	$60.00	$60.00		W1-1,9
1022	Rent	07/31/06	$550.00	$550.00		W1-1,9
1023	Vendor	08/09/06	$400.00	$400.00		W1-1,10
1024	Supplies	08/09/06	$40.00	$40.00		W1-1,10
1025	Utilities	08/25/06	$60.00	$60.00		W1-1,10
1026	Rent	08/31/06	$550.00	$550.00		W1-1,10
1027	Supplies	09/05/06	$40.00	$40.00		W1-1,11
1028	Utilities	09/25/06	$60.00	$60.00		W1-1,11
1029	Rent	09/30/06	$550.00	$550.00		W1-1,11
1030	Vendor	10/06/06	$400.00	$400.00		W1-1,12
1031	Supplies	10/08/06	$40.00	$40.00		W1-1,12
1032	Utilities	10/25/06	$60.00	$60.00		W1-1,12
	Subtotals		$8,190.00	$8,190.00		

Joe Buck, Business Checking Account   **Schedule 5, page 2**
2006 through 2007   **Check Analysis**

Check #	Payee	Date	Amount	2006	2007	Reference
	Subtotals		$8,190.00	$8,190.00		
1033	Rent	10/31/06	$550.00	$550.00		W1-1,12
1034	Supplies	11/07/06	$40.00	$40.00		W1-1,13
1035	Utilities	11/25/06	$60.00	$60.00		W1-1,13
1036	Rent	11/30/06	$550.00	$550.00		W1-1,13
1037	Utilities	12/25/06	$60.00	$60.00		W1-1,14

Joe Buck, Business Checking Account (continued)   **Schedule 5, page 2**
2006 through 2007   **Check Analysis**

Check #	Payee	Date	Amount	2006	2007	Reference
1038	Rent	12/28/06	$550.00	$550.00		W1-1,14
1039	Vendor	01/09/07	$520.00		$520.00	W1-1,15
1040	Utilities	01/25/07	$60.00		$60.00	W1-1,15
1041	Rent	01/31/07	$550.00		$550.00	W1-1,15
1042	Utilities	02/25/07	$60.00		$60.00	W1-1,16
1043	Rent	02/28/07	$550.00		$550.00	W1-1,16
1044	Supplies	03/05/07	$40.00		$40.00	W1-1,17
1045	Utilities	03/25/07	$60.00		$60.00	W1-1,17
1046	Rent	03/31/07	$550.00		$550.00	W1-1,17
1047	Utilities	04/25/07	$60.00		$60.00	W1-1,18
1048	Rent	04/30/07	$550.00		$550.00	W1-1,18
1049	Supplies	05/02/07	$40.00		$40.00	W1-1,19
1050	Vendor	05/12/07	$500.00		$500.00	W1-1,19
1051	Utilities	05/25/07	$60.00		$60.00	W1-1,19
1052	Rent	05/31/07	$550.00		$550.00	W1-1,19
1053	Utilities	06/25/07	$60.00		$60.00	W1-1,20
1054	Rent	06/30/07	$550.00		$550.00	W1-1,20
1055	Utilities	07/25/07	$60.00		$60.00	W1-1,21
1056	Rent	07/31/07	$550.00		$550.00	W1-1,21
1057	Supplies	08/08/07	$40.00		$40.00	W1-1,22
1058	Vendor	08/08/07	$500.00		$500.00	W1-1,22
1059	Utilities	08/25/07	$60.00		$60.00	W1-1,22
1060	Rent	08/31/07	$550.00		$550.00	W1-1,22
1061	Utilities	09/25/07	$60.00		$60.00	W1-1,23
1062	Rent	09/30/07	$550.00		$550.00	W1-1,23
1063	Supplies	10/01/07	$40.00		$40.00	W1-1,24
	Subtotals		$17,170.00	$10,000.00	$7,170.00	

Joe Buck, Business Checking Account   **Schedule 5, page 3**
2006 through 2007   **Check Analysis**

Check #	Payee	Date	Amount	2006	2007	Reference
	Subtotals		$17,170.00	$10,000.00	$7,170.00	
1064	Utilities	10/25/07	$60.00		$60.00	W1-1,25
1065	Rent	10/31/07	$550.00		$550.00	W1-1,26
1066	Utilities	11/25/07	$60.00		$60.00	W1-1,27
1067	Rent	11/30/07	$550.00		$550.00	W1-1,28
1068	Utilities	12/25/07	$60.00		$60.00	W1-1,29
1069	Rent	12/28/07	$550.00		$550.00	W1-1,30
Totals			$19,000.00	$10,000.00	$9,000.00	

Schedule 5 is a listing of all of the checks drawn on Joe Buck's business account for the periods under investigation. It is, in fact, a recreated check register for the account, identifying the check numbers, payees, dates of issue, and amounts. The schedule allows for a comparative analysis of business expenses to the business books and records.

The comparison to the business books and records is important in determining whether there are claimed business expenses that had to be paid in cash. Remember that cash expenditures, even for deductible business expenses, are added into the cash expenditures in the bank deposits and cash expenditures method of proof. A sample of how the amounts for cash business expenses are determined is contained in schedule 8, the adjustments schedule.

Adjustment items that are considered in the analysis of checks drawn on an account are checks written to cash and for deposit to other accounts, as transfers. In our example, there are no adjustment items to consider in this account.

In doing the checks analysis, unusual items or those that do not fit the nature of the account (personal items purchased through a business account) may provide valuable leads to other financial transactions in the investigation. Checks issued to a certain payee may lead to cash purchases from the same payee and increase the provable income.

Joe Buck, Personal Checking Account **Schedule 6, page 1**
2006 through 2007 **Checks Analysis**

Check #	Payee	Date	Amount	2006	2007	Reference
2143	Restaurant	01/05/06	$220.00	$220.00		W1-25,26,27
2144	Clothing	02/15/06	$1,540.00	$1,540.00		W1-25,26,28
2145	Gasoline	03/01/06	$17.00	$17.00		W1-25,26,29
2146	Restaurant	03/06/06	$170.00	$170.00		W1-25,26,29
2147	Cash	05/02/06	$5,000.00	$5,000.00		W1-25,26,31
2148	Restaurant	05/07/06	$300.00	$300.00		W1-25,26,31
2149	Clothing	06/06/06	$2,100.00	$2,100.00		W1-25,26,32
2150	Gasoline	06/28/06	$17.00	$17.00		W1-25,26,32
2151	Restaurant	07/04/06	$70.00	$70.00		W1-25,26,33
2152	Cash	08/01/06	$3,500.00	$3,500.00		W1-25,26,34
2153	Restaurant	08/04/06	$210.00	$210.00		W1-25,26,34
2154	Groceries	11/20/06	$200.00	$200.00		W1-25,26,37
2155	Gasoline	11/21/06	$16.00	$16.00		W1-25,26,37
2156	Gifts	12/02/06	$4,200.00	$4,200.00		W1-25,26,38
2157	Gasoline	12/20/06	$20.00	$20.00		W1-25,26,38
2158	Cash	01/14/07	$6,000.00		$6,000.00	W1-25,26,39
2159	Restaurant	01/22/07	$240.00		$240.00	W1-25,26,39

Joe Buck, Personal Checking Account (continued)   Schedule 6, page 1
2006 through 2007   **Checks Analysis**

Check #	Payee	Date	Amount	2006	2007	Reference
2160	Restaurant	01/31/07	$160.00		$160.00	W1-25,26,39
2161	Gifts	02/13/07	$620.00		$620.00	W1-25,26,40
2162	Gasoline	02/22/07	$15.00		$15.00	W1-25,26,40
2163	Restaurant	03/27/07	$170.00		$170.00	W1-25,26,41
2164	Restaurant	04/04/07	$210.00		$210.00	W1-25,26,42
2165	Clothing	05/13/07	$2,800.00		$2,800.00	W1-25,26,43
2166	Restaurant	07/28/07	$160.00		$160.00	W1-25,26,45
2167	Gifts	11/30/07	$4,000.00		$4,000.00	W1-25,26,49
2168	Cash	12/14/07	$6,000.00		$6,000.00	W1-25,26,49
2169	Gifts	12/18/07	$4,100.00		$4,100.00	W1-25,26,49
2170	Restaurant	12/26/07	$170.00		$170.00	W1-25,26,49
	Totals		$42,405.00	$17,580.00	$24,825.00	

Jane Doe—Second Bank Checking Account   Schedule 7, page 1
2006 through 2007   **Checks Analysis**

Check #	Payee	Date	Amount	2006	2007	Reference
1200	Joe Buck	04/12/06	$2,200.00	$2,200.00		W13-1,2,6
1201	Cash	05/03/06	$4,000.00	$4,000.00		W13-1,2,7
1202	Cash	06/28/06	$4,000.00	$4,000.00		W13-1,2,8
1203	Cash	07/03/06	$4,000.00	$4,000.00		W13-1,2,9
1204	Cash	07/21/06	$4,000.00	$4,000.00		W13-1,2,9
1205	Dress shop	08/01/06	$580.00	$580.00		W13-1,2,10
1206	Furrier	08/01/06	$6,000.00	$6,000.00		W13-1,2,10
1207	Jeweler	08/01/06	$180.00	$180.00		W13-1,2,10
1208	Cash	11/15/06	$4,000.00	$4,000.00		W13-1,2,13
1209	Cash	11/24/06	$4,000.00	$4,000.00		W13-1,2,13
1210	Cash	12/07/06	$4,000.00	$4,000.00		W13-1,2,14
1211	Cash	01/10/07	$4,000.00		$4,000.00	W13-1,2,15
1212	Cash	02/10/07	$4,000.00		$4,000.00	W13-1,2,16
1213	Cash	04/10/07	$8,000.00		$8,000.00	W13-1,2,18
1214	Cash	06/10/07	$8,000.00		$8,000.00	W13-1,2,20
1215	Airline	07/02/07	$1,240.00		$1,240.00	W13-1,2,21
1216	Cash	08/10/07	$8,000.00		$8,000.00	W13-1,2,22
1217	Cash	09/18/07	$1,000.00		$1,000.00	W13-1,2,23
1218	Cash	10/10/07	$8,000.00		$8,000.00	W13-1,2,24
1219	Import shop	12/03/07	$250.00		$250.00	W13-1,2,26
1220	Cash	12/10/07	$8,000.00		$8,000.00	W13-1,2,26
Totals			$87,450.00	$36,960.00	$50,490.00	

In schedules 6 and 7, the adjustment items needed to accurately compute income using our method are highlighted. In most cases, there will be substantially more items that need to be considered in the adjustments. For those cases, separate schedules are prepared for each category of adjustment. The simplicity of our example allows for the individual items to be listed in the adjustments schedule (schedule 8).

Again, the other checks written would provide additional leads to other potential expenditures such as the jeweler, furrier, airline ticket purchase, and the import shop. For our example, we will say the leads showed these payments to be the only purchases made.

Joe Buck and Jane Doe   **Schedule 8, page 1**
2006 through 2007   **Adjustments Computation**

Item	Year		2006	2007	Reference
Cash on hand		$2,000.00	$2,000.00		W5-1 W6-1
Cash on hand		$212.00	$212.00		W5-1 W6-1
Total cash on hand		$2,212.00	$2,212.00		
Transfers from Bus. Acct.	2006	$24,000.00	$24,000.00		Schedules 1&2
	2007	$24,000.00		$24,000.00	Schedules 1&2
Transfers from Doe Acct.	2006	$2,200.00	$2,200.00		Schedule 1
Total transfers		$50,200.00	$26,200.00	$24,000.00	
		Checks to Cash			
Buck Pers. Acct. 2147	2006	$5,000.00	$5,000.00		W1-25,26,31
2152	2006	$3,500.00	$3,500.00		W1-25,26,34
2158	2007	$6,000.00		$6,000.00	W1-25,26,39
2168	2007	$6,000.00		$6,000.00	W1-25,26,49
Doe Acct. 1201		$4,000.00	$4,000.00		W13-1,2,7
1202		$4,000.00	$4,000.00		W13-1,2,8
1203		$4,000.00	$4,000.00		W13-1,2,9
1204		$4,000.00	$4,000.00		W13-1,2,9
1208		$4,000.00	$4,000.00		W13-1,2,13
1209		$4,000.00	$4,000.00		W13-1,2,13
1210		$4,000.00	$4,000.00		W13-1,2,14
1211		$4,000.00		$4,000.00	W13-1,2,15
1212		$4,000.00		$4,000.00	W13-1,2,16
1213		$8,000.00		$8,000.00	W13-1,2,18
1214		$8,000.00		$8,000.00	W13-1,2,20
1216		$8,000.00		$8,000.00	W13-1,2,22
1217		$1,000.00		$1,000.00	W13-1,2,23
1218		$8,000.00		$8,000.00	W13-1,2,24
1220		$8,000.00		$8,000.00	W13-1,2,26
Total checks to cash		$97,500.00	$36,500.00	$61,000.00	

The bank deposits and cash expenditure method of proof requires that certain items be considered to ensure that all income is accounted for and that no item making up the income is counted more than once in the computation. In our example case, we have several of the items that need to be adjusted for in any bank deposits and cash expenditures computation.

Cash on hand is the first item considered in our adjustments schedule. In a more complicated case, the starting point would have to be established and a determination made as to the cash available at the beginning of the periods under investigation. Cash available to the subject of the investigation prior to the periods could be deposited during the periods in the computation. Cash could also be used later for a purchase, and cash expenditures are added to our income figures in the computation. For these potential reasons, the subject is given credit against income to ensure that the cash was accounted for correctly.

The second category includes transfers of funds from one account to another and cash withdrawals that could be redeposited or used to make cash purchases that are included in the computation. Transfers are funds already deposited once to get into an account, and then transferred to a different account where they are counted again. Removing the transfers and cash withdrawals eliminates the possibility of counting amounts as income more than once.

The last category in the adjustments schedule is the total of checks written to cash. The same logic is employed in viewing these items as being the potential source of cash expenditures that are added to the net deposits computed. If the checks to cash exceed the total of cash expenditures and cash deposits documented during any of the periods in the computation, the amount credited to the subject can be limited, up to the amount of cash expenditures and cash deposits.

As you can see, even in a simple example like this, the supporting schedules play an important role in organizing and combining similar transactions to simplify the presentation to a judge or jury for purposes of litigation. The last schedule in our bank deposits and cash expenditures case is the summary schedule or appendix, which ties together all of the financial information obtained during the investigation.

Joe Buck and Jane Doe 2006 through 2007		Bank Deposits and Cash Expenditures Computation			Appendix A
Item	2006	2007	2006	2007	Reference
Deposits					
Buck business account			$41,400.00	$40,000.00	Schedule 1
Buck personal account			$24,000.00	$24,000.00	Schedule 2
Buck savings account			$8,200.00	$7,000.00	Schedule 3
Doe checking account			$90,200.00	$147,800.00	Schedule 4
Gross deposits			$163,800.00	$218,800.00	

continued

Joe Buck and Jane Doe (continued)

| | | Bank Deposits and Cash Expenditures | | Appendix A |
| **2006 through 2007** | | Computation | | |
Item	2006	2007	2006	2007	Reference
Less:					
Cash on hand			$2,212.00	$0.00	Schedule 8
Transfers			$26,200.00	$24,000.00	Schedule 8
Checks to cash			$36,500.00	$61,000.00	Schedule 8
Net deposits			$98,888.00	$133,800.00	
Add:					
Motorcycle			$32,000.00		W17-1,2
Business expenses	$14,000.00	$16,000.00			W15-1,2
Less: Paid by check	$10,000.00	$9,000.00			W15-1,2
Cash expenses	$4,000.00	$7,000.00	$4,000.00	$7,000.00	
Income			$134,888.00	$140,800.00	
Less: Reported income			$24,000.00	$24,000.00	W15-1,2
Unreported income			$110,888.00	$116,800.00	

Appendix A is the summary schedule that presents the entire financial investigation in a concise and easy-to-read format. All of the deposits are added together to determine the gross deposits for each time period under investigation. Adjustments are subtracted from gross deposits to account for monies available from the time prior to the investigation (cash on hand in our example) and deposits that could be duplicated in the computation (transfers, cash withdrawals, redeposited items, and checks to cash). The results are the net deposits for each time period. Additional funds, not entering the bank accounts, used by the subject are then added to the account for income that was never deposited. The result being the least amount of income the subject had to have earned in each of the 2 years we investigated. The income that the subject admits to or has previously reported is then subtracted. The difference is the amount of unreported income determined by the indirect method of proof.

In our example case, we have established the sale of narcotics as a likely source for the unreported income. We have also shown the likely intent to conceal the income by keeping it in a bank account in the wife's maiden name and in another state. The investigation would go much further in gathering additional information relative to the elements of the crime for sale of narcotics charges to be brought against Buck and Doe. The investigation would also open the door to expanding the investigation to include Buck's supplier, the users frequenting the tattoo parlor, and any other individuals that may be associated in the drug network.

Additional surveillance could now be justified to identify more potential customers that frequent the parlor at different times and on different days of the week. Interviews of the customers that are regular visitors at the parlor and do not stay long enough to get a tattoo would be interviewed. The potential for obtaining direct testimony on purchases of narcotics from Buck or Doe expands as the number of customers identified increases. Follow-up investigation would also be justified in tracing the movements of Buck and Doe when they travel. The lack of banking activity indicates that they close for several weeks in the summer and again around the Thanksgiving and Christmas holidays. There is also a follow-up potential on the airline expense, by identifying the destination and the duration of their trip. Additional assets may have been acquired in previously unknown locations, and additional cash expenditures may also be found.

The extent of the indirect method of proof investigation is only limited by the time and resources of the investigator or the investigation team. The initial investigation may lead to the development of cases in other geographic locations and on a variety of other potential targets.

Once the investigator is comfortable that sufficient evidence has been obtained to support a conviction on the charges, the case is then taken to the report writing phase. This aspect of the investigation will be discussed in Chapter 18.

The Net Worth and Personal Expenditures Case

15

The net worth and personal expenditures method of proof is most often used when personal records for the subject are not available, or they are inaccurate or incomplete. This method began in criminal investigations of federal tax violations. Cases in which an individual's illegal activities are not readily apparent, or in cases where the individual is well insulated or removed from direct involvement in the illegal activity, are often investigated using the net worth and personal expenditures method of proof.

A person who gains financially from an illegal activity by providing financing or services to those persons actually carrying out the crimes may never have direct involvement in the criminal acts, and may derive substantial financial benefits from his or her participation. The financier for a drug distribution ring, the jeweler who modifies the appearance of stolen gems, the money launderer disguising the nature of illegal proceeds, and the fence who sells the stolen goods are all indirectly involved in criminal activity. The risks involved in their participation are usually minimal, but the rewards are substantial. It is often the discovery of these facilitators of crime that leads to the identification and conviction of those involved in the criminal enterprise.

Indirect methods of proof used in investigating financial dealings can also be a benefit in situations in which the criminal activity generating the money is taking place in a different jurisdiction. The individual may have ties to a criminal activity in California and be enjoying the proceeds in West Virginia. The financial investigation can trace the money back to the source and establish the culpability of the individual for participation in the criminal acts. In one case in New Mexico, the subject conducted his illegal activities overseas in various locations along the Pacific Rim. He was using the illegal gains to establish a private estate in New Mexico. The financial investigation showed that he had invested millions of dollars in the development of his estate over a 3-year period. The alleged illegal activities in several foreign countries were used as the likely source of income for the indirect methods case.

The net worth and personal expenditures method gained favor in investigations of organized crime cases, and was reviewed by the U.S. Supreme Court in *Holland v. United States.* The *Holland* case sets out the parameters for this indirect method of proof. Again, all of the concerns expressed by the Court in using an indirect method of proof must be addressed by the financial investigation.

The net worth and personal expenditures method of proof looks at how money can be used in a different perspective than that covered in Chapter 14. It relies on the logical position that monies received by an entity (individual, corporation, or organization) can only be used in limited ways. Money can be invested in assets, used to pay off debts, or spent to purchase items. In other words, the entity can acquire assets, reduce liabilities, or spend the money on perishable items.

The summary schedule for this method, in Appendix A, tracks the financial activity conducted over a period of time through the assets an entity acquires and disposes of, the liabilities the entity increases or decreases, and the personal expenditures the entity makes. In the bank deposits method (Chapter 14), we focused our attention on cash expenditures made during the periods under investigation. In net worth method, the focus is on the personal expenses made by the subject whether in cash or by check. The method presumes that any business expenses will offset the profits available to the subject for personal use.

Because the method is based on the aforementioned areas of financial activity, the amounts reflected can include only the actual cost of items and expenses. The appreciable value of investments cannot be attributed to the entity as income. For example, if an individual buys a collectible coin for $50.00, and the coin increases in value over 2 years to $100.00, the asset is listed at the cost of $50.00 in each year of computation that the individual keeps the coin. Only purchases and sales affect the overall computation of income in the net worth and personal expenditures method of proof. Assets are included in the computation for the period when they were acquired, and removed from the computation when they are sold or traded in.

The following section is a case scenario we will use in the preparation of the schedules needed for a net worth and personal expenditures case.

Case Summary

John Fawn owns and operates a donut shop in town. He purchased the business in 2004 and has operated the shop for the past 3 years. An anonymous informant called in to state that Fawn is living a lifestyle "way above" his means. He is spending a lot of money on expensive items and nightlife, which he could never afford by running a donut shop.

The cursory investigation shows:

1. A public records search showed that Fawn purchased the donut shop in April 2004 for $200,000.00. He financed $180,000.00 of the purchase price on a 20-year mortgage.

2. Department of Motor Vehicles (DMV) records showed that Fawn purchased a 2002 Ford Taurus in 2002 for $16,000.00 and transferred the vehicle to his daughter in 2006. In 2005, he purchased a 2005 Jeep Grand Cherokee for $38,000.00, and in 2006 he purchased a 2006 Lincoln for $46,000.00. There were no liens filed against these vehicles.
3. Fawn is 46 years old. He married Clare in 1980, and their daughter was born in 1981. He divorced Clare in February 2004 and remarried in April 2004. His current wife, Gayle, is 23 years old and not employed.
4. In 2006, Fawn and his new wife purchased a newly constructed house for $275,000.00. They obtained a mortgage for $250,000.00 to purchase it. A drive by the house showed that they had landscaped it and added a large deck off the back of the house.

Further investigation into the background of Fawn and his wife discovered that he had worked in bakeries from his senior year in high school up till the present. His first wife, Clare, is a nurse and works in the local hospital. His current wife, Gayle, has never been employed. Neither Fawn nor Gayle has any criminal record.

The divorce settlement records provide the following information:

Assets	
House: 100 Maple St.	$180,000.00
2001 Chevrolet Impala	$10,000.00
2002 Ford Taurus	$7,000.00
Stocks and bonds	$24,000.00
Cash in banks	$12,000.00
Home furnishings	$8,000.00
Total assets	$241,000.00

Liabilities	
Mortgage (as of 4/1/04)	$2,583.00
Car loan (Ford Taurus)	$3,500.00
Credit card balance	$217.00
Total liabilities	$6,570.00

The cash in banks is to be used to pay off all liabilities; the remainder to be divided equally between Clare and John ($2,715.00 each). The house, 100 Maple Street, and the home furnishings will be quitclaimed by John to Clare. The Chevrolet Impala goes to Clare, and the Ford Taurus to John. The stocks and bonds are to be sold and the proceeds divided equally ($12,000.00 each). Each of the respondents is to keep his or her personal effects. The court ordered no alimony or child support payments.

After reviewing the information, a determination is made to further investigate John Fawn's financial activities. The minimal financial status shown for him in the divorce settlement, coupled with his recent financial acquisitions, supports the information received from the anonymous informant. Further investigation reveals:

1. Fawn has worked as a baker for many years. His salary over the past 3 years has been $34,000.00 in 2001, $35,500.00 in 2002, and $37,000.00 in 2003.

2. Fawn had gross sales from his donut shop of $60,000.00 in 2004 and $80,000.00 for each of the years 2005 and 2006. His net income from the business was $35,000.00 in 2004 and $45,000.00 for 2005 and for 2006.

3. He purchased both new vehicles from local car dealers. Both purchases were made by paying cash in full. He made the $20,000.00 down payment on the donut shop with a cashier's check issued from First Bank of Windsor. The down payment on the new home purchase was done in the same manner.

4. The First Bank of Windsor provided copies of the cashier's checks. They were issued from an account in the name of Easy Street Ltd. The checks were authorized by J. Faun, an authorized representative of the company. The balance in the account was $1,300.00 and had not changed since the second cashier check was issued. The account was opened in January 2004. A photograph of John Fawn was identified as being a photo of the John Faun who opened the account. Employees at the bank remembered Fawn as a regular customer who made cash deposits to several business accounts at least two and sometimes four times a month. The deposits were in cash and usually between $6,000.00 and $9,000.00 each. The business names for the accounts were obtained.

5. Canadian corporate records identified the owners of the 10 accounts at First Bank of Windsor. Background checks on these individuals disclosed that they were members of an organized crime family. Letters rogatory were sent, and the records of the 10 accounts and Fawn's account were obtained for the years 2004 through 2006.

6. Analysis of the bank records showed cash deposits, beginning in January 2004, of several thousand dollars each. The deposits made to Fawn's account were exactly 5% of the amounts deposited into the other 10 accounts. The deposits to the 10 accounts continued through 2006. Deposits were only made to Fawn's account until sufficient funds were available to issue the two cashier's checks.

7. Both Fawn and Gayle declined to participate in interviews or to provide any information.

The following information was obtained through surveillance, a mail cover, and third-party interviews:

1. Fawn and Gayle go to an exclusive restaurant almost every Thursday night. On Friday afternoons, Fawn drives across the bridge into Windsor and goes to the bank. Gayle shops at the most exclusive stores in town. They attend exclusive shows and have an elaborate nightlife. They receive mailings from jewelry stores and very expensive gift shops in New York. They also receive airline advertisements, and a United Airlines preferred customer and frequent flier newsletter.
2. Fawn receives Pilot and Travel magazines. Gayle receives several catalogs, and received a letter from a plastic surgeon's office. They also received statements from a stock brokerage firm.
3. The third-party interviews resulted in the identification and documentation of several personal expenditures that each had made over the past 2 years. Other interviews identified investments made in Aspen, Colorado. (For our purposes, the individual expenditures will be identified in the schedules that follow.)

We made the analogy that indirect methods of proof are similar to comparing photographs of the subject's financial condition over periods of time. To understand the difference between the bank deposits method and the net worth method, think of the bank deposits method as a group photograph of the debits and credits to bank accounts, and the net worth method as a single photograph of the subject's financial picture at the end of each of the periods being investigated.

The financial value of assets, liabilities, and expenditures are included in the net worth and personal expenditures computation at their cash value at the close of each period under investigation. If an asset is sold during the period, its value changes to zero. Similarly, if a liability is paid off, its value becomes zero. Personal expenditures are included in the period in which they were acquired.

The following is an example of the schedules that would be used in the net worth and personal expenditures analysis for our case example:

John and Gayle Fawn 2004 through 2006	Assets Net Worth and Expenditures			Schedule 1
Item Description	12/31/04	12/31/05	12/31/06	Reference
Cash on hand	$14,715.00	$0.00	$0.00	W1-1
Cash in banks	$4,300.00	$26,300.00	$1,300.00	W2-1
100 Maple St.	$0.00	$0.00	$0.00	W1-1, W3-1
New house	$0.00	$0.00	$275,000.00	W3-2

continued

| John and Gayle Fawn (continued) | Assets | | | Schedule 1 |
| 2004 through 2006 | Net Worth and Expenditures | | | |
Item Description	12/31/04	12/31/05	12/31/06	Reference
Donut shop	$200,000.00	$200,000.00	$200,000.00	W3-3, W4-1
Stocks and bonds	$12,000.00	$28,000.00	$35,000.00	W5-1
Ford Taurus	$16,000.00	$16,000.00	$0.00	W6-1
Jeep Cherokee	$0.00	$38,000.00	$38,000.00	W7-1
Lincoln	$0.00	$0.00	$46,000.00	W6-2
Colorado Condominium	$0.00	$200,000.00	$200,000.00	W8-1
Total Assets	$247,015.00	$490,300.00	$795,300.00	

Our computation begins with including assets and liabilities for the starting point or base year, 2004. As the base year is not one of the periods charged against the subject, expenditures for that period are not included. In our example, we can assume that the information contained in the divorce settlement is an accurate representation of Fawn's assets and liabilities at the time of the divorce. The proceedings would be an admission of the subject under oath for the court proceedings. All that would be needed to establish 12/31/04 as the starting point for the computation would be to add any assets acquired and liabilities incurred from the date the divorce was final through the end of the year.

Cash on Hand

The divorce settlement showed that John Fawn was to receive 50% of the sales proceeds from the sale of stocks and from the cash in banks after paying off all liabilities. The stock sale would net Fawn $12,000.00, and his share of the cash in banks would be $2,715.00, that is, a total of $14,715.00. Because no evidence was obtained to indicate any cash on hand for the following periods, this $14,715.00 is included in the starting point period and shown as zero balances for the years under investigation.

This results in a reduction of the total assets between 12/31/04 and 12/31/05. The effect on the computation is to give Fawn credit for the cash being available to purchase assets, pay off liabilities, or make expenditures in the subsequent periods. If the amount of cash on hand exceeded all payments made by Fawn in 2005, the difference would be carried forward to 12/31/05 and credited against the income shown in the computation for 2006.

Cash in Banks

The amounts listed for the year-end balances of cash in banks would be derived from the records obtained on Faun's (Fawn's) account with the First Bank of Windsor. Bank account balances, in an indirect methods computation, must be reconciled to the end of the period (in this case, year-end) to ensure that the amounts are accurate. Any checks outstanding or deposits in transit need to be accounted for before the balances are put into the schedules. For our example, we will assume that the reconciliation showed the balances included in the schedule of assets.

House: 100 Maple Street

The house is placed on the schedule with zero balances throughout the computation. It can be shown in this manner to assure the reader that all leads were followed in establishing the starting point, even those that do not affect the computation. The investigator may choose to omit the asset as it has no affect but would then be required to address it in the narrative of the investigative report. By including it in the schedule, the numbers allocated to the asset (zeroes) reflect that it was in existence in 2004 but disposed of prior to the year's end.

New House

The investigation shows that Fawn and Gayle purchased their new house for $275,000.00 in 2006. The purchase price is used to record the asset in the computation. This amount is the actual price of the property. Any encumbrances against the property will be shown and accounted for in the schedule of liabilities. If permanent improvements were made on the property and fully documented the value could be increased according to the actual costs of the improvements. Appreciation of the property or increases in assessed valuation is not considered because the purpose of the computation is to show the application of funds received during the time periods under investigation.

Donut Shop

Fawn purchased the donut shop in 2004 for $200,000.00. Again, this is the actual price paid by Fawn. The same handling of permanent improvements, as in the new house, would apply here. Because Fawn acquired the property in 2004 and has held ownership throughout the year 2006, the amount shown for each year remains constant at $200,000.00. For tax investigations there would be adjustments made to income to allow for depreciation and other offsets to the income generated by business property.

Stocks and Bonds

Because Fawn's prior investments in securities were liquidated for the divorce settlement, these amounts represent his investment in a new brokerage account. The information gained through the mail cover mentioned earlier would have provided the lead that uncovered this new account. The amounts shown in the schedule are the actual funds invested in the account. He would have invested $12,000.00 in 2004, $16,000.00 in 2005, and $7,000.00 in 2006. There were no withdrawals, so the balance shown in the computation reflects an increase in the asset from year to year. Again, the asset is listed by its actual cost to Fawn. Gains and losses in value have no effect on the computation unless stocks are purchased or sold.

Ford Taurus

The Ford Taurus was purchased by Fawn prior to the years considered in the computation and was held by him until he gave it to his daughter in 2006. The cost of the vehicle when it was initially purchased would be the amount used in the computation. This amount would be obtained from the dealer who transferred the title to Fawn on the date the vehicle was acquired.

Jeep Cherokee/Lincoln

Both these vehicles would be included in the year they were purchased at their total cost to Fawn. Because he kept possession of both vehicles throughout the years under investigation, they remain in the computation through the end of 2006.

Colorado Condominium

This asset was discovered from the follow-up on leads obtained from third parties who disclosed the Fawns' extensive travel to Colorado. The asset purchase would be documented through public property records and an interview of the seller of the property.

The total amount of assets for each of the periods in the computation will be carried to the summary schedule, just as the summaries were reflected in the appendix in our example of the bank deposits and cash expenditures computation in Chapter 14.

The next schedule needed in the computation will identify all of the liabilities of John and Gayle Fawn, and any changes in the amounts owed from year to year. Just as assets are listed at actual cost, liability amounts are shown initially at the actual proceeds amount and carried forward at the payoff amounts for consecutive periods.

John and Gayle Fawn 2004 through 2006	Liabilities Net Worth and Expenditures			Schedule 2
Item Description	12/31/04	12/31/05	12/31/06	Reference
Mortgage, donut shop	$175,000.00	$163,000.00	$149,000.00	W9-1,2

John and Gayle Fawn (continued) 2004 through 2006	Liabilities Net Worth and Expenditures			Schedule 2
Item Description	12/31/04	12/31/05	12/31/06	Reference
Mortgage, new house	$0.00	$0.00	$250,000.00	W10-1,2
Mortgage, condo	$0.00	$120,000.00	$0.00	W11-1,2
Credit card balance	$0.00	$125.00	$275.00	W15-1
Total liabilities	$175,000.00	$283,125.00	$399,275.00	

The mortgage amounts shown in the liabilities schedule reflect the principal balance due on the last date in the respective time period. Payment of interest and taxes, normally included in a mortgage payment, are added as expenses for the period in which they were paid. Those items do not decrease the debt established by the mortgage agreement.

The mortgage balance on the donut shop would decrease each year as a part of the monthly payments were applied to the principal. The schedule reflects that no principal was applied to the mortgage on the new house. The schedule also shows that the mortgage obtained to purchase the Colorado condominium was paid in full during 2006.

The credit card bills for Fawn and Gayle were paid in full each month. The amounts shown in the schedule represent the outstanding balance, which had not as yet been billed as of year-end. A reconciliation of the credit card account would be prepared in the same manner as the bank account reconciliations.

The third schedule in our example is the recording of documented expenditures for each of the periods under investigation. Because such expenditures hold no value after the initial purchase, they are included as cost for the period in which they occurred.

The expenditures included in the schedule have to be fully documented as to amount and to ensure that they were actually made by the subject. The expenditures included are limited to personal expenditures. Business expenses (being deductible) are not included in the net worth and personal expenditures method unless part of the scheme to conceal the income includes manipulation of business records. In those cases, a separate computation for the business is made.

John and Gayle Fawn 2005 and 2006	Personal Expenditures Net Worth and Expenditures			Schedule 3
Item Description	2005	2006	W/E#	Reference
Utilities, CO	$1,500.00	$1,600.00		Schedule 3A
Property tax	$3,000.00	$3,200.00	W16-1	
Interest	$3,800.00	$7,800.00	W17-1	
Symphony	$500.00	$500.00	W18-1	
Concerts	$750.00	$1,250.00	W19-1	

continued

Item Description	2005	2006	W/E#	Reference
John and Gayle Fawn (continued) 2005 and 2006	**Personal Expenditures** Net Worth and Expenditures			**Schedule 3**
Tailor	$3,125.00	$3,600.00	W20-1	
Dressmaker	$4,500.00	$4,900.00	W21-1	
Watches	$0.00	$22,000.00	W22-1	
Airline tickets	$1,200.00	$1,800.00	W23-1	
Restaurants	$4,400.00	$6,500.00		Schedule 3B
Ski equipment	$5,200.00	$0.00	W24-1	
Ski-lift passes	$600.00	$600.00	W25-1	
Car rentals	$180.00	$220.00	W26-1	
Lawn care	$200.00	$450.00	W27-1	
Utilities, new house	$0.00	$2,000.00	W28-1	
Auto maintenance	$600.00	$800.00	W29-1	
Spa visits	$1,200.00	$1,600.00	W30-1	
Eyeglasses	$500.00	$0.00	W31-1	
	$31,255.00	$58,820.00		

The expenditures schedule lists all of the personal expenditures made by the subject or subjects of the investigation that can be proven for litigation. To be included, the expenditures have to be independently documented. To do this, the investigator needs to contact each of the vendors with whom the subjects had financial transactions. Leads for the contacts are found throughout the investigation. Every document, interview, and observation has the potential to develop new leads. The investigation will never account for every penny spent by the subjects, but sufficient expenditures can be found by reviewing the items people spend money on every day.

For presentation in court, it is nice to be able to show that illegal or unreported income was used to acquire luxury items that the average juror cannot afford. To introduce the evidence in court, the investigator must adhere to the rules of evidence in obtaining the proper documentation and have a competent witness to introduce each document.

Our example schedule of expenditures shows the witness and the exhibit reference, as well as the description and cost of the item. The more items that are documented, the more complicated the schedule becomes. In cases where there are several similar items (utilities and restaurants in our example), sub-schedules may be made to present the amounts in an aggregate form.

The last schedule in our example is the summary schedule that puts the entire investigation into perspective: Appendix A. The summary will determine the net worth for each of the periods under investigation. The prior period net worth will be subtracted from each of the periods under investigation. The result will be the increase or decrease in the net worth of the subject from one period to the next. Personal expenditures will then be added to each period net worth increase or decrease. The result is the least amount of income the subject had to have received during the respective time period.

Legitimate or reported income for the respective period is then subtracted to determine the amount of illegal or unreported income. If sufficient amounts are determined by the computation, the investigator may move on to preparing the case for court. If any of the periods that the investigator hopes to charge against the subject are minimal in amount, he or she may want to continue canvassing for additional personal expenditures. Investigators do not need millions of dollars, but they have to establish sufficient harm to charge a subject. A $10.00-a-month embezzlement is not going to tie up the court's time.

John and Gayle Fawn 2005 and 2006	Net Worth and Personal Expenditures Summary			Appendix A
Item	2004	2005	2006	Reference
Assets	$247,015.00	$490,300.00	$795,300.00	Schedule 1
Less: liabilities	$175,000.00	$283,125.00	$399,275.00	Schedule 2
Net worth	$72,015.00	$207,175.00	$396,025.00	
Less: prior net worth		$72,015.00	$207,175.00	
Increase/decrease		$135,160.00	$188,850.00	
Add: expenditures		$31,255.00	$58,820.00	Schedule 3
Corrected income		$166,415.00	$247,670.00	
Less: reported income		$45,000.00	$45,000.00	W34-1
Additional income		$121,415.00	$202,670.00	

The preceding schedules organize the evidence for the investigator and allow for deductions to be drawn from the analysis. In our example, the correlation between the cash deposits made by Fawn to his own account and the total deposits to the other accounts at First Bank of Windsor is a strong indication that Fawn was laundering money for the other account holders. Such information becomes a valuable tool in interviewing the subject. An individual involved on the fringes of a larger criminal enterprise may be willing to talk when faced with additional criminal charges of conspiracy.

The last schedule provided is the list of witnesses and exhibits used in the report recommending the prosecution of the subject. In conducting an indirect method of proof investigation, voluminous records are analyzed and reviewed. There can be scores, if not hundreds, of witnesses required to introduce the documents into evidence and explain their importance in court.

Organizing the witnesses and evidence is just as important as assembling the financial computations. The list of witnesses is used to identify the competent witness to introduce the documents, identify those that a witness will introduce, provide the location of the evidence in the files, and provide a synopsis of the witness' testimony. Due to the length of time needed to complete this type of financial investigation, it is important to have as much identifying information about the witness as possible. The following is an example of how a list of witnesses would look for our net worth and personal expenditures computation. A sampling of witnesses is provided to reflect the construction of such a list used in these kinds of cases.

John and Gayle Fawn **Net Worth and Expenditures**	**List of Witnesses**		**Page 1**
	Witness	Exhibit	Description
1	Allen Ace, Divorce Court Clerk 1234 Main St., Mytown (123) 222-2222	1	Divorce Court File #32143, John, Clare Fawn 04/18/04
2	Joe French, Representative of First Bank of Windsor, 12 Lake St. Windsor, Ontario (321) 111-2222	1	Signature card and statements for account #54321
		2	Signature card and statements for account #54322
		3	Signature card and statements for account #54323
		4	Signature card and statements for account #54324
		5	Signature card and statements for account #54325
		6	Signature card and statements for account #54326
		7	Signature card and statements for account #54327
		8	Signature card and statements for account #54328
		9	Signature card and statements for account #54329
		10	Signature card and statements for account #54330
		11	Signature card and statements for account #54331
		12	Cashier check #9990, 2004
		13	Cashier check #12220, 2006
3	Registrar of Deeds, County 21 First Ave., Mytown (123) 222-1122	1	Deed to 100 Maple St., Mytown
		2	Deed to New House, Mytown
4	Ron Glazer 3224 West Street, Mytown (123) 222-4321	1	Records of the sale of Donut Shop
5	Jim Buymore, Gamble Agency 333 Second, Mytown (123) 222-6565	1	Brokerage account records of J. and G. Fawn

John and Gayle Fawn (continued)   **List of Witnesses**   **Page 1**
Net Worth and Expenditures

	Witness	Exhibit	Description
6	C. U. Coming, Fords-R-Us	1	Sales records for Ford Taurus
	777 Skyline, Mytown	2	Sales records for Lincoln
	(123) 222-9000		
7	G. I. Joseph, Cheap Jeeps	1	Sales records for Jeep Cherokee
	800 Skyline, Mytown		
	(123) 222-8008		
8	Registrar of Deeds, Ski County	1	Deed to condominium
	32 High St., Skiington, CO		
	(333) 423-1110		
9	Representative of Last Bank	1	Mortgage file for Donut Shop
	1005 Yeti, Mytown	2	Mortgage file for New House
	(123) 222-2334		
10	Rep. of Sticky Mortgage	1	Mortgage file for condominium
	12222 Hwy 2, Skiington, CO		
	(333) 423-7768		
11	Rep. of Mytown Gas Co.	1	Gas account, new house, Mytown
	1244 Craft, Mytown		
	(123) 222-4561		
12	Thom Thumb, Manager	1	Sales records, 2 watches
	Thumb Jewelers, West Mall		
	Mytown, (123) 222-3311		
13	Representative of the ski resort	1	Receipts for motel rooms
	Skiington, CO (333) 423-9997	2	Ski lodge lift receipts
		3	Pro shop receipts for equipment

The remaining witnesses would be listed in a similar fashion. Telephone numbers and e-mail addresses are also included to ensure that witnesses at time of trial can be located. Each exhibit would be fully described to ensure that all trial exhibits for a specific witness are included. Sometimes it is necessary to have one witness introduce a document even if others will testify about it.

The list of witnesses organizes the case for presentation in court in the same way that the schedules are used to organize the evidence. The list should be set up to provide the reviewer or prosecutor with a suggested order for presentation in court. The sequence of witnesses should follow a logical progression in how to build the case for a jury. The investigator should list the witnesses in the order required to create the picture of the financial activity of the subject.

Witnesses can be organized to provide the proof needed for convincing a jury that the elements of the crime have been met and that the subject caused the crime to be committed. Witnesses who will provide evidence and information as to the various segments of the subject's financial activities should also be grouped together to ensure a logical flow to the financial presentation.

The investigator must not get lost in the volume of financial activity being documented and presented. All the aspects of criminal culpability must be established for the case to be successful. At the same time, it is necessary to ensure that the investigation and the report recommending prosecution show how the investigator met all the judicial requirements for use of the indirect method of proof.

The investigator becomes the artist who paints the canvas of the crime to show to the jury. There are several ways in which to make a logical presentation of evidence that will clearly show the criminal activity of a subject. It is up to the investigator to decide how to present that evidence.

Chapter 18 will discuss the preparation of the case report. This report is used to review and verify the legal requirements for purposes of prosecution; it is also used as a guide for the prosecutor to understand the case, become comfortable in its merits, and suggest how to proceed.

Indirect Methods in Tax Investigations

16

The origins of indirect methods of proof in financial investigations are rooted in tax investigations. The development of forensic accounting practices using an acceptable scientific method of inquiry became a necessity as tax policies and procedures became more and more complicated.

Since every government requires financial support to exist, each taxing authority attempts to collect all of the taxes due on income, sales, or other basis for taxation. To retain a level of public confidence in the taxing system, it is necessary for them to ensure that everyone subject to the tax accurately report their bases (income, sales, etc.) and pay their tax liability.

On the other hand, everyone that is required to pay taxes wants to ensure that they are paying the least amount required by law. Here is where the temptation to evade and defeat the tax laws comes into play. In the United States with its uncertain and fluctuating tax rates, ever-changing taxable and nontaxable items, varying categories of deductible and nondeductible items, and a myriad of loopholes to be discovered and utilized, forensic accounting techniques have become a necessity to decipher the complexities of financial manipulations designed to defeat the tax system.

Forensic accounting techniques began being applied in the United States in the early 20th century when the government required additional revenues to pay for World War I debts. The government continued to expand with the transition to bureaucratic government, and the financial crises of the 1920s and early 1930s helped to make the federal income tax a permanent revenue generator. As the tax code and regulations expanded, a whole new service industry developed in the areas of accounting, investment advising, and finance. As the complexity of tax reporting and payment increased, the temptation to avoid and defeat the system increased.

These changes also expanded the criminal field of financial violations. Here was a relatively safe way for individuals and business entities (criminal or legitimate organizations) to increase their wealth and status through fraudulent financial manipulations. No violence or intimidation was necessary to steal from others or to cheat them out of their money; all it took was a sharp pencil and a sharper mind.

Since tax crimes are often referred to as victimless crimes through the eyes of legal systems, the courts have seen fit to adjust the penalties in sentencing by reducing the potential time of incarceration and focusing on financial penalties. However, the taxing authorities and those who try to comply honestly with the tax laws are, in fact, the actual victims in these types of violations. In most states, the penalty for robbing a convenience store of a few hundred dollars by threat of harm could carry a sentence of 3 to 10 years in prison. If you evade the payment of $70,000.00 to $100,000.00 in taxes, you might receive a sentence of 3 months to a year (the maximum penalty for a federal tax felony is 5 years, but it is rarely handed down by the courts).

Since the decision whether to commit a crime is usually based on a risk–benefit analysis, it is easy to see that if the perpetrator has the option of a crime of violence or a financial crime involving fraud and deception he or she will choose the latter. Therefore those that are in a position to commit a white collar crime and have the mental propensity toward criminal behavior will follow the path of least resistance and minimal risk.

Types of Tax Crimes

There are two main categories of criminal tax violations: (1) evasion of the payment of tax and (2) failure to file the required tax forms and information. In the United States, the statutory requirements for income taxes are contained in Title 26 of the United States Code. Title 26 USC Section 7201 defines the statutory provisions for the attempt to evade and defeat federal income taxes. Title 26 USC Section 7203 provides the same information for failing to file tax returns and return information. The elements for each violation are given, along with the respective maximum penalties. Both categories require that the suspect of the crime have knowledge of the requirements and the willfulness or criminal intent to commit the violation. These requirements are a key factor in successful prosecution. These requirements are also the main focus for the presentation of a defense in criminal tax cases.

Although there are relatively few criminal tax statutes, the methods used to circumvent and defeat these statutes are endless. Just as the crime scene investigation shows how the end result (the crime) took place, forensic accounting shows how the perpetrator ended up with the financial gains from the financial fraud that took place. Indirect methods of proof go to the result of the criminal violation without having to explain all of the complex regulatory tax provisions and simplify the results or fruits of the crime for presentation to a judge or jury. For criminal prosecution, the indirect methods give the perpetrator the benefit of all legitimate deductions, credits, and allowances for nontaxable receipts. This allows the prosecution to show the judge or jury that the government (taxing authority) is minimizing the dollar amount of the criminal tax violation. In the same sense, all technical adjustments that would be detrimental and increase the tax liability of the perpetrator are removed from the criminal computation and left for auditors to include into the civil assessment of the tax due and owing.

As stated earlier, there are only two ways for businesses or individuals to underreport their earnings: understate the actual income or overstate the expenses that offset the income. These are the most common ways to evade and defeat the payment of tax liabilities. They are also the most common means for reducing the reported income so as to not be required to file tax returns at all. Oftentimes the criminal tax violation is based on the reporting of a portion of the actual income in an attempt to defeat a portion (usually a large portion) of the true tax liability. In other cases, an entire source of income, legal or illegal, is omitted from the tax return. In these cases the investigator must identify the likely source of the alleged understatements to be able to successfully prosecute the criminal violation.

Understating Income

For the subject of the investigation that generates income from the sale of goods and services, customer payments come in various forms such as by check, debit or credit card, or cash. Since businesses are required to keep track of sales and accurately record and report gross receipts, there are usually multiple copies of the information pertaining to each transaction. If sales are recorded at multiple locations (i.e., two or more sales registers), sales from one or more registers may be omitted from gross daily receipts in the books and records of the business operation.

If the subject operates a business with substantial cash receipts (bars, bookstores, convenience stores, restaurants, coffee shops, etc.), cash sales may go unreported in part, or in illegal businesses in total.

If the business has several different categories of goods and services that combine to generate the business income, one or more of the categories may be omitted from the business books and records to conceal unreported income. As an example, a boat marina can have boat sales and rentals, tours and fishing junkets, equipment sales and rental, and a snack bar and bait shop; the income from any of these could go unreported.

Concealment of receipts can also be accomplished from the other perspective by failing to include those receipts that are generated by a specific customer base. In businesses that supply services (advertising, consulting, cleaning, maintenance, repairs, etc.), certain customers or accounts may be omitted and the income generated from those accounts omitted from gross receipts.

If the business is of an illegal nature (narcotics, stolen property, kickbacks, usury, extortion, etc.), all of these receipts will be unreported or laundered to appear as legitimate receipts to avoid the admission of participating in the illegal activity.

If the business is engaged in aiding and abetting other criminal activities (money laundering, fencing stolen goods, bribery or extortion), a portion of the receipts may be reported as legitimate income; however, the true source of the receipts will be falsified. The basic criminal tendencies of people involved in this type of activity would make it unlikely that a complete and accurate reporting of income would be made. Under United States law expenses related to the generation of illegal income are not deductible for tax purposes. Again, the indirect methods of proof show the least amount of income that the entity acquired during specific time periods. In doing so, these methods do take into account business expenses in whatever business is being investigated and filter down to the net gains of the suspect. For criminal prosecution purposes the judge or jury is shown the net wealth increases without having to establish the elements of the criminal activity that generated the profits. This simplifies the prosecution and weighs heavily in showing the investigation has given every benefit to the suspect and still is able to prove the tax violation beyond a reasonable doubt.

Overstating Expenses

In businesses that use a variety of products and supplies, and maintain a wide range of accounts in their reporting practices (convenience stores, grocers, electronics outlets, office supply stores, etc.), expenses may be padded to deduct more than the business actually paid for the goods and services. Another method of overstating expenses by these businesses would be to create one or more fictitious vendor accounts and write off the amounts they want to divert to personal use.

In businesses that provide services (maintenance services, consulting and advisory services, repair services, etc.) a wide range of miscellaneous expenses may be overstated. The larger the clientele of this type of business, the smaller the padding of expenses per client is required to facilitate the underreporting of taxable income. The adage of theft by fraud is often applied; steal a lot from a few or steal a little from a lot. This can also apply to the overstatement of expenses. Either application of the fraud can result in a substantial understatement of income.

Most businesses use a standard system of accounting to record their business activities, and tax laws require that all aspects of the business be documented to support the information used to prepare and file income tax returns. Not all business income and expenses involve the exchange of cash. Items such as inventory and depreciation have a direct effect on the computation and reporting of taxable income. The year-end inventory evaluation of a business is compared to the opening inventory to account for the amount of products that were sold during the year. It is also used to determine the cost of the goods sold in manufacturing and retail sales. Since most business audits do not go into the actual business location at the end of each reporting period, inventory verifications have to be based on the books and records of the business, or independently verified through suppliers. Manipulation of inventory figures can be a means of falsifying actual business income.

Depreciation is another "book" entry that can be manipulated to reduce reported taxable income. Since depreciable business assets can remain on the books and records of a business for several years, the basis for computing depreciation expenses can be manipulated to reduce reported income. Fictitious depreciable items may also be included in the books and records to decrease reported tax liability. In one case, collusion between related businesses resulted in the same depreciable equipment being used to claim depreciation deductions by three different companies. These assets were heavy equipment depreciable over a 20-year useful life expectancy. When the investigator asked to see the equipment, the equipment was moved from business to business in an attempt to justify the depreciation deductions. The investigator was able to go back 9 years to the original purchase of the equipment and verify from the equipment manufacturer that only one of each of the items was actually purchased (a direct benefit from following all the leads available).

These are only a few of the methods that people use to defeat income tax statutes and regulations, but overstating deductible expenses or failing to include all of the income are the foundation for most income tax violations. Income taxes are not the only form of taxation that is targeted for evasion. Sales taxes, excise taxes, luxury taxes, and any other tax imposed reducing profits are all vulnerable to fraud and deceit in reporting and payment. Also, any form of taxation used to provide incentives through tax credits or used to reduce or eliminate an industry or product through increased taxation or special fees are ripe areas for manipulation and fraudulent practices.

Underreporting sales in an attempt to evade the payment of income taxes necessitates the underreporting of sales taxes. This "double dipping" of fraud constitutes two related violations under two different taxing authorities. Sales taxes, due to the relative simplicity of computing the taxes due and owing, are far more limited in the schemes used to defeat the tax. As an example, a bar waters down its drinks to customers, which allows the bar to sell more than the inventory figures would show in the business books and records. The bartenders fail to report the sales ($0.00 sales rung up on the registers) in the same amount as the extra drinks being sold resulting in a percentage of unreported sales.

Excise taxes are applied to specific products (gasoline, alcohol, tobacco, etc.) and contract labor charges. These taxes can be reduced by falsifying transactions between buyers and sellers. As an example, if a building contractor is willing to take one half of the payment for a home improvement project in cash, he understates his income by not reporting the cash portion on the job and the homeowner benefits by a cost reduction of half the excise taxes that should have been paid.

In the same manner but on a much grander scale, luxury taxes can be manipulated to avoid paying the add-on portion of the tax. This type of fraud again involves collusion between the buyer and seller with either a falsification of the actual price or having the amount needed to go below the dollar criteria for the tax being paid separately in cash or as a kickback. In these instances the investigator has to determine the culpability of both parties and allocate the tax to the correct person having the actual liability. Let's take an example in which a person wants to buy a yacht. If a luxury tax of an additional 10% is assessed on purchases over $500,000.00 and the yacht costs $750,000.00 the seller would be required to pay an additional $25,000.00 on the purchase. If the seller agrees to write up two sales at $499,000.00 and $251,000.00, no luxury tax would be applied to the purchase. The seller might require a kickback of part of the $25,000.00 or assist in the fraud to make the sale. Either way, both the seller and the buyer have committed violations. The investigator also has to ensure that the $251,000.00 "sham" sale was reported as income by the seller.

Other Tax Crimes

Governments use taxation and regulation for several other purposes outside of generating revenue. Higher tax rates, surcharges, and fees may be placed on certain businesses and industries to discourage the growth of those businesses. Tax credits, reduced tax rates, and tax deferments may be placed on other businesses to encourage growth and expansion of those businesses. Individuals may be given tax credits for low income, energy efficiency, furthering education, or by making certain purchases. Other industries receive preferential treatment for capital improvement or for size or expansion.

Each of these aspects of taxation and regulatory policy is also subject to fraud when people try to take unqualified benefits or avoid required penalties. There are also those crimes that take advantage of the large number of returns and transactions that any taxing authority has to handle. Keep in mind that the taxing authority needs to maintain public confidence that the system is administered fairly and that the greater number of people who are required to file returns, the lower the tax rates that are necessary to fund public programs. Following are some examples of tax crimes that do not fall under the common categories of evasion or failure to file tax returns.

Tax-Related Crimes

Criminals will often try to take advantage of areas in which they feel there is little or no scrutiny. Through technological advances, taxing authorities are able to check the mathematical and formulative accuracy of tax returns being filed. It is more difficult for them to be timely in responding to fraud schemes that employ the filing of multiple false returns that claim minimal refund amounts.

False Returns

False filing schemes involve the falsification of earning statements showing wages and taxes withheld. The statements and subsequent returns use a false identity and identification number to give the appearance of a legitimate tax return. The returns will take care to ensure that each return qualifies for and claims any lucrative tax credit. Hundreds and even thousands of these returns are then submitted for small refunds. The hope for the criminal is that the refund checks will be issued and cashed before the taxing authority can identify the fraud. The criminal enterprise will then relocate and often try the same scheme the next year using different names, identification numbers, and locations for the false returns.

One scheme involved three individuals. One individual paid poor people in various neighborhoods $10.00 for each identification card they obtained and used a library typewriter to prepare false W-2 (earnings statements) forms claiming income and tax withholding. Another individual prepared the false returns attaching the false W-2s and handled the mailing to two different return processing centers. The third individual (a convicted forger) signed each of the returns. This group filed over 120 false federal tax returns. They added the bonus of filing over a hundred false state returns. The scheme netted them more than $400,000.00, and the subsequent conviction netted several years in prison.

False Preparer Schemes

Not all tax return preparers are honest and trustworthy. Schemes have been identified in which the preparers will falsify deductions to generate larger tax refunds for their clientele. The preparer will usually benefit from word-of-mouth advertising (one client tells friends and relatives about getting a larger refund by using the preparer, and the publicity spreads). The preparer will usually charge the clients a percentage of the anticipated refund for the tax preparation service. The difficulty in this type of investigation is that the clients are unaware that falsification has occurred on their returns based on the certification of the preparer. It is also difficult to explain that the client is responsible for the corrected tax due and owing on the identified false returns. Skill and tact is required to gain their cooperation to be witnesses in subsequent criminal litigation. It helps when the clients realize that the preparer is trying to place the criminal culpability on them.

One scheme involved a preparer who had been preparing false returns for a 3-year period of time. He inflated itemized deductions (primarily contributions, medical expenses, casualty losses, and miscellaneous deductions). His clientele were mostly low-income workers who rented homes or apartments in the poorer neighborhoods of the city. One witness (client) remembered being asked if she had a balcony on her apartment and if she kept any plants on it in the summer. The client said she did. The preparer added a farm schedule to her return showing a $2,500.00 farming loss. Further investigation showed that a substantial number of his clients had similar losses on their returns although none of them lived outside the city or owned any rural property.

Tax Shelter Schemes

A tax shelter scheme is designed by perpetrators to convince their clientele that they have discovered how to use a new tax "loophole" to reduce or eliminate the payment of tax on income. There are a wide variety of schemes that have been used over the years and new ones are concocted as the old ones fail. The preparation and development of the scheme is usually quite elaborate to present the façade of being a legal and legitimate tax planning program. The scheme may involve little known portions of tax law that are taken out of context or presented in an incomplete fashion so as not to show the restrictions that make it useless to the client. Some of the schemes have involved living trusts, investment write-offs, tax credits for new technology or scientific research, and any other financial aspect that can be sold as a way to keep your income and take "paper" losses to shield the income from taxation.

The perpetrator in this type of scheme will provide what is purported to be all the necessary forms and instructions that the client will need to avoid the payment of taxes. The forms will usually be legitimate but the instructions for their use will direct them to misuse the paperwork when clients file their tax returns. The packages are sold to the clients well before the tax returns will be due to be filed. Once official scrutiny falls upon the client returns, the perpetrator(s) will leave the area and often start anew in a different location.

In one example the perpetrators rented a very nice office and office equipment, and posted false finance degrees on the walls. They gave seminars (the sales pitch) at a luxury hotel. The scheme was the sale of trusts, which they said could divert regular income into nontaxable withdrawals. They sold more than 800 trust packages at $1,000.00 each. A few clients asked for official verification of their packages, which led to an investigation. The scheme was uncovered as the perpetrators were planning to move out of town.

These are just a few examples of the types of financial crimes that are committed relating to taxation. The investigator should always be aware that whenever a scheme is uncovered and a successful prosecution follows, others wanting to commit a similar fraud will be deterred. Also, if one avenue for fraud is closed off, those determined to commit this type of fraud will find or invent new schemes. Tax-related crimes also require multijurisdictional cooperation and investigation.

Unique Aspects of Criminal Tax Investigations

17

The use of indirect methods of proof began in the United States in the investigation of criminal tax violations. As early as the turn of the 20th century, taxing authorities were seeing more instances of tax fraud and the use of more complex schemes to facilitate the fraud.

As covered earlier, the U.S. Supreme Court decision in *Holland v. United States* established the acceptability and the parameters for the use of the net worth and expenditures method of proof for criminal prosecution. The Court allowed the prosecution and conviction for criminal tax violations based solely on circumstantial evidence as long as the scientific method of inquiry could be clearly demonstrated to the judge and jury. Indirect methods of proof have expanded in scope to cover the investigation of illegal activities and have proven invaluable in linking the criminal to the fruits of his or her crimes.

Since the use of indirect methods of proof is relatively new in the area of jurisprudence, it is only natural that they have evolved through a series of appeals and reviews. In establishing the requirements for their use, courts have refined the use of indirect methods by placing unique circumstances and restrictions on the government (taxing authority) when they are applied to criminal tax cases. These unique aspects follow the fact that tax crimes are a unique form of financial fraud. There are three general areas in which tax crimes differ from the financial crimes perpetrated by con men and thieves.

First, tax fraud is committed directly against the government taxing authority. The state becomes the primary victim. However, the result of tax fraud is indirectly transferred to the taxpaying public since the tax revenues are used to finance programs and governmental functions set in place for the benefit of the general public. It is similar to the situation where three people share the cost of rent on an apartment and one fails to contribute their share, the other two must make up the difference.

Second, the computation of tax due and owing is prepared and submitted by the individual or entity subject to the tax as opposed to a standard flat rate fee or assessment by the government. Due to this circumstance, there is little corroboration for the accuracy of the computation unless an official audit of the subject is authorized and conducted. If you have ever put yourself on a diet or exercise program you fully understand the difficulty in personal self-regulation.

Third, and probably most important, tax computations involve a wide variety of special circumstances and adjustments that are not applicable in the general criminal financial investigation. There are special regulatory provisions and differing treatments applied for specific groups, businesses, industries, and individuals. Adjustments to the tax computation may involve the level of income, the passive or active nature of income, excluded or deferred portions of income, prior tax-period allowances, varied income rates, and several other unique situations. Tax computations are also set to account for deductible items that may be limited by a dollar amount cap, a set requirement to exceed a percentage of gross income limitation, or other level of income regulations. There are also certain restrictions and qualifications set for the claiming and receipt of tax credits that may come and go year to year.

Due to these unique distinctions, financial investigators need to ensure that they have given consideration to all of the regulatory and current court modifications that apply to each individual investigation. It is not like the criminal investigation of a crime such as embezzlement where the amount embezzled is known and all that needs to be done is to determine who had financial gain beyond their legitimate earnings. In the same way that a seasoned tax preparer or certified public accountant needs to know and understand as much as possible about their client's business, employment, investments, expenses, and financial activity to prepare a complete and accurate return, the investigator is required to learn these things during the course of the investigation. By the end of the investigation the investigator should know more about the historical financial activity of the subject of the investigation than the subject can remember. Information on the business and employment can be readily obtained through a little research and some interviewing of third parties. For the investigator, the determination of the subject's financial activity is the result of a complete and thorough investigation.

In a criminal tax evasion investigation it is best to begin by verifying as much of the information that has been volunteered by the subject on the returns that have been filed. If returns have not been filed, then the investigator must get the reasoning that the subject used for not filing from the careful use of interviewing techniques. Keep in mind that not every person may be required to file returns. These initial steps in the investigation are the same techniques that civil auditors would use to verify information received from the subject. Courts have developed and accepted the premise that the rational person will not do anything that is to their detriment intentionally. In relation to taxation the premise is that an individual will claim all of the deductions and benefits allowed by the tax code. For civil purposes this relieves the auditor from having to seek out additional benefits for the taxpayer. Since criminal conviction carries the penalties of loss of freedom and finances, the investigator cannot accept this premise completely. The investigator must ensure that any information developed during the investigation that has a beneficial effect on the subject must be included in computing the criminal liabilities. This same logic would be applied for any mistakes on the returns that could be attributed to "honest" mistakes. In cases involving corporations, partnerships, and joint ventures, the investigator must not only determine the amount of unreported income but also ensure that the proper allocation of that unreported income is made to any and all of the parties involved in the fraud. Oftentimes this allocation will weigh heavily on the jury when separate trials are given to multiple conspirators.

Therefore, the onset of the criminal tax investigation would be to verify the information provided by the subject on the returns by analyzing the source documents and materials used by the subject to prepare the returns. These are the same steps that the civil auditor would use when reviewing the returns under a civil audit of the taxpayer. If major discrepancies are discovered, the case must then be considered for criminal investigation. Oftentimes various indirect methods of investigation are used to corroborate the discrepancies as mentioned in Chapter 11.

Additional Steps Needed in Tax Cases

The following information is based on U.S. federal income tax regulations and filing procedures. The theory and practicality behind the additional steps needed for criminal prosecution of tax crimes will be consistent based on tax law variations for any national, state, or regional taxing authority.

The first difference between criminal tax cases and general financial crimes is the lack of a physical victim to present to the judge or jury. In this sense, the prosecution loses the advantage of having a victim to testify or be presented to the court to show personal harm and garner sympathy and empathy during the litigation process. To compensate for this disadvantage, the criminal financial investigator should take extra care to emphasize the *mens rea* or evil intent of the perpetrator of the tax fraud. There are unique factors that should be explored and developed to enhance the presentation of criminal intent for tax cases that would rarely be present or apply to general criminal investigations. In general criminal investigations, the criminal history of the defendant plays an important role in providing leads, establishing a criminal mind-set, and showing a possible *modus operandi*.

In tax cases, other criminal acts (unless they are the source of the unreported income) are barely relevant to the case and most often will not be admissible in the case presentation. Repeat criminal tax offenses by an individual or group of individuals are unusual, especially if the first offense was successfully prosecuted. Instead, the typical criminal tax case will cover an extended period of time (successive filing periods). Once discovered, the tax fraud will be prosecuted for any and all periods within the statute of limitations. Once an offender has been prosecuted and punished for tax fraud (receiving a monetary fine and incarceration), a second attempt at fraud by the same offender will usually be completely unrelated to the prior crime. Therefore, establishing a pattern of criminal tax fraud over a series of consecutive tax reporting periods can serve to replace prior criminal conduct and strengthen the presentation of criminal intent. A judge or jury will find the defense of innocent or unintentional error difficult to accept if the defendant is shown to have repeated the same fraudulent acts over and over again. This is accentuated by the fact that in most tax fraud cases the perpetrator will increase the amount of the fraud in each subsequent period (not being caught the first, second, or third period in a row emboldens the offender), believing that their scheme is foolproof and that they will never get caught. It is also common that as the fraud proceeds increase, the expenditures that are made with the proceeds will become more extravagant and luxurious. Most jurors and judges have a set lifestyle based on their regular income, and are quick to notice and remember leaps in the spending habits of the defendant. These factors are a key part of the criminal tax case and need to be fully developed and highlighted in the report by the financial criminal investigator.

The second major difference between tax and other general crimes is that the subject under investigation provides the foundation for the tax case. A large portion of the evidence that will be used in the criminal tax case comes directly from the subject's admissions on the filed return. Unless the suspect in a general crime investigation confesses to the crime, the investigator must develop all of the evidence independent of the subject. Tax returns, on the other hand, are prepared and filed based on the information that the taxpayer submitted voluntarily to the taxing authority. The presumption of legal interpretation is that an individual will not willfully provide false information that is detrimental to his own cause.

Many people are confused by the use of the term "voluntary tax system." To paraphrase one district court judge in the United States, he explained the terminology to a jury like this:

> A voluntary tax system is like a traffic stop sign. The sign does not force you to stop, but rather make the decision as to whether or not to stop voluntarily. However, if you don't stop, you have committed a violation of the law.

Therefore, the taxpayer has an obligation to submit the necessary information to the taxing authority that is needed to determine if a return has to be filed, and if so, how much of a tax liability is due and owing. In this sense the taxpayer actually provides the basis and origin of the criminal tax investigation. This is also the foundation to determine the extent of the fraud since the taxpayer is the one who can falsify or omit information from the return. For these reasons, all avenues of investigation and all leads developed must be followed through to their conclusion to ensure successful criminal prosecution.

The last major difference between tax and other criminal investigations is that the investigator is responsible for including, deleting, or correcting all of the taxpayer's information and preparation in determining the corrected tax due and owing. The indirect methods of proof establish the least amount of income that was received for each tax period, but adjustments have to be made to ensure that the investigator is not overlooking any of the items that affect the correct computation of the tax due and owing. Knowing the correct income amounts for each period can affect other line items and schedules on the returns. It may also lead to changes in mathematical factors such as percentages applied to deductions and credits as well as the correct tax rate that applies. In many cases, the taxpayer is required to file more than one return for each period or include an additional schedule to the return (i.e., business, personal, corporate, partnership). Due to the level of complexities that apply to the specific subject under investigation, the investigator must be up to date on the methods and requirements for filing all applicable returns and be able to merge the related return information. In short, the investigator must be a good return preparer as well as a financial criminalist. This also requires the investigator to make himself or herself aware of the filing requirements and procedures for each of the periods under investigation (tax laws are fluid in nature and subject to changes from period to period).

Since every taxing authority has its own forms and statutory provisions for filing returns and paying tax, we will review the general areas of concern for the financial investigator. First, it is necessary to review the general way that income tax returns are prepared. The following will apply to all forms of income tax returns, business and personal. I will use the category identification for items on the personal return, but the same type of items will apply to business returns using a different set of category titles.

There are usually several steps involved in the preparation of income tax returns. The preparation generally begins with adding up the gross income for the tax period. Any amounts that are offsets to income or the nontaxable portions of the gross income amounts are removed. Adjustments are then made to determine an *adjusted gross income.* For individual tax returns, the gross income would include items such as wages, interest and dividends, capital gains, and so forth. The adjustments to arrive at an adjusted gross income amount would include any deductible expenses such as education expenses, moving expenses, alimony payments, and individual retirement account deductions. Once the adjusted gross income is determined, personal deductions are deducted to arrive at the taxable income. This is the amount that the completed indirect method analysis will be compared to to determine the extent, if any, of unreported income.

For business income tax returns, similar steps are taken. The gross receipts from sales or services rendered during the tax period are compiled. Any returned items are removed from the total. For manufacturing and retail sales businesses, the cost of the goods sold are also removed. Any other sources of income are added in and the result is the gross income for that business during the respective tax period. Other types of businesses and industry, such as farming and rental income, will make the same type of computations although the terminology of the income and adjustment categories may vary. If the business is a taxable entity (subject to return filing, tax determination, and payment) there still may be portions of the income that flow through to the individuals owning or operating the business. In other cases, the income from the business may be computed on a separate schedule that is attached to the individual's tax return. The amounts from these schedules are usually identified line items that are added into the gross income for the individual's return.

In many cases, the unreported income uncovered through the use of the indirect methods of proof are concealed or omitted from the legitimate business dealings of the subject of the investigation. For this reason, it is necessary for the investigator to be familiar with all of the aspects of the subject returns to be able to specify the method used to understate the income. Remember that the indirect method of proof requires that a "likely" source of income or unreporting of income be identified. In most cases where there is the receipt of illegal income, the subject will fail to report all of the illegal proceeds or add a small portion of the illegal proceeds to the return as "other income."

After all of the return information is verified or corrected, the actual computation of tax is prepared. The indirect method of proof will provide the comparisons necessary for the determination of the unreported income for each of the returns. Before tax can be computed, the investigator must apply all of the adjustments to the adjusted gross income needed to bring the indirect computation down to a corrected taxable income amount for each year. These adjustments include removing any nontaxable sources of income such as tax-free interest and dividends, the dissipation of a cash hoard, additional loans (third-party loans not disclosed during the investigation and personal undocumented loans), inheritances, and so forth.

After the corrected taxable income (what should have been originally reported) has been established, the last step in the process is to compute the tax. At this point the investigator becomes the accountant and needs to review the tax preparation for each relative time period or year covered by the investigation. Since tax rates and return preparation guidelines change over time, it is imperative that the investigator applies the rules for each period individually. This will also help to ensure that the correct tax is determined based on the increases to income. A new tax rate, the elimination or addition of tax credits, and limitations on deductible items are some of the considerations that have to be taken into account.

The corrected tax due and owing then becomes the baseline for computing the actual understatement of tax. The reported tax due for each period is subtracted from the corrected tax for that period, and any applicable penalties on the alleged understatements may be shown for informational purposes. Penalties and interest can be shown for internal agency review and to apprise the prosecutor of the total impact of the investigation. They are applied until the case has been successfully prosecuted.

Keeping in mind the understanding that indirect methods of proof in financial investigations show the least amount of income or receipts that the individual or entity had to have received, tax cases require that the computation be reduced to show only the taxable portions of that income. The additional steps needed to prepare and present a criminal tax case are shown in the following example.

	First Year	Second Year
Corrected income (indirect method)	$247,000.00	$312,000.00
Adjustments (for Nontaxables)		
Cash hoard (base year)	$9,000.00	$0.00
Personal loan (uncle)	$0.00	$6,000.00
Gift (grandparents)	$0.00	$8,000.00
Corrected adjusted gross income	$238,000.00	$298,000.00
Less		
Itemized deductions	$8,550.00	$10,200.00
Exemptions	$5,000.00	$5,000.00
Corrected taxable income	$224,450.00	$282,800.00
Corrected tax due	$56,112.00	$61,200.00
Reported tax	$4,800.00	$5,700.00
Additional tax due and owing	$51,312.00	$55,500.00

In this example, the additional tax due and owing would represent the amounts of tax evaded by the subject of the investigation. The tax determined to be due and owing would be the amount used in the indictment. The amounts of unreported income would be referenced in the presentation of intent to show the scope and size of the nontaxed benefit to the subject, and establish the method used by the subject to commit the tax violation.

The Case Report

18

We have compared the use of indirect methods of proof to a picture of the financial dealings of the individual under investigation. As the old adage goes, *a picture is worth a thousand words*. As we have seen in the previous chapters, the schedules organize the financial transactions and can consolidate a *thousand* transactions into a single schedule. The case report for indirect methods of proof provides the narrative explanation of the schedules.

As indirect methods of proof are built out of circumstantial evidence, the investigator must be able to show how the evidence proves the allegations of the crime. The report shows the reviewer and the prosecutor how the investigation was conducted and how the circumstantial evidence provides proof beyond a reasonable doubt that the subject committed the crime. The report becomes the roadmap to convince the prosecutor, the grand jury (for felony charges), and eventually the judge and jury as to the relationship of the evidence to the crime in a logical and sequential way.

The case report is prepared in a similar fashion to a research paper. The presentation needs an introduction, the body of the report, and a conclusion. In a research paper, the introduction tells the reader what is to be covered in a brief overview. The body of the paper lays out the details in depth to convince the reader of the premise. The conclusion presents what the reader should learn from the presentation and the logical conclusions that must be drawn from the evidence in the report. We will discuss the three sections and what is needed in each to assemble a complete presentation of the facts.

Introduction

The report needs to introduce the reader to the subject material that will be presented. The investigator should include the pertinent information that will identify the subject, the type and time frame of the investigation, the type of charges that are recommended, and the method of proof being used in the investigation. Many offices will have a set standard for this information, such as a template or guide to the presentation. If this is not available, it is a simple matter to construct one and use it as a cover page to the report. Information used to identify the case would include the subject's name, the case or investigation number, the address, social security or other identifying number, the periods under investigation, the recommended charges against the subject, and the date of the report.

The next step would be to present the purpose of the report. Using the case example from Chapter 15, the introduction could be set forth as follows.

This report relates to the alleged violation of the money-laundering statutes, failure to report income derived from money laundering on state and federal tax forms, and the filing of false Custom declarations, during the years 2005 and 2006, by John and Gayle Fawn. John Fawn would receive currency at various restaurants in town and take the currency across the border into Canada. He would then deposit the currency into 10 various accounts. He would also deposit 5% of the cash into an account of his own, which was under a variation of his name. A total of $51,000.00 was deposited to Fawn's account during the years 2004 through 2006. The report will show that this was a small portion of the proceeds Fawn received for transporting the currency and filing the false Customs declarations. In reality he made more than $320,000.00 during the years 2005 and 2006. Both he and his wife benefited from the unreported income derived from the money-laundering scheme.

Recommended Charges

The next section of the report would provide definitions of the relevant aspects to the case, and the identification of the subjects and pertinent information as to their history. For our example, it would look like this.

John Fawn; Two (2) counts of tax evasion, One (1) count of conspiracy to launder money, Ninety (90) counts of filing false Custom declarations, One (1) count of money laundering

Gayle Fawn; Two (2) counts of tax evasion, One (1) count of conspiracy to launder money

In addition to the number of counts and the statute description, the numerical statue references would be included for each respective violation. Example: Title 18 USC Section 371, for conspiracy.

History of Subjects

Names: FAWN, John and Gayle
DOBs: 01/01/63, 02/02/81
SSNs: 123-45-6789, 987-65-4321
Address: New House, Mytown, 2006
Prior addresses: 1201 Elm, Apt. 4, Mytown
Children: None; John—adult daughter from first marriage

Marital status: John—divorced from Clare 2004, married Gayle 2004
Military service: None
Occupations: Baker, housewife
Reputation in community: Good
Criminal history: None

The history section can be presented in outline form, but any explanation for an item should be included. This section should provide any and all relevant information about the subjects. It can include any other information that would help to give the reader a familiarity of the subject's history and background. It should include the positive items (a prosecutor wants to know if he or she is going to face difficulty in trial on character witnesses) as well as negative items (the prosecutor would also want to know if the subject had prior convictions for similar crimes). The prosecution must be advised as to any potential obstacles it may have to overcome in advance. The fact that the subject received the Medal of Honor and two Purple Hearts should not be first discovered when the defense begins its case.

Positions in community organizations, fraternal organizations, benevolent societies, and public service should be documented and introduced in this section of the report. Any evidence used in providing information in the report should be noted in footnote form after the item is presented. This is important for all aspects of the report from the introduction to the case narrative. If the information on dates of birth is derived from driver's license information, the witness for the licenses and copies of the licenses should be referenced. Example: (W33-1,2). This allows readers to go to the evidence and review the accuracy of any of the statements made in the report, or to clarify any item to their satisfaction.

Business History

As we are presenting a financial case, it is necessary to include a section on the business history of the subjects. In this section, all of the pertinent information on the legitimate financial activities of the subject should be described in sufficient detail for the reader to understand. Any illegitimate or unreported income will be addressed in the body of the report and the conclusions. As an example, the Fawn report would include a section like this.

John Fawn currently owns and operates the Donut Shop. He worked in bakeries from his senior year in high school and until he purchased the Donut Shop in 2004. Gayle Fawn has never been employed. She is now the co-owner of the Donut Shop with her husband John. John made a new financial start after his divorce from Clare in 2004.

Theory

The next step in the introduction would be to present the theory of the case. In this section, the investigator has the latitude to present how he or she views the evidence collected during the investigation and how he or she interprets that evidence. This section of the report expands on how the investigator interpreted the evidence, and the logic behind the conclusions the investigator has made as to who, what, where, when, and how the criminal acts occurred.

The theory section should address each element of the criminal charges recommended, and should identify the harm done to the victims. In the case of money laundering, the harm done is in the failure to comply with regulatory provisions and the potential for concealing illegal gains on behalf of others. Tax charges would identify the taxes evaded. In both situations, a substantial harm will most likely be required to convince the prosecutor to go forward.

The theory section for our example case on John and Gayle Fawn could be prepared as follows.

John Fawn was divorced in February 2004. He left the marriage with approximately $14,000.00 and a paid off 2002 Ford Taurus. By the end of the year he was a business owner who had amassed a net worth of $72,000.00. He remarried shortly after his divorce, to Gayle. She had no assets of her own to add to the marriage union. She has never been employed and was living in an apartment her parents had rented for her. Their only reported legitimate income came from the operation of the Donut Shop and totaled $45,000.00 per year. Over the course of the following two years, the Fawns increased their net worth to almost $400,000.00 and made purchases of more than $90,000.00.

The income they used to improve their holdings and lifestyle was derived from a 5% commission that John Fawn received on laundering funds for a local organized crime family. He would take U.S. currency into Canada and deposit the funds into 10 accounts controlled by the organized crime family. He also deposited some of his 5% cut into an account that he opened under a variation of his own name.

Fawn would receive the money to be laundered on Thursday evening while dining out with his wife. He would transport the currency by car through Customs. When asked if he had anything to declare, he would respond no, and if asked to complete a Customs declaration, he would write in an amount between $100 and $200 for currency taken across the border. He deposited $51,300.00 into his Canadian account and withdrew the funds in the form of two cashier's checks, each for $25,000.00. He used these funds to purchase property. During the years 2005 and

2006, Fawn transported and laundered more than $8,000,000.00. The proceeds from his involvement were used by him and his wife to purchase a new home, a condominium, new vehicles, custom clothing, jewelry, and to take very nice vacations.

The investigation will show that John Fawn willfully transported undeclared currency into Canada in an attempt to conceal the nature of the funds on behalf of others residing in the United States. The agreement in the conspiracy to launder the funds is implied in the actions Fawn took on behalf of the 10 foreign account holders. The investigation will also show that John and Gayle Fawn knowingly failed to report the income derived from the money-laundering conspiracy. Finally, it will show 90 trips with undeclared currency taken by John Fawn.

The theory section shows how the investigator pieces together actions and events to present a plausible explanation as to the method used to commit the crime, and ties the related crimes into the story. This provides the reader with an understanding of what to look for as the evidence is presented and to evaluate the evidence in relationship to the criminal charges that are proposed.

Venue

The next item addressed is that of venue for prosecution of the criminal acts. Financial investigations often contain overt acts that could be used to establish venue in multiple jurisdictions. It is necessary that the investigator present all of the factors that could establish venue in all the jurisdictions involved. The investigator should then present the factors that support the reasoning behind the selection of venue. Venue will usually be instituted in the most logical location for facilitating a trial. The place of residence of the subjects, the location where there is a substantial number of the witnesses, and the location in which any of the parts of the crime occurred are all considered in establishing venue. Using the Fawn case, the venue section could be presented like this:

Venue may lie in the judicial district of Mytown, where the subjects reside, own, and operate a business, maintain their bank accounts, and from which their tax returns were filed (could be state, federal, or local assessments). Venue may also lie in the judicial district of Skiington where the subjects purchased a condominium and made substantial use of the illegal proceeds. It is recommended that venue be instituted in the judicial district of Mytown.

Starting Point

After providing the introductory information needed in the report, the narrative turns to an explanation of the evidence presented. In using an indirect method of proof, it is useful to address the restrictions placed by the courts on using the method. The starting point is one requirement that the courts stressed independently of the financial computations and should be addressed in its own section of the report. All of the evidence used in establishing the starting point for the investigation should be presented, and all of the judicial concerns should be addressed directly. The Supreme Court decision in the *Holland* case states the judicial concerns about using the net worth method and is a good reference for this section of the report.

The following is an example of how the starting point could be presented in the John and Gayle Fawn scenario.

John Fawn is a baker. He was married to Clare Fawn in 1979 and divorced in February of 2004. After the divorce, he received his portion of the property settlement, which consisted of $14,715.00 and a 2002 Ford Taurus. He remarried in April 2004 to Gayle Fawn. From April until year-end, he and Gayle accumulated a net worth of $72,000.00. Gayle Fawn has never been employed and brought only personal effects into the marriage. Clare Fawn stated that she hired a detective agency to check on the property acquired during her marriage, and she believes that the divorce settlement is an accurate statement as to all of her holdings with John as of February 2004. John Fawn reported earning $35,000.00 from his ownership of the Donut Shop (acquired in 2004), and $45,000.00 each year thereafter.

December 31, 2004, is used for the starting point in the net worth and personal expenditures computation. This date allows the computation to show only the income of John Fawn. His first wife was employed in 2004 prior to and after the divorce. The divorce settlement provides an accurate reflection of Fawn's net worth as of February 2004, and the investigation was able to bring that net worth forward to year-end. Beginning the criminal computation with the year 2005 allows for presentation of the majority of the acts of money laundering and a much simpler presentation of the tax evasion charges. Fawn began his business ownership in 2004, and his first two full years of operation were 2005 and 2006. This choice of starting point allows the subject full credit for cash on hand from the divorce settlement to begin the computation.

Likely Source of Income

The evidence will show that John Fawn received 5% commission on the money he transported to Canada for the organized crime family. It will show that he willfully failed to report more than $8,000,000.00 in currency to Customs officials, and gained more than $400,000.00 from this illegal activity.

Evidence of Intent

An integral part of any criminal case is to establish the intent of the subjects to commit the crime or crimes being charged. This aspect of the investigation should also receive specific attention in the final investigative report. Because intent is a determination of the state of mind of the subject, the investigator should include all the actions of the subject that would infer an intent to commit the crime. This would include both the actions taken and the failure to take the proper actions. Often, the investigator will have to present a series of circumstantially proven events in proper sequence to convey the inference of intent. Using our example, it could be presented in this manner:

John Fawn transported U.S. currency in amounts ranging between $40,000.00 and $100,000.00 into Canada between May 2004 and December 2006. He made these trips 90 times over the 2½-year period. On each of these occasions he failed to report having currency in excess of $3,000.00 to U.S. Customs officials. As early as June 17, 2004, he completed a Customs declaration form and stated he had less than $3,000.00 in currency with him. Over the next 30 months he made the statement in writing 18 more times.

John Fawn knew of his obligation to report the currency he was transporting and willfully failed to do so. Once in Canada, he kept 5% of the currency he had smuggled into Canada for himself, then deposited his percentage to a bank account with First Bank of Windsor. He made an attempt to conceal the account by changing the spelling of his name on the account signature card. He made 12 cash deposits to this account. The total amount of currency he smuggled into Canada exceeded $8,000,000.00, which he laundered by depositing it to 10 other bank accounts controlled by the organized crime family.

The evidence shows that John and Gayle Fawn used cash to pay for most of their purchases during this time in an attempt to conceal their illegal income. The Fawns failed to report the illegal income on their tax returns and began making substantial purchases out of the state to avoid suspicion over their newfound wealth. It is evident that both John and

Gayle Fawn knew the income was illegal, and both attempted to keep the source hidden from detection, especially by the government. The Fawns made more than $400,000.00 during the 2½ years, hardly an amount that could be forgotten about or overlooked.

Any other topics that the investigator believes should be addressed can be included in the introductory portion of the report. Any topic in history or background that could impact the investigation can be given its own section for narrative explanation.

Evidence

Once the "Introduction" is complete, the investigator will provide a full presentation of the evidence to be used in support of the recommendations being made in the report. In our example scenario on John Fawn, the evidence section of the report could be separated into evidence of unreported income, money laundering, and conspiracy, or be addressed altogether under the single heading of "Evidence." The following is an example of how the evidence narrative could be presented. We will not address every item from our example case on the Fawns but provide a representative sampling.

Assets

Cash on Hand
John Fawn was given credit for $14,715.00 in cash on hand for the base year 2004. This amount was the total he received from his divorce settlement. None of his expenditures in 2004 was considered to offset this amount.

Cash in Banks
John Fawn opened an account with First Bank of Windsor in March 2004. He used the name J. Faun but was identified by bank personnel as the same individual. Handwriting analysis of the account signature card and Fawn's handwriting exemplars confirm that he signed to open the account. This account had reconciled year-end balances of $4,300.00, $26,000.00, and $1,300.00 for the years 2004 through 2006, respectively.

100 Maple Street
This was the home that John Fawn and his first wife, Clare, had at the beginning of 2004. Clare received the house in the divorce settlement in February 2004. It is included for informational purposes at $0.00 balances to show that Fawn retained no interest in the property in computing the opening net worth starting point.

Ford Taurus

John Fawn purchased a Ford Taurus for $16,000.00 in 2002. He received the car in the divorce settlement. There were no liens against the vehicle. In 2006 he transferred title to the car to his daughter. It is carried at cost in the computation for the years 2004 and 2005. The vehicle is removed from the schedule for 2006.

Liabilities

Mortgage: Donut Shop

John Fawn purchased the Donut Shop in 2004 for $200,000.00. He obtained a mortgage on the property for $180,000.00. The principal balances for the years ending 2004 through 2006 are included in the computation. Related expenses for taxes and interest are included in the schedule of expenditures.

Mortgage: Condominium

Fawn purchased a condominium in Colorado with his wife in 2005. They purchased the property for $275,000.00. They obtained a mortgage on the property for $175,000.00. The balance of principal owed on the mortgage as of 12/31/05 was $120,000.00. The mortgage was paid off in November 2006.

Expenditures

Watches

In 2006, John and Gayle Fawn purchased matching gold watches for a total cost of $22,000.00. Both subjects were wearing the watches when asked for interviews in 2007.

Spa Visits

John and Gayle visited the Eden Spa during 2005 and 2006. The spa visits cost $400.00 each. They visited the spa every 3 months, with a total of three visits in 2005 and four visits in 2006.

As you can see from the examples given, the narrative explanations and descriptions of the evidence follows the construction and sequence of the schedules prepared for the case. Every item contained in the schedules should be commented on, even if only to say that no further explanation is necessary. Within the explanations of the evidence, the relevant witness and exhibit references should be included so that the reader can verify the investigator's figures and follow the logic behind the handling of the items. Be sure to include all the references to evidence that apply to each item in

238 Criminal Financial Investigations

your schedules. Also, provide the reader with line references to each of the schedules for the amounts being discussed in your evidence section. In the case of a purchase of property, you may need to include all of the witnesses and exhibits that verify the amounts you have shown in the schedule, and all of the witnesses that will testify to the transaction during litigation. In the Fawn scenario, assets would be addressed, then liabilities, and then expenditures. The summary schedule, or appendix, will be explained in the conclusions and recommendations section at the end of the report.

Defense of Subject

After all of the evidence shown in the schedules and used to support the investigator's allegations is addressed, the next step is to provide the reader (usually the prosecutor assigned the case) with any potential problems or difficulties that occurred during the investigation, and how these obstacles were overcome to reach the recommendations in the report. A separate section to address any concerns is beneficial in showing that all leads were followed and that the investigator is being completely honest in his evaluation of the evidence to be sufficient to gain a conviction. In a financial investigation, the defenses are much more subtle than in a crime of violence. All of the financial activities of the subject are presented in sequence. It is difficult for the subject to say he or she was not at the scene of the crime or that he or she has an airtight alibi. Any defenses presented during an interview with the subject or uncovered during the investigation that have potential to fit the charges against the subject must be addressed. The defenses may be as intricate as the indirect method of proof and use similar circumstantial evidence. The best defense is to present something that the investigator has not considered or would have difficulty in refuting under the time pressure of a trial. The familiarity that the investigator gains with the subject's actions, movements, habits, and financial dealings provide the best tools needed to discredit a defense. By the time the investigation is complete and ready to go to trial, the investigator will know more about the subject's finances than the subject can remember.

The section of the report that addresses the potential problems is often referred to as the defense of subject section. The investigator must include any defenses presented by the subject or other witnesses. The investigator should also include any potential defenses that would likely be brought up at trial. The prosecutor needs to have the same confidence in the factual quality of the report as the investigator. The prosecutor must also be able to gain at least the basics in understanding the logic and reasoning used in the investigative report. The common defenses of a cash hoard and a lack of intent are already discussed in the earlier sections for cash on hand and intent. There is no need to repeat those arguments unless they have been made by the subject. We will again use the Fawn scenario to demonstrate how this section of the report could appear.

Both subjects declined interviews, so no defenses were presented on their behalf. The possibility of a defense that a cash hoard was available would be refuted by the testimony of Clare Fawn and the divorce files maintained by the county. In addition, the availability of a cash hoard would not require frequent trips across the border for access to the funds, and the regularity of the trips and the deposits to Fawn's foreign account indicate that one large source of funds was never available. The 1-year delay in paying off the mortgage on their Colorado condominium also indicates that the money became available with the periodic laundering payments.

1. The jeweler stated that the Fawns jokingly said they received an inheritance from a rich uncle when asked how they could afford such fine watches. Both family histories were traced. John Fawn has two aunts and no uncles. Only one aunt was married. Her late husband (Fawn's uncle-in-law) passed away 6 years ago in a nursing home. His widow lives with a friend and receives Social Security payments for her livelihood. Gayle Fawn has two uncles, both of whom are alive and well.
2. When the curiosity of their neighbors became evident in regard to their newly available wealth, the Fawns spread the rumor that they won the money from a Powerball lottery ticket. Lottery records were checked, and neither of the Fawns cashed winning lottery tickets above the amounts required to be claimed through the lottery headquarters. In addition, no winnings were reported on their tax returns. Clare Fawn stated that she and John never played the lottery while they were married.
3. If gifts or personal loans are claimed to be the source of funds shown in the computation, the Fawns would need to bring in a member of the organized crime family to present this defense. It is unlikely that any member of the family would be willing to sacrifice themselves for the Fawns. Seven of the members are facing their own investigations for the funds that Fawn deposited into their accounts with First Bank of Windsor.

Conclusions and Recommendations

The last section included in the investigative report would be the conclusions and recommendations section. As in any good research paper, the introduction lets the reader know what the report is about, the body gives the evidence found to tell what the report is about, and the conclusion retells what the report is about and what the writer (investigator) believes should be done with the information.

The conclusion portion of this section will restate the criminal activity shown by the evidence in the report, through the perceptions and logic applied by the investigator. The recommendations portion will restate each recommended charge and the specifics that support the charges. We will again use the Fawns for our example. Note that in a case with two potential defendants, the charges are separated as they relate to each of the individuals who are being charged.

The evidence shows that John and Gayle Fawn entered into an agreement with members of the organized crime family to illegally transport U.S. currency into Canada by failing to report the currency and filing false declarations with the U.S. Customs Service. In so doing, they attempted to launder the currency and conceal it from taxing authorities. The scheme ran from April 2004 through the end of 2006, and a total of approximately $8,000,000.00 was laundered during this time. The Fawns received 5% of the total laundered funds for their part in the conspiracy. The share they received was used to improve their personal lifestyle and provide them with luxury items they could not otherwise afford. John Fawn attempted to conceal their proceeds from the scheme by opening a foreign account himself and depositing some of their share into that account. He made a veiled attempt to conceal the account by using a misspelling of his name on the account signature card.

The Fawns failed to report any of the income derived from their part in the money laundering scheme on their tax returns for 2004, 2005, and 2006. Their gains totaled approximately $400,000.00 over this time period.

It is recommended that John Fawn be charged with 90 counts in violation of federal Customs laws for failing to report the transportation of currency in excess of $3,000.00 out of the country and filing false Customs declarations on 18 of these occasions.

It is further recommended that John Fawn be charged with 90 counts of money laundering and 1 count of conspiracy to launder money on behalf of the organized crime family. The currency he transported was picked up at various locations in town on Thursday evenings and taken across the border on Fridays. The money was deposited into 10 different nominee accounts under the control of seven members of the organized crime family. On each occasion he received 5% of the total funds as his fee for doing the money laundering.

It is also recommended that John Fawn be charged with two counts of tax evasion for failing to report the income derived from the scheme on his tax returns for 2005 and 2006. The 2004 tax year has not been included due to the fact that John Fawn was in two marriages during the year, and presentation of the split year might lead to confusion for a jury. Civil authorities will still be able to recoup the taxes due for 2004.

It is recommended that Gayle Fawn be charged with 22 counts in violation of federal Customs laws for failing to report the transportation of currency in excess of $3,000.00 out of the country, for those occasions when she traveled to Canada with her husband and failed to acknowledge the money being taken into Canada.

It is further recommended that Gayle Fawn be charged with 90 counts of money laundering and 1 count of conspiracy to launder money on behalf of the organized crime family. She shared in the knowledge of the scheme, the overt acts of money laundering, and the financial benefits of participating in the scheme.

It is also recommended that Gayle Fawn be charged with two counts of tax evasion for failing to report the income derived from the money laundering on their joint returns for the years 2005 and 2006.

It is also recommended that criminal forfeiture proceedings be considered on the assets acquired by the Fawns using the illegal income from the money laundering scheme. The assets to which these funds can be traced specifically are included as an addendum to this report.

The examples that are provided in this chapter are recommendations. There is no format that is set in stone. The investigator should find a way to meet all of the indirect method's requirements in a manner that they can be comfortable within the report. The only requirements for the report are that it includes all of the necessary evidence to support the charges and that the presentation be simple and logical enough to be accepted by a judge or jury. We used a criminal case for our examples, but the same methodology can be applied to civil litigation, internal security and control, and business applications for the determination of acquisition costs and debt settlement. The criminal application for the indirect methods was used because the requirements for proof are more stringent. The investigator has the discretion to assemble the case to meet whatever criteria are needed.

Preparation for Trial

19

Several things have to be done to prepare the financial investigation for presentation in court. As in any project, the better the planning and preparation, the greater the likelihood of success. There are several stages involved in preparing the case for trial, and it may take weeks or even months to complete the necessary preparation. During this time the investigator and the prosecutor must work together to plan the best way to provide a clear and convincing courtroom presentation.

Packaging the Evidence

After completing the report, the first priority in preparing for trial is to ensure that all of the evidence referenced in the report is packaged in a way that is easily accessible for review and presentation. A financial investigation can involve hundreds of witnesses and thousands of documents. Organizing the evidence in advance of trial is crucial to maintaining the flow of information during the prosecution's presentation, to being ready for redirect examination, and to responding to defense witnesses on cross-examination. Investigators need to develop a method they are comfortable with and that allows them to retrieve any item of evidence quickly when it is needed.

One of the easiest ways to organize the evidence is to create a separate file for each witness. Inside the file would be memoranda of the witness' statements, and the documents and evidence that the witness will introduce in trial. It is also beneficial to have a background sheet on the witness with contact information, his or her relationship to the subject (if pertinent), the documents and exhibits that the witness will introduce, and any relevant information as to competency of that witness. Witnesses can be numbered in the order they appear in the investigative report. This will allow the prosecution to follow the steps that the investigator took in building the case against the subject. Similarly, the exhibits that the witness will introduce should follow the order presented in the report. The witness will introduce all of the documents he or she is responsible for, even if these are to be testified to by subsequent witnesses.

Once the witness and exhibit folders are prepared, they should be packaged together as a single collection. This can be accomplished by using cartons designed to hold either legal or letter-size folders. The investigator continues to have the responsibility for the security and maintenance of the chain of custody of the evidence. This allows for easy movement of the exhibits, and secures their storage throughout the trial preparation and trial. The original evidence files should be copied and at least two sets of copies made. One set will be used as work copies for trial preparation, and one will be ready to provide to the defense for discovery.

Although the investigator is the creator of the case and often a key witness at trial, the prosecutor has the final word in the sequence for the presentation of the evidence in court. The attorney has the knowledge and courtroom experience to determine the proper sequence of witnesses. This expertise can cover the habits of the judge assigned the case in taking breaks, recessing for lunch, and when the court day will end. The attorney may shuffle some of the witnesses to maximize the flow and continuity needed in presenting the case. Within this scope of expertise, alterations to the investigator's organizational plan often occur. The investigator needs to adjust the evidence to accommodate any changes that arise, again to ensure ready access to the evidence. This may involve changing the order of the witness folders or obtaining a different competent witness to introduce an item of evidence. Constant communication between the investigator and the prosecutor will also allow the investigator to bring to light any problems that changes may cause. This is a joint effort, and cooperation and discussion are required to ensure the best product.

Grand Jury Presentation

The time and resources needed to complete a financial investigation using an indirect method of proof usually restricts the application to felony violations. Law enforcement agencies as well as business internal security and civil litigators need to be efficient in managing resources, and often strive to get the most "bang for the buck." This does not supersede official duties or, in the case of law enforcement, the sworn duty to serve and protect, but it is always an administrative concern. Society is not best served if $100,000.00 in resources is applied to investigating a $900.00 shoplifting case. Civil remedies for recovery are in place to protect the community from these types of offenses. As intricate felony charges are the usual fare for indirect methods of proof investigations, the case is first presented to a grand jury to secure the indictment, and regular law enforcement techniques are sufficient to charge the perpetrator.

The grand jury presentation allows the prosecution to present all of the facts and evidence obtained in the investigation to the jury panel. The grand jury then decides whether the case merits going to trial (a true bill) or not (a no bill). The defense does not participate in this proceeding, and the prosecutor can present the case through the investigating agent without calling other witnesses. This also provides a dress rehearsal for the presentation of the case.

In the presentation to the grand jury, the investigator may be called to provide a recap of the entire investigative process, and be required to describe and explain the evidence and testimony obtained throughout the investigation. Once the investigator is sworn in and introduced to the grand jury panel, he or she will respond to the questions posed by the prosecutor and any questions that arise from the panel. For indirect methods of proof, it is beneficial and therefore customary for the investigator to explain to the grand jury the method being applied and why it was selected in the specific case. The investigator needs to be able to explain the method in terms that can be readily understood by the wide variety of grand jury members. He or she also needs to assure the grand jury that the legal requirements imposed on the use of the method to ensure its accuracy and to protect the innocent were met.

Grand jury panel members are selected in the same manner as trial jurors. They are part of the local community, usually selected from voter registration records. They will have various levels of age, gender, race, education, financial status, business acumen, and attitudes toward law enforcement. For these reasons, the investigator must be completely familiar with all of the aspects and nuances of the investigation, and be able to answer a wide variety of questions.

Pretrial Conferences

Once the indictment is returned, the actual trial preparation begins. The usual sequence is to have a planning conference with the prosecuting attorney. The prosecutor will review all of the evidence and decisions that will be made on what questions to ask each witness, the order in which the questions will be asked, and how potential problems with the witness or the evidence will be addressed. At this time the contact information for each witness will be updated for preparation of the trial subpoenas, and the prosecution team will prepare a schedule of pretrial conferences for those witnesses who will be supplying critical evidence and testimony.

The prosecutor will usually attack the evidence in the same way that the defense will most likely attack it. The investigator should field the scrutiny and provide adequate responses. If difficulties are found in any of witnesses' testimony or the documentary evidence, this is the time to iron out any problems.

During this time the defense will file its motions and ask for discovery. The investigator is usually responsible for making sure that the defense receives copies of all the evidence and other material they are entitled to receive. In addition, the prosecution team will want a complete set of copies of the evidence to use as working copies. The working copies should be the only documents used in pretrial planning and conferences. The original set of exhibits should be secured and protected from contamination until they are introduced into evidence during the trial. At this time the prosecution will request, through motions, the defense's proposed list of witnesses. The investigator will find out as much as possible about each of these witnesses and help the prosecutor anticipate the relevance of these witnesses to the defense's case.

Pretrial Interviews

Shortly before the trial is to begin, pretrial interviews will be scheduled for the witnesses that the prosecution intends to call to the stand. These interviews provide a dual purpose in presenting the case in court. First, they relieve the anxieties that the witness may have about testifying in court. The prosecutor will explain the procedures that will take place and go over the questions that will be asked. Second, the witnesses will have the opportunity to review any prior testimony given to the investigator and to refresh their memory by reviewing any documents they provided as evidence. It will also help them renew their familiarity with the documents they will use to give their testimony and introduce in court. This will usually be the first time that the witness meets the prosecutor. The investigator should make the introduction and be present during the interview for advice, explanations, and as a familiar face for the witness.

The prosecutor will use these interviews to evaluate the witnesses' credibility and anticipate their performance in the trial. Together, the prosecutor and investigator will decide on whether a witness' anticipated testimony needs to be strengthened with other witnesses or whether it is sufficient enough to stand alone. Remember that there are usually several witnesses to each transaction who can discuss the transaction through testimony in court. In many cases, the witness will bring the original documents to be used as evidence (included in the trial subpoena). The witness will provide those records and documents in court pursuant to the subpoena, and these documents will supersede the backup documents obtained during the investigation as the actual trial exhibits.

If the subjects of the investigation provided any testimony to the investigator, the investigator will be a witness in the trial as to the statements made. The prosecutor will also prepare the investigator as a witness in the same manner as the other witnesses. As the investigator is most familiar with the case, this preparation is usually much less formal. If the investigator is not to be used as a witness in the case, an expert witness on indirect methods will be used to summarize the financial schedules in the case computations. Even if the prosecution does not intend to call the investigator as a witness, it is likely that the defense will. This gives the defense the opportunity to challenge the investigator's impartiality and competence.

The expert witness will be given sufficient time to review the investigative report and ask any questions pertinent to the computations. If the expert is uncomfortable with any of the deductions drawn by the investigator or the prosecutor, these areas will be modified or corrected to the satisfaction of the expert witness. The expert witness will be responsible for providing an easily understood explanation of the evidence that shows the culpability of the defendants. The pretrial interview will cover both the direct testimony on the case and evidence, as well as an anticipated or "mock" cross-examination to ensure that the case is solid and ready for trial. Usually, an expert witness will provide a written summary of his or her qualifications to the court and the defense. Both the judge and the defense may ask any questions as to the expert's qualifications when he or she is offered as an expert in the trial.

At this point, the case is ready for trial. Coordinating and accommodating the witnesses needs to be handled pleasantly and efficiently. Out-of-town witnesses need to be provided with rooms and meal expenses, and the prosecution needs to ensure that enough witnesses are available so as not to delay the trial. Often a witness coordinator will assist in facilitating this aspect of the trial.

The Trial

The standard procedures for criminal cases are followed from the filing of motions to the turning over of the case to the jury. A few items are unique in the presentation of indirect methods of proof cases. The prosecution will usually file a motion to have the witnesses excluded from the courtroom until after they have testified. This is to prevent the testimony of one witness from having an effect on the testimony of another.

The prosecutor will ask for an exception to this motion for the case agent and the expert summary witness, if one is used. The prosecutor will request that the case agent be present throughout the trial at counsel's table to assist in the presentation. The expert summary witness must be present in the courtroom throughout the trial (usually in the spectator area).

The expert will prepare his or her own schedules and computations based on the evidence as it is introduced and accepted by the court. These are the schedules that the expert will use in providing the summary of the case testimony. To ensure a complete and accurate summation, the expert must be present during the entire trial. The expert summary witness will also note the evidence accepted by the court independently to support his or her testimony at the end of the case presentation.

During the trial, the investigator should follow the questioning of each witness, using the pretrial interview fact sheet, to ensure that all of the documents and testimony is obtained before the witness is excused. Another option is to use a copy of the list of witnesses and exhibits, and to check off the documents as they are offered and accepted into evidence. The investigator should also note any questions that the prosecutor should ask before closing the witness' testimony and assure the prosecutor that all of the exhibits needed were introduced.

Special attention should be given to the testimony of the witnesses on cross-examination. The investigator should offer suggestions for redirect questioning and be able to locate any of the exhibits the prosecutor requests for redirect questioning. The same procedures are followed throughout the case in chief and become very important for cross-examination during the presentation of the defense case.

Due to the complex nature of a financial case and the volume of witnesses and exhibits, these trials often take weeks or months to complete. The work of the prosecution team does not end when the court is adjourned for the day. The team meets after court to review and analyze what occurred during the day and plan the strategy for the following day. Each evening is similar to the halftime break in a football game; adjustments are made to facilitate the case presentation. The prosecutor, investigator, and the expert witness are all involved in analyzing the daily results and progress of the criminal case. If an additional witness is identified and needed, the investigator must obtain that witness' accessibility to appear in court in the evening, during breaks, or get assistance in locating and subpoenaing the witness.

After the defense has presented its case and rested, the prosecution will call any rebuttal witnesses to negate information or claims made by the defense during its presentation. The trial plan for this phase of the trial is usually prepared during the defense's presentation and solidified in the evening conferences. Again, if new witnesses are needed for rebuttal, they must be located and served a subpoena to appear. If time is available (lunchtime, evenings, and weekends), the same steps are followed that were used in preparing the initial set of witnesses.

Once the case presentation is complete, the jury will retire for deliberation. The prosecution will have custody and control of the evidence admitted for the case, and the prosecution team will be required to provide any of the evidence the jury asks for to assist them in their deliberations. The next step is to anxiously await the jury's decision.

Standard procedures are followed after a conviction. The evidence is turned over to the court, the witnesses are paid and released from the subpoenas, and the sentencing process begins. The judge will request a presentence report from the probation department. Probation will interview both sides in the case. The report will then be filed with the court.

Innovative Applications

20

New areas have emerged in which the use of indirect methods of proof in the investigation of financial activities have gained prominence. The worldwide expansion of international white collar crimes, corporate manipulations, and the global concerns relating to terrorism has shown the need for competent criminal financial investigators. The size and scope of white collar financial crimes, such as the Bernie Madoff case, the "oil for food" scandal, the recent corruption discovered in several government agencies and subsidized companies, and the money flow supporting terrorist organizations around the world, have pushed financial investigating to the forefront of most law enforcement and security agencies.

Corporate fraud has resulted in the inflation of consumer goods and a reduction in product quality. Investment and consumer fraud has eaten away at retirement investments, adversely affected public costs for insurance, and raised consumer fears on advertising veracity and product safety. Financial fraud through charitable and business entities has been found to support and pay for terrorist activities that include training and recruitment.

In many of these cases relatively new laws have been written to recover as much as possible of the ill-gotten gains from major financial fraud schemes. In addition, being able to follow the money and stop its flow to terrorist organizations has been a major tool used by governments in the War on Terror. This chapter will show how the use of indirect methods of proof and forensic accounting techniques can be applied to counter at least the financial harm from these emerging areas of fraud and corruption. The three primary applications are forfeiture, money laundering, and the freezing of currency being used and directed toward terrorist operations.

Forfeiture

Forfeiture statutes are divided between civil and criminal litigation. Civil forfeiture is used to take property used in the commission of a crime or acquired from the commission of a crime. For example, if a person uses their car to commit a burglary and to remove the stolen property, then it can be seized and forfeited through civil litigation. Criminal forfeiture is brought about by a governing authority against property as a punishment for criminal behavior. In either instance, indirect methods of proof and forensic accounting techniques are a valuable tool in identifying and quantifying the property to be forfeited.

These methods are most often used in criminal forfeitures when substitute asset provisions have been codified in the respective laws. Substitute asset provisions allow for the government to trace illegally obtained funds over time, and seize and forfeit assets that have been obtained with the money that can be tied to the illegal activity. The concept applied is that illegally obtained or unreported income keeps its original nature no matter how many times it is used to acquire new items of value. If $100,000.00 is taken through fraud and used to purchase gold coins, and the coins are sold to purchase a yacht, the $100,000.00 yacht becomes the result of the initial fraud and is subject to forfeiture. Tracing the funds, or following the money, is achieved through the application of indirect methods and forensic accounting investigative techniques. As examples:

1. The financial investigation of a health care provider discloses that false claims have been filed and paid over a 3-year period. The false claims resulted in a minimum harm of $1.2 million (minimum harm determined by the indirect method of proof on the business operation). The illegally obtained funds were used by the two owners of the business to buy some new equipment for the business and the rest split between the two for the purchase of personal assets. The illegal proceeds were traced by following the money by preparing net worth computations on the two owners. The net worth computations revealed that $500,000.00 went to each of the two owners. Their shares of the false claim proceeds were used to purchase two new vehicles each, gold coins, jewelry and other personal items, as well as $120,000.00 in new business assets.

   The financial investigation now becomes the starting point from which the money can be followed to see where it is currently. Personal and business assets are often in a state of change or transition. Older assets are sold or traded in to acquire newer assets to keep the items up to date or to add new items to one's inventory of lifestyle improvements. Since the false claim proceeds came in the form of checks to the business, the checks were cashed or deposited to bank accounts, and the funds used by the two owners.

   Each owner reported legitimate income. The substitute provision would then allow for the forfeiture of assets that were acquired with the fraudulent receipts. If these assets are still in the possession of the two owners, they could be subject to forfeiture. If they have subsequently been converted to new or different assets, the substitute provisions would allow the government to file the forfeiture against the new assets. The logic behind the statutory provisions is that none of the new assets could have been acquired from any legitimate income and therefore the perpetrator is not entitled to keep the assets. If any assets were acquired over the amount of legitimate income, these assets could be subject to forfeiture since the only source for the additional funds would be the false claims income. The vehicles, coins, and jewelry could be subject to the forfeiture proceedings if it could be shown that the funds used to acquire these assets had to have been generated by the false-claim fraud scheme.

2. The investigation of an individual reveals that through corporate embezzlement, the individual stole $480,000.00 over 2 years. The embezzlement is discovered 3 years after it occurred and is successfully prosecuted. The embezzler has used the proceeds to enhance his lifestyle. Any assets that have been identified through the financial investigation as being purchased with the proceeds are then traced to the current holdings of the perpetrator. By following the money through various asset conversions, it was shown that the bulk of the embezzled funds were eventually used to purchase a duplex in Florida that was used as a winter home. Under the substitute asset provisions of the forfeiture law, the Florida property would be subject to forfeiture proceedings.

In this case, if the known amount of the financial crime was less than the cost of the substituted asset (the Florida property), the property could still be seized, forfeited, and then sold to obtain the amount of money decided upon by the court.

Depending on the statutory provisions, either part or all of the funds used in the acquisition of a substitute asset may need to be shown as generated from the illegal acts or fraud committed. The respective statutes will also define the criminal violations necessary as a precursor to the initiation of the forfeiture action.

Money Laundering

The term *money laundering* applies to the attempt to change the appearance of funds from an illegal action to that of legitimate financial gains. This can apply to the proceeds from any financial fraud, any illegal source of funds, or just the failure to report legitimate income for the purpose of facilitating tax fraud. Money laundering can be done in a variety of ways. Offshore bank fronts, dummy corporations, and intricate banking transfers and manipulations have all been used to try to give illegal funds a legitimate appearance, to conceal the nature of the funds from taxable to nontaxable sources, or to hide the true origin of the funds. Indirect methods of proof and forensic accounting techniques can help the investigator to follow the money backward in time to discover its true nature or forward to identify the persons involved in facilitating the money laundering scheme.

If someone has made the decision to violate laws for personal gain and taken the time to develop, implement, and maintain an elaborate fraud scheme or criminal enterprise, it only stands to reason that they will want to maximize their gains and have it appear to have been generated from honest hard work or good fortune. If the scheme has operated for any period of time, the individual will have enjoyed a rising level of status in the community and will do whatever is necessary to avoid having the new social and financial status tainted by fraud and deceit.

Since most fraud schemes are relatively intricate, the major fraud artist spends the majority of his time keeping the scheme concealed and running smoothly. Due to this fact, those conducting major fraud schemes and multi-million dollar tax schemes do not have the time or expertise to formulate an adequate money laundering scheme with which to conceal their gains. This has resulted in the birth of a new criminal industry: money laundering. A new criminal element skilled in financial record keeping, and national and international financial regulation have set up shop to accommodate drug cartels, organized criminal enterprises, and the larger financial and tax fraud perpetrators. For a fee ranging between 2% to 10% of the money laundered, they transform the nature and character of the monies made through these activities.

The small time or financial crime beginner or the individual tax evader does not have the contacts, business acumen, or resources to employ a professional money launderer. Although the fraud scheme being perpetrated may involve substantial amounts of money, it would pale in comparison to cases such as Bernie Madoff, the major drug cartels, organized crime, and international corporate fraud. That does not stop them from taking various steps to conceal the true nature of their receipts or to rely on the hope that their scheme will go unnoticed. This does not preclude the investigator from pursuing money laundering charges in conjunction with the primary charges for the financial crime. The subject must however meet all the element provisions of the money laundering statute. The definition of money laundering is relatively short and simple: Any actions that are designed to hide or alter the nature, origin, ownership, or control of money to avoid reporting requirements under laws or regulations; or to conceal the fact that the money was obtained by unlawful means.

How do these violations look when being performed by the financial criminal? Several methods have been used to attempt to achieve this goal. To hide or alter the money, an individual may divert the funds to an offshore bank or company, and withdraw the money in the form of loans on which no actual repayments are made. An individual may also open a bank account in a false name or use a nominee (an account opened in the name of a relative or acquaintance over which they have full control). The money is thereby concealed as to true ownership and monies taken back out are altered to look like a gift or personal loan, which also falsifies the origin of the funds. A fictitious business may be created through which the monies are put in and subsequently funneled back to the individual. This may also be done to give illegally obtained funds the appearance of being acquired through legitimate business dealings.

Most governments regulate the movement of currency to monitor and control the distribution of their currency. In the United States, currency transaction reports (CTRs) are required to be filed by financial institutions for cash transactions in excess of $10,000.00. Also, U.S. Customs requires that anyone carrying more than $3,000.00 in currency declare the money on their Customs declaration prior to traveling outside of the country. Violation of either of these requirements can be considered a criminal violation and prosecuted under money laundering statutes.

Failing to report currency being taken outside of U.S. borders facilitates the use of offshore banking and corporate fraud schemes. The funds are moved offshore, given the appearance of legitimate financial transactions and then brought back in for use by the violating parties. The amounts of currency involved in major illegal activities are great. Drug cartels and organized criminal enterprises amass billions of dollars in U.S. currency each year. The criminal activities deal primarily in cash to keep from generating more of a paper trail, and their customers and victims use cash to conceal their involvement in criminal behavior. To move these amounts of currency, these groups will most often use professional money laundering operations and cooperative employees of legitimate international banking institutions.

Violators of these money laundering provisions may be caught in the act by Customs or Coast Guard personnel. In many cases however, the violations will be discovered through financial investigation of those involved when the money is returned to the United States and put to use on lavish lifestyles. The financial investigator must keep in mind that risking prosecution and incarceration to gain millions of dollars is of no value if the perpetrator cannot use and enjoy the fruits of the crime. The indirect methods of proof help the investigator to identify not only the illegal or unreported monies being received but also to identify those involved in laundering the money. Once a laundering enterprise is identified, it opens a whole field of new investigations by identifying the customers and clientele of the money launderers.

So as not to be misunderstood, not all offshore financial institutions are involved in money laundering. Many major banks have international offices to accommodate an expanding global economy. The use of sham-type offshore financial institutions is patterned to look like a legitimate institution, and investigative steps are needed to determine their legitimacy. Fictitious offshore financial institutions are also used to perpetrate fraud against investors and customers by offering interest rates and benefits that sound too good to be true; and they are too good to be true.

The manipulation of currency within the national borders is also a problem for enforcement and taxing authorities. Those involved in individual fraud schemes, tax fraud, or at the localized levels of organized criminal activities need to try to hide and conceal the nature, origin, and ownership of their cash as well. Cash transactions by individuals in excess of $10,000.00 are rare within current banking operations, and stand out to bank employees. When the legislation for currency reporting was enacted, criminals were quick to adapt. A flurry of activity began in which multiple deposits of less than $10,000.00 were made. This was either done by one individual going to the one bank several times a day or to several bank branches on the same day, or by having several individuals go to the bank with single deposits under the $10,000.00 reporting limit. This operation became known as "smurfing."

The laws were modified to include multiple transactions that totaled more than the dollar limit within a short period of time. One early case involved a drug dealer at the "street" level who wanted to buy a small apartment complex for $297,000.00. This individual went to his bank three times a day for 11 consecutive days depositing $9,000.00 at each visit. The laundering case was established and the no-down-payment purchase of $297,000.00 was a major asset in the indirect method of proof. Another rather innovative scheme was set up by a major independent jeweler. His scheme was to have the individual give him the money. He would then give the customer jewelry valued at the amount of 10% less the amount of money to be laundered (his commission for laundering). The individual and his wife or girlfriend would wear the jewelry and travel to Germany where he had an associate who would buy back the jewelry and allow the customer to deposit the funds in a foreign account. Gold coins have also been used to take money outside the country. American gold coins (valued at bullion market prices) would be taken outside the country and the Customs declaration would show no currency over $3,000.00 under the guise that the "face value" of the coins would only be $1.00 per coin and they had less than 3,000 of them. Under this thinking, 100 gold dollars could be sold overseas for more than $100,000.00.

Examples of attempts to conceal the origin of the money would include the case of an individual who created a dummy corporation. He included the corporation as one of his suppliers for accounting purposes and made regular payments to the corporation as part of his skimming operation. He kept the amounts regular to avoid suspicion. When he wanted to take the money for his personal use, he would issue a loan from the corporation to himself and use the money for his personal benefit. This not only helped him to evade the payment of taxes on his business (increasing reported expenses to the dummy corporation) but also allowed him to conceal the skimmed funds. Another example was a bank investment officer who handled the sale of certificates of deposit to the bank customers. She would issue new certificates to the customers she thought would not withdraw from or cash their certificates. Rather than make the redeposit she would keep the money for herself. She would then transfer the money to an out-of-state account in her deceased sister's name.

Money laundering can also be done by taking illegal receipts and running them through as income from a business. Many criminal organizations will purchase businesses that deal primarily with cash customers such as bars, restaurants, grocery stores, and service businesses. They will then make deposits into the business checking accounts and record the deposits as legitimate income. The case of the bank that was requiring kickbacks on high risk loans from their customers comes to mind. In that case the monies were reported by one of the coconspirators as income from his restaurant (the restaurant operated at a sufficient loss each year to keep the funds from being taxed). This concealed the true nature and origin of the money and was only uncovered and quantified when the indirect methods and forensic accounting techniques were employed.

As examples:

1. Information has been received that three individuals are living lavish lifestyles with no apparent means of support. The net worth method reveals that each of these individuals has unexplained income of more than $1 million for each of the past 3 years. Further investigation establishes illegal narcotics trafficking as the likely source of the unreported illegal income. The income reported by these three is shown as consulting fees totaling $30,000.00 per month going to each of them. The consulting fees come from ABC Financial, a Panamanian corporation. The investigation reveals that ABC Financial was incorporated in Panama 4 years ago and that the same three individuals are the officers for the corporation. The company has no actual customers and only the three employees. The money laundering occurs with the deposit of illegal funds (narcotics sales receipts) into the account of ABC Financial and again as the funds are paid to the three individuals as consulting fees. In addition to the money laundering charges, the unreported narcotics trafficking income (the amount over and above the $360,000.00 per year) can be proven through the use of indirect methods and used for prosecution of tax evasion charges. This also opens up the potential for the pursuit of seizure and forfeiture of the illegal proceeds from the narcotics trafficking operation, and may identify other players in the narcotics ring.

2. An individual operates an air charter service. His business records indicate that he makes about $120,000.00 a year hauling freight and passengers between Florida and countries in or bordering the Caribbean. An indirect method of proof shows that he has more than $300,000.00 in net worth increases each year. Further investigation shows that none of the customers identified in his business records exist. The cargo manifests indicate that he makes deliveries to foreign countries, but only transports passengers on return flights. Federal aviation records show that he makes flights three times a week. The investigation then reveals that he has bank accounts in four countries that do not have extensive financial banking regulations. The result of the investigation is that he is transporting currency out of the country and depositing it to various accounts held by drug dealers, fraud artists, tax evaders, and others. He receives a 5% fee for laundering the funds. Since the bulk of his income is from cargo (the few passenger fees are accurately reported), the amounts determined by the indirect method can be used to extrapolate the amounts of laundered funds (5% of the understated income each year).

Financial Investigating and Counterterrorism

The increase in terrorist actions around the world in the past two decades has raised concerns by governments in how to address the problem and maintain security for their people. A major factor in the capabilities, recruitment, and longevity of terrorist organizations is the flow of money needed to finance and sustain the terrorist groups. Several steps have been taken to cut off the funding to these organizations.

To recruit members to a terrorist organization, the organization has to maintain a steady flow of propaganda to keep their message in the minds of the people. This can be accomplished through radical speech by charismatic individuals, keeping a media staff at work publishing its propaganda in print or through the Internet, and by conducting dramatic attacks that will whet the appetite of the news media and be televised and talked about around the world. Once individuals are recruited, they require resources to reinforce their conversion. The recruits need to be removed from the general population to insure that they do not lose their enthusiasm and resolve. They also need to be fed, clothed, housed and supported at least as well, and usually better, than the lives they left behind. The last major task is to train them for their acts of violence and equip them to carry out their attacks.

Terrorist organizations also need a safe haven in which to formulate their plans and house their operational structure. This is achieved by acting as "hired guns" for rogue nations that either cannot carry out the offensive attacks against a perceived enemy or that want to retain anonymity from the attacks and have plausible deniability diplomatically in the world community. A more frightening new development has been the alliance of terrorist organizations with major international drug cartels around the world. This alliance stems from the common goal of wanting governments to have to deal with a constant state of chaos, and to be viewed as weak and incapable of protecting their populations. Terrorist actions by narcotics cartels have been constantly increasing in an attempt to secure and expand their operations and to allow them to function without impediment from enforcement agencies. The constant fighting and bloodshed in Afghanistan has been primarily fueled by the drug production that has been a mainstay of their economy.

When you analyze the financial aspects of the tragedy that occurred in the United States on September 11, 2001, the cost for this devastating attack seems minimal. Investigation has shown that the cost to place, train, and support the terrorists for 18 months was less than $500,000.00. However, the costs to al-Qaeda for training and recruitment are substantially more. The funding used to sustain and grow these terrorist organizations is generated from a wide variety of sources. As touched on earlier, some governments are willing to pay terrorist groups to conduct acts of terrorism covertly on their behalf against a common enemy. Narcoterrorists fund terrorist actions to insulate themselves against government interference with their illegal activities and to intimidate the people in their areas of operation. The terrorists themselves will use organized crime tactics such as kidnapping, arson, and extortion to finance their operations.

There are also several more subtle ways in which funds are funneled into terrorist organizations. Terrorists have become more sophisticated and use sham charities, humanitarian organizations, and corporations to generate profits and solicit contributions. Sometimes they will disguise their cause and receive funds from legitimate charities without revealing the true use of the funds to the donor. They will also create or use existing ethnic, religious, or racial organizations to further their terrorist activities. Because of these innovations, it has become more important for enforcement and regulatory agencies to be able to utilize sophisticated forensic accounting techniques to turn off the flow of money to terrorist groups.

In response to the increasing threat of terrorism around the world, many governments have taken steps to provide the means of freezing and confiscating funds that are directed to these radical organizations. Steps have also been taken to penalize legitimate financial institutions for the lack of due diligence in dealing with substantial monetary transactions. The problem lies in being able to determine intent on the part of the contributing party and being able to quantify the amounts that were sent or intended to be sent to terrorist organizations. Although the indirect methods of proof were originally designed to identify tax fraud schemes, they were subsequently adapted to assist in the prosecution and punishment of those involved in financial crimes. Now they are not only available but also extremely valuable in the area of counterterrorism. Following the money is essential in cutting off the financial resources of terrorist groups and can help identify those who are sympathetic to their causes.

Most of the books written on terrorism, counterterrorism, and homeland security point out the great need to stop the flow of money to terrorist organizations but fail to address what tools, methods, and practices can be used to accomplish this goal. The Middle Eastern subbanking system referred to as the *Hawala* is often talked about as an undetectable means for the transfer of funds without a paper trail. This would be true if the investigator was limited to direct evidence of financial dealings. An example of this system would appear like this: An individual in Tehran has $10,000.00 they want to send to Boston. They would contact a member of the Hawala and give them the money. This member would contact another member in Boston to distribute the funds from their holdings that are already in the country. This member would have people in Boston wanting to transfer funds back to Tehran. Both members (Boston and Tehran) would only keep their records until the amounts balanced. If further transactions occurred a new accounting would begin. In reality, the only paper trail would be an accounting of receivables and payables.

As you can see, money is never moved outside of the two cities. This might appear as a foolproof way to defeat banking, finance, and cash reporting laws and regulations. Terrorist organizations need large amounts of money to keep their groups functioning, and they need additional large amounts to acquire weapons, equipment, and supplies. Even under the most idealistic circumstances and if any individual had the extraordinary means needed, individuals that are willing to violate and circumvent the laws are not going to have enough trust in their associates not to keep a record of all of their receivables and payables. There is no honor among crooks.

In addition, the money is of no use unless it can be used to purchase items and pay bills. Since terrorists do not exist in a cloistered environment, they need to make their acquisitions from businesses not owned and operated in the terrorist camp. This is where the forensic accounting techniques come into play. Legitimate businesses, even when they dabble in illegality, will still create the same type of falsification of their records to cover the transactions. These methods can trace the funding forward and back to identify the players involved in the support group for the terrorist organization. Although the investigations will most likely carry a heavy cost in time and manpower, the results can more than make up for the intensive amount of work applied.

As radical groups and organizations become more sophisticated, the ability to monitor and analyze financial transactions become of greater importance. Crimes of all sorts, financial or otherwise, are done with the purpose of gaining more power and control. In the case of terrorism, part of the quest for power is hoped to be achieved through the dissolution of the existing authority of government so as to be able to take that authority for themselves. Every criminal investigator and financial analyst should be familiar with the methodology and understand the benefits of indirect methods of proof.

Index

Y